SHADOW BODIES

Black Women, Ideology, Representation, and Politics

JULIA S. JORDAN-ZACHERY

RUTGERS UNIVERSITY PRESS

New Brunswick, Camden, and Newark, New Jersey, and London

Library of Congress Cataloging-in-Publication Data

Names: Jordan-Zachery, Julia Sheron, author.
Title: Shadow bodies : black women, ideology, representation, and politics / Julia S.
    Jordan-Zachery.
Description: New Brunswick : Rutgers University Press, [2017] | Includes
    bibliographical references and index.
Identifiers: LCCN 2017014955 (print) | LCCN 2017027077 (ebook) | ISBN
    9780813593418 (E-pub) | ISBN 9780813593432 (Web PDF) | ISBN 9780813593401
    (cloth : alk. paper) | ISBN 9780813593395 (pbk. : alk. paper)
Subjects: LCSH: African American women—Social conditions. | Feminism.
Classification: LCC E185.86 (ebook) | LCC E185.86 .J6733 2017 (print) |
    DDC 305.48/896073—dc23
LC record available at https://lccn.loc.gov/2017014955

A British Cataloging-in-Publication record for this book is available from the British
Library.

♾ The paper used in this publication meets the requirements of the American National
Standard for Information Sciences—Permanence of Paper for Printed Library
Materials, ANSI Z39.48–1992.

www.rutgersuniversitypress.org

Manufactured in the United States of America

CONTENTS

PREFACE

It is an interesting time for me to be writing this book—both politically and personally (I recognize that this divide is not rigid). I start with the political side of this story. I am an immigrant Black woman living in the United States at the transition of the Barack Obama administration. As was the case when he was first elected, and emphatically more so today, I find myself pondering the question: What does the election of the U.S. president, regardless of social location and political affiliation, mean for Black women within and outside of the United States? Will any of these administrations, particularly the 2017 one, substantively respond to Black women? Additionally, I find myself pondering: What do Black women want? Who speaks for Black women—is it people like me who walk the halls of the academy or is it service providers like my mother? Why does it feel like these two groups of Black women seemingly do not talk, or maybe they do and could it be that some of us are simply unaware?

Simultaneously, I am raising a young Black woman. This is a young woman who is active on Twitter and who considers herself an "intersectional feminist" (I'm like: Why not just say *Black feminist*? But that intergenerational conversation of Black gender consciousness is another book) and who swears by Beyoncé's visual album, *Lemonade*. My daughter thinks that Twitter is a great platform for activism—hashtag activism—and that Beyoncé embodies what it means to be Black and female in the twenty-first century. Needless to say she is ready to get in "formation." As I watch her political identity develop and blossom, I am fascinated by how the emergence of her political consciousness is heavily influenced by cultural representations in the era of social media, and in the context of the presidency of Barack Obama. But I wonder.

What does it mean for Black women to get in formation in a political context that has generally ignored them or that has been unresponsive although Black women have shown themselves as a primary voting bloc? How for example, does #sayhername translate into a political agenda that manifest itself in specific policies? *Shadow Bodies* does not address these questions directly, but by centering the positionality of the Black women's body it serves as a springboard for helping us think through this intersection of political and cultural representation. It does so by asking: How do discursive practices, both speech and silences, support and maintain hegemonic understandings of Black womanhood, thereby rendering some Black women as shadow bodies? This is a historical study spanning the time frame 1997–2007. It looks at different platforms of Black women's speech in hopes of understanding how Black gendered corporeal inscriptions, such as displayed in Beyoncé's *Lemonade* and that embody #sayhername, influence who speaks for Black women, who gets included in such speech, and the responses advanced in response to the Black female body.

This analysis helps us to better understand Black female bodies' materiality as a site for the intersection between the political and cultural realms. In this sense, *Shadow Bodies*, via an analysis of the scripting of the Black female body, affords us a theoretical framework that stretches beyond the time frame of the study and beyond the modes of talk included in the analysis. The theoretical framework permits an analysis of places of dissent and convergence, for analysis of the space between Beyoncé's formation and the political treatment of Black women because it is an analysis of race–gender boundaries. By considering discursive structures and rhetorical devices I offer insights into structures of ideology and power that might simultaneously converge and diverge in the political and cultural spheres. This then allows for a deeper understanding of what it means when Black women get in formation—both culturally and politically—and how said formation is responded to by political elites across a wide spectrum of identities.

This is a book about what often goes unsaid, silences. I attempt to show how the silences can be more revealing than what is often vocalized. In exploring these silences, I often found myself growing increasingly frustrated. I was frustrated because "normal" social science did not afford me with an approach for understanding silence, yet the strength of the analysis was judged by these methods. I often heard that you have to show it, not simply tell it. But how do you show silence, the absence of something? So I had to fight against a type of silencing that exists in academia—the unwritten rule of reproducing what is already in existence. As I wrote, I was simultaneously analyzing the politics of silencing while experiencing it on a very personal level. For example, an editor told me that I did not include sufficient materials from Black feminist politics. This dumbfounded me, as I offer a historical evolution of Black feminist works on representation and public policy and voice within the field of political science by Black critical (female) scholars. After pushing back on this claim, I later learn that the editor felt that I had failed because I needed to do more with one "celebrated" and popularly known Black female author. My response was: How do you dismiss the critical work done by the other scholars to privilege the work of one more popularly recognized individual? I mention this experience because I want us to think of the types of scholarship that are allowed to be published and how this process can be a form of silencing, thereby curtailing how we understand the Black political woman. As you read this analysis, I encourage you to think of the various manifestations of silence, the moments where shadows are produced. Hopefully, you will use this analysis to continue to explore the various manifestations of silence and how we can collectively resist such. It is this collective effort that will bring us closer to the liberation of Black women and others who find themselves oppressed. It is because of my commitment to freedom that I persevered and wrote this book.

SHADOW BODIES

INTRODUCTION

In your silence
Every tone ...
Is heard.

—Langston Hughes, "Silence"

My mother's experiences as a mental health nurse stand at the center of my interest in HIV/AIDS, domestic violence, and mental illness, and their intersection.
From my mother's experiences I learned of how the three are intertwined and
difficult to separate when treating the mentally ill, for example. My mother, for
35 years, was a mental health nurse in Barbados. She played an instrumental role
developing the community mental health program. Additionally, for several
years she was the nurse in charge of the outpatient clinic. As a young girl, I would
travel with my mother around the island, as she brought mental health treatment
to those who were in need and who, for various reasons, could not make it to the
clinic or the hospital. My mother cared deeply about all of her patients, but she
was particularly passionate about the treatment of two populations—children
and women. In her words, these were the two groups who tended "not to be
heard" by those in power. She used her position and her voice to question, to
challenge, and to empower women to fight, for themselves and their children, so
that they could be heard.

In addition to being trained as a mental health nurse, my mother was also
trained as a drug counselor. As drug use became increasingly prevalent she
found herself having to address the intersection of mental illness and substance abuse. This was again the case as incidences of HIV/AIDS emerged on
the island. She saw intimately the relationship between race, class, gender, and
mental illness, HIV/AIDS, and domestic abuse. There are a number of stories
my mother told that I found myself reflecting on as this project developed. One
involved a 15-year-old girl who was sexually molested by her stepfather. He
molested her for a number of years and when she turned fifteen, in response
to the molestation, the young woman ingested rat poison. She was hospital-
ized and later had to participate in psychiatric care for her attempted suicide. As
part of her attempts to cope with and respond to the abuse, the young woman
turned to sex and would have sex with multiple partners, which in turn fueled

her cyclical experiences with psychiatric care. I also remember my mother telling the story of one woman whom she characterized as "the nicest woman you could know," who was suffering from mental illness in an abusive relationship and who later contracted HIV from her husband. She would say, "That poor woman didn't stand a chance." By saying, "didn't stand a chance" my mother was addressing how societal structures and stigmas coalesced in this patient's treatment and her lived realities. She often spoke of how class played a major role in what some patients had access to and even how they were treated. For my mother, it was impossible to separate her patients' identity, as Black, primarily indigent women who were HIV positive, who suffered a mental illness, and/or who were abused. My mother was speaking to the subjectivity of Black women and the political and policy responses.

I did not always understand or appreciate the types of relationships my mother spoke to and how she was speaking to concepts such as intersectionality, stigma, identity, positionality, and silence. It would be years later that I would reflect on why my mother would say that the women, such as the ones described above, "didn't stand a chance." It was not my mother's failure to see their humanity; she did what she could to ensure that such women received the best care possible (I have written previously of how she often defied authority to ensure that patients receive adequate care [Jordan-Zachery, 2013]). Instead, she was reflecting on how some bodies were treated by those in power. As my research interests focused on intersectionality, I found myself pondering this question: Why are some bodies treated in particular ways? Particularly, I wondered why some bodies, those that are not only marginalized by race, class, and gender, but also by "illness," treated in particular ways.

Years later my recollection of my mother's talk on the intersection of HIV/AIDS, domestic violence, and mental illness and the impact on the Black community and Black women specifically led me to ask: How do Black women talk about how these issues affect their material lives? To my dismay, my initial research on Black women's talk on these issues yielded nothing, or at best a sliver of what I hoped to find. My initial project focused on Black female congresswomen's talk on HIV/AIDS and Black womanhood. The original data revealed that the women spoke volumes about HIV/AIDS. However, most of the talk (as I discuss in chapter 4) focused on either the impact of AIDS outside of the United States or on recognizing organizations or individual actions within the United States. It was not necessarily the lack of talk; it was more how Black women talked about the issues and who tended to be excluded from the talk that caught my attention and led to my frustration. Ignored in the talk, for example, were lesbian Black women who were also HIV-positive. Left out of the conversation was how patriarchy and poverty, for example, contribute to the spread of HIV among Black women in the United States. This is what I mean by silence—the absence of some bodies and frames from the discourses on HIV/ AIDS, mental illness, and domestic abuse. Given this, I decided to abandon the project. After all, how could I write about nothing?

But then it struck me, "nothing" was my data: it was the silence that needed to be analyzed. This occurred to me when I taught a class called "Lost Bodies." This class focused on how some bodies are included and/or excluded from the body politic. During one of our conversations I asked students: How might we explain the silence around transgender HIV/AIDS youths of color? In response to my question I searched existing literatures but was not often satisfied with what I could find—especially among political science research. There was not a lot of theorizing on the concept of silence and particularly on Black women and silence. As Trinh T. Minh-ha argues (1990, pp. 372–373), "Within the context of women's speech silence has many faces. . . . Silence is commonly set in opposi- tion with speech. Silence as a will not to say or a will to unsay and as a language of its own has barely been explored." Silence serves as an index of identity and as such should be analyzed.

On the surface, what appeared to be nothing is actually something. The silences are the data. I recognize, in the words of Picard (1948/1952, p. 24), that "speech came out of silence . . . and in every silence there is something of the spoken word." As I thought about the silences around HIV/AIDS, domestic vio- lence, and mental illness I began to wonder: Do Black women not care about issues such as domestic violence? And were there factors that constrained not only if they spoke about all three issues, but also how they could speak about them and who could speak?

To explore these questions, I rely on an interdisciplinary array of concepts and theories, garnered from Black feminist thought—specifically intersection- ality, muted group theory, and body studies—to analyze and explain the dif- ficulties of seeing, reading, and writing the bodies of Black women who have HIV/AIDS, who have been abused, and/or who suffer from mental illness. Black feminist theory, muted group theory, and body studies afford me a sys- tematic framework for uncovering, analyzing, and explaining silences and the resulting shadow bodies. What they provide to this study is a combined way of understanding the positionality and representation of Black womanhood and its intersection with HIV/AIDS, domestic violence, and mental illness. Inte- grating these theoretical insights also permits me to understand the implica- tions of this representation, which is influenced by the ideologies surrounding power relations between Black women. As I argue, silence operates as a form of discourse and subsequently embodies ideologies of power. Consequently, both speech and silence should be explained in order to ascertain the embed- ded implicit meanings and assumptions that allow us to understand what my mother was referring to when she said one of her patients "did not stand a chance." Combined, they allow me to explain how some black female bodies become shadow bodies.

Ronald Jackson's (2006) analysis of how the Black masculine body is treated in popular media offered me a way to conceptualize and explain the silences evident in the talk of Black women and the resulting shadow bodies. Jackson, using the concept of scripting, explains why the Black masculine body tends to be negativized and punished. Scripting suggests that all bodies are surfaces that can be written on; thereby, carrying cultural assumptions and understandings of how the body should behave and perform. As such, the body as corporeal text serves as a discursive tool in which meanings may be extracted. As I discuss in more detail later, I ground the analysis in two dominant scripts, the *Ass* and *Strong Black Woman*. I argue that these dominant scripts are the mechanisms that allow Black women to avoid confronting the stereotype of the sexually permissive Black woman (*piece of ass* script, for example) and support the belief in the script of the *Strong Black Woman*. Given the functioning of these scripts in determining the prototypical Black woman, those who are HIV-positive or who have AIDS, those who are suffering some form of mental illness, and those who are abused by their partners fail to live up to the expectation of the Black woman as the "guide" of the Black community since they are not fit, physically at a minimum, to lead the Black community. Scripts ascribed to Black women's bodies reveal fractures and moments of solidarity as they "proscribe normative behaviors" (Johnston, Larana, & Gusfield, 1994, p. 12). Consequently, the scripts ascribed to Black women's bodies become an important factor for understanding the positionality of Black women vis-à-vis Black women. Scripts allow for an understanding of how "discreet silences" are employed, thus showing the link between silence and power—that is, how some bodies become shadows.

Shadows suggest the absence of light; however, there can be no shadows unless there is light. This captures the positionality of Black women who are affected by HIV/AIDS, domestic violence, and mental illness in the talk of Black women. The notion that these women are shadow bodies does not suggest that they are completely absent, but exist in a space in-between—a space of both proximity and separation. Some Black women are rendered *shadows* of other members in the Black community as they are often vaguely represented. They are rendered invisible or visible based on the rays of illumination that are cast on them. Finally, shadows emerge only relative to the presence of someone else; they are there but never seen for themselves. I understand shadow bodies as both an analytical and conceptual framework. Doing such allows for a better understanding of how shadow bodies provide a means of analyzing the relationship between scripts, talk, silence, and representation. In terms of a conceptual framework, shadow bodies permit us to see how silences function as a type of logic used in the rhetoric of Black women. As Becker (1995, p. 6) writes, "Each people leaves some things unsaid in order to be able to say others." This is the work of shadow bodies, through the analysis of the functioning of the *Ass* and *Strong Black Woman* metascripts, in Black women's politics, I reveal what is left unsaid so that something else may be stated.

Why the *Ass* and *Strong Black Woman* metascripts? My decision to focus on these two metascripts is multidimensional, and it grew out of Koenig (n.d., p. 3) description of metanarratives. Accordingly, metanarratives "(1) are so pervasive that they can be used in almost any situation, and (2) possess a superior credibility, in that it has moved beyond empirical scrutiny." This analysis is only meant to be suggestive, not exhaustive, so I am not proposing that these are the only two scripts ascribed to Black women's bodies. Second, in an attempt to delimit the study, I focus on two of the most prominent scripts relevant to the policy foci selected. Third, the metascripts were selected given their relationship to longstanding stereotypes about Black women, so that they would form the basis of a common point of departure; thereby permitting my theorizing to transcend disciplines and as such bolster the cross- or multidisciplinary reach of the analysis. The use of these scripts is sometimes unconsciously discussed in analyses of the functioning of stereotypes and images of Black womanhood. Consider for example, the Mammy image, which is an outgrowth of the strong woman script, and the Jezebel image, which is an outgrowth of a subscript of the *Ass* meta-script (see chapter 2). Finally, I strive to provide a model of how such research can be done.

Shadow Bodies: Black Women, Ideology, Representation, and Politics asks: How do discursive practices, both speech and silences, support and maintain hegemonic understandings of Black womanhood, thereby rendering some Black women as shadow bodies? In this sense, this work builds on the long history of Black feminists and others who critically engage questions of identity, positionality, democracy, voice, and belonging in their writings (Collins, 1991; Roberts, 1997; Smith, 1995). Mae King, in 1973, wrote on the "policy of invisibility" of Black women in the United States. King explored how stereotypes, images, and myths result in the marginalization of Black women. She concludes, "it should be emphasized that although the stereotyped images of black women are generally devoid of reality, this actuality hardly diminishes their effectiveness in achieving the political power purposes that they serve" (p. 22). K. Sue Jewell (1993) extends, in part, the argument made by King by honing in on public policy and its relationship to the often-negative construction of Black womanhood. In her analysis of how the media deploys negative images of Black women in relation to government policy and public perceptions, Jewell shows how such images perpetuate the marginalization of Black womanhood and how the use of such images in effect silence the voices of these women.

Scholars such as Ange-Marie Hancock (2004) and I (Jordan-Zachery, 2009) continue to explore this relationship between the social construction of Black womanhood, the policy process, and silence. Hancock, like Jewell, focuses primarily on what was once known as "welfare," and I consider how policy makers rely on negative images of Black women to inform not only welfare but also crime and family policies. Using two central ideas—"public identity" and "politics of disgust"—Hancock argues that the negative public identity of Black women resulted in the 1990s Welfare Act that not only marginalized and punished all poor mothers but also muted their voices and lived realities from the alleged democratic process that resulted in the reforms. My research shows how policy that is reliant on the negative construction of Black women limits the options and resources available to them.

Extant research (some of which I referenced above) has analyzed the damaging forces (or what Collins refers to as the controlling images in the matrix of domination) that undergird black women's marginality. Additionally, prior scholarship analyzes the functioning of stereotypes and culture and how they work to demobilize (or mobilize) Black women. Similarly, this work continues this by analyzing how scripts (the wellspring of stereotypes) are deployed in the framing of social issues and policy and how such deployment results in demobilization and marginalization.

There is a tendency in the literatures discussed above and in similar works to analyze Black women's positionality via a state-centered focus and to show how Black women mobilize in response to interlocking oppressive structures. What is often left underexplored is how such demobilization (or mobilization), along gender, class, and sexuality axes plays out within the Black community. This is the point of departure of this analysis.

There are some theoretical openings within Black feminist scholarship, particularly among political scientists, that begin to explore the intragroup politics of identity, meaning making, and representation within the U.S. Black community (Alexander-Floyd, 2007; Berger, 2004; R. N. Brown, 2008; Cohen 1999; Fogg-Davis, 2006; Isoke, 2013). As in the case of prior research, these researchers analyze how some populations within the Black community, and Black women specifically, become visible and how they are able to speak within Black politics. My work resonates with this particular expanding body of research. Specifically, this research aligns with Cathy Cohen's (1999) assessment of cross-cutting issues within Black politics. Like Cohen, I highlight the ways in which individuals of particular identities within the Black community are not embraced within cross-cutting issues. I extend Cohen's research by showing the mechanisms, the scripts ascribed to Black women's bodies, by which cross-cutting issues are constituted. This of course is a consistent theme among Black feminist political scientists and Black feminist researchers more generally. In addition to building on the work of Cathy Cohen, this work also builds on the theoretical underpinnings of Michele Berger's (2004) work. Berger discusses the ways in which HIV-positive women and those with AIDS are stigmatized. She looks at how intersectional stigma marks these women's bodies and traces alternative definitions of understanding agency to broaden our conceptualization of Black political participation. Similarly to Berger, I work within a theoretical framework, shadow bodies (which is similar to Berger's conception of intersectional stigma), that is designed to encompass the multiple forms of oppression—race, class, gender, and sexuality—and stigma (the ways in which people are socially defined as *nonprototypical*) to explain political behaviors. Berger shows how the social identity of women, who make up her study, was defined by intersectional stigma and how this manifested in the restriction of resources and opportunities to which these women could avail themselves. Like Berger, this research advances understandings of the ways in which differences (real and perceived) cut across an individual's identities and affect access to social resources and opportunities, including political representation.

Similarly, Ruth Nicole Brown (2008) in her work exposes ways in which Black girlhood is not embraced either by Black political scientists as a whole or by those who study girlhood in general. Brown, using the voices of girls, shows how they fight for visibility and to be heard in the context of hip-hop culture. According to Brown (2008, pp. 1–2), Black girls have to carve such space for representation because "narratives created about Black girls without our input never seem to recognize our worth, our value, and our power." Her work challenges the erasure of the study of Black girlhood and also the often imposed subjectivity of Black girls that sees them as negative and in need of "fixing" and "controlling." My research extends Brown's by analyzing how narratives result in invisibility and the muting of some populations.

Cohen, Berger, and Brown situate their work within the larger questions of identity, demobilization, mobilization, and representation. In *Shadow Bodies*, I pick up many of these themes, such as identity and mobilization, visibility and invisibility, omission and gaps, commonly discussed among Black feminist researchers and among those who critically analyze Black women's politics, across multiple disciplines. This work looks at the functioning of scripts ascribed to Black women's bodies in the framing of social issues and how such functioning renders some bodies invisible in Black politics in general and Black women's politics specifically. In the vein of this growing body of work, I explore how Black women who are HIV-positive or have AIDS, who are domestically abused, and/or who suffer from mental illness emerge as political subjects in the (political) talk of Black women. *Shadow Bodies* extends this literature by situating the process of meaning making and Black female subject formation within the policy making process. This works moves us beyond chronicling the impact of the negative construction of Black womanhood within a state-centered context and instead centers the mechanisms that result in marginalization and invisibility within the community of Black womanhood. In this work I seek to better understand what I term the intragroup performance of intersectionality as a way to understand the silences that produce some Black women as shadow bodies within Black women's politics.

I use the notion of intragroup performance of intersectionality as a means of separating this exploration from others that tend to focus on how Black women experience interlocking systems of oppression—race, class, gender, and sexuality (such as that conducted by Jordan-Zachery, 2009 or Harris-Perry, 2011)—and research that focuses on how researchers should conduct intersectional analyses (see Hancock, 2004; McCall, 2005; Strolovitch, 2007; Weldon, 2006). Additionally, this analysis while similar in nature is also different from research that considers how Black women respond to stereotypes in their political behavior (N. E. Brown, 2014a; Harris-Perry, 2011) and how public policy is influenced by stereotypes of Black women (Jordan-Zachery, 2009; Hancock, 2004). How this work differs from these, beyond its focus on the intragroup performance of intersectionality, is that it is focused on scripts and not stereotypes per se. It is somewhat easy to conflate the two—scripts and stereotypes—but there is a difference. Stereotypes, which are outgrowths of scripts, represent beliefs towards a group that are based on over generalizations and prejudgments that are applicable to all the groups' members. In contrast, scripts serve as mechanisms used to express beliefs and values that define our roles in the world and how we should "play" these roles. Scripts are learned patterns of framing and interpreting not only an individual's behavior but also the behavior of others. Consequently, scripts can work to enhance, or limit, in this case, the groups' strategies of action (see Karst 1995). Similar to Lau (2009, p. 902) I consider scripts as the "product of aggregating stereotypes."

I look at how Black women actually engage scripts in their representation of Black women and how the scripts ascribed to the body influence their behavior. Few studies use intersectionality to understand the intragroup performance of intersectionality across cross-cutting issues (those issues thought of as affecting only a subsection of the community), thus leaving us with unanswered questions, such as: How do marginalized women with "access" to power perform their intersectionality in terms of advocating on behalf of other marginalized women, particularly of their racial group? To take up this issue, I analyze how Black women in power—congressional representatives; those who write in the name of Black womanhood; Black female bloggers; and publications that construct themselves as speaking to Black women, *Essence* and *Ebony* magazines—talk about and frame these issues. Research suggests that Black congresswomen's policy deliberations are influenced by their sense of race-gender collective identity (N. E. Brown, 2014a; Smooth, 2014) and their desire to serve as a voice for the voiceless regardless of boundaries. As such, I would expect them to speak on behalf of the women who serve as a backbone of this study. I would also expect the officials to speak on their behalf, especially if others are not speaking for the women and if, for various reasons, they cannot speak for themselves. There is limited research on Black female bloggers, but from what does exists, I would also expect that this group of women would actively speak on behalf of those who have been rendered less visible in public discourses; the same is to be expected of *Essence* and *Ebony* magazines (this is explored in chapter 3). This book pushes the boundaries of intersectionality by focusing on intragroup behavior and its relationship to policymaking in particular and political behavior more broadly. This allows theorists and students of Black feminism and intersectionality, and those who study power in general, to expand our understanding of what Crenshaw (1989) refers to as political intersectionality.

My approach, therefore, focuses not only on which Black women are allowed to speak and the content of their speech, but also, and perhaps more importantly, on who is silenced or marginalized and to what extent. "To understand the true impact of a marginalized status we must search out the subtle ways in which inequalities are defined, maintained, and heightened" (Cohen, 1993, p. 60). The silences I encountered represent a subtle way in which Black women marginalize other Black women. My research reveals, among other things, that protectionist logic is a persistent feature that limits Black women's liberation efforts.

Why these three issues in particular? A quick look at the statistics reveals the answer. At first glance the data may appear dated; however, when possible I use such data in an attempt to match the time frame of the study, 1997–2007. This allows the reader a sense of the context, if only partially, of Black women's talk on these issues. Regarding HIV and AIDS, data suggest that:

- Black women represent more than a third (35 percent) of AIDS diagnoses among Blacks (Black men and women combined) in 2008; by comparison, White women represent 15 percent of AIDS diagnoses among Whites in 2008 (Kaiser Family Foundation, 2010).
- In fact, among the factors that affect health status among African Americans—such as inadequate health insurance and limited quality care— poverty appears to be a primary underlying factor and, as such, contributes to the risk for HIV infection among African American women in the South. While poverty is associated with increased risk for multiple adverse health outcomes, it is typically not directly addressed in public health interventions (Stratford, Mizuno, Williams, Courtenay-Quirk, & O'Leary, 2008, p. 10).
- Chronic poverty, residential segregation, and sex roles may combine to propel some women into the informal economy—including trading sex for commodities and for survival needs such as housing and food—and greatly influence their relationships with children and intimate partners. Some impoverished women use illicit drugs, such as crack cocaine and heroin, which greatly increases the risk for HIV/AIDS (Stratford et al., 2008, p. 11). Women and girls of color—especially Black women and girls—bear a disproportionately heavy burden of HIV/AIDS. In 2007, for female adults and adolescents, the rate of HIV/AIDS diagnoses for Black females was nearly 20 times as high as the rate for White females and nearly 4 times as high as the rate for Hispanic/Latino females (Centers for Disease Control and Prevention, 2010).

While the data are not always consistent, they hint at the fact that Black women are disproportionately affected by domestic violence (Hampton & Gelles, 1994; Rennison & Welchens, 2000). Domestic violence, according to the Black Women's Health Imperative, is the number one health issue faced by African American women (Avery, 1990). Consider the following:

- Homicide is the leading cause of death for young African American women ages 11 to 24 (Centers for Disease Control and Prevention, 1997).
- Spousal homicide rate among African Americans is 8.4 times more than for Whites (Salber and Taliaferro, 1998).
- The Office of Justice Programs reported in 1998 that rates of nonlethal intimate partner violence were higher among African American females than Caucasian females (quoted in Campbell, Sharps, Gary, Campbell, & Lopez, 2002).
- Among women, being Black, young, divorced or separated, earning lower incomes, living in rental housing, and residing in urban areas are all associated with higher rates of intimate partner victimization (Campbell et al., 2002).

The picture of Black women and mental illness seems to be the least articulated, in comparison to HIV and AIDS and even domestic abuse. Data are scant at best for understanding the complexity of Black women's experience. From what is available, it is shown that:

- Non-Hispanic Black women and girls (11 percent) report higher rates of depression than non-Hispanic White women and girls (8 percent) (U.S. Department of Commerce & Office of Management and Budget, 2011, p. 44).
- Caucasians experience depression more often, but African American and Caribbean women experience greater severity and persistence (National Alliance on Mental Illness, 2009, p. 1).
- African American women had the highest rates of schizophrenia, generalized anxiety disorder, somatization, and phobia during a one-year period. Phobia was the most frequently occurring mental disorder among African American women. With a few exceptions, African American women express the highest levels of psychological distress (Brown & Keith, 2003b, p. 25, p. 41).
- Obesity among Black and Hispanic women is significantly higher than among White women. In 2009, 11 percent of non-Hispanic White women reported being in fair or poor health, compared to 18 percent of Hispanic women and 21 percent of Black women (U.S. Department of Commerce & Office of Management and Budget, 2011, p. 40).
- Additionally, we are told that age, particularly being young; marital status (being unmarried); and socioeconomic status (lower socioeconomic status) increases Black women's vulnerability to mental illness (see Keith, 2003).

What is lacking in our data collection is how these illnesses/issues are intertwined in the lives of Black women. So for example, there is no data on Black HIV/AIDS female cases that is also aggregated by experience with domestic violence and/or mental illness. Thus, we have a vacuum for understanding the depth and breadth of how Black women are affected.

To examine these issues, I analyze discussions between 1997 and 2007 on blogs, in the speeches of Black congresswomen, and in mainstream media among Black women talking about HIV/AIDS, mental illness, and domestic violence.[1] I study the relationship between the scripting of Black women's bodies and the "Black" female response, via 18 Black congresswomen's talk—that involved analyzing the discourses of women who were in office to determine how they frame the issues and the women who are impacted (for a list of the women who inform the study, see Table A.1 of the Appendix). I also investigate the pages of *Essence* and *Ebony*, two popular magazines devoted to Black women (I choose these magazines because they are relatively comparable, as a result of their historical presence and their similar publication cycles, see chapter 3). The analysis of blogs takes place within the time frame 2006–2010 (some of the blogs existed prior to this time, but 2006 represents the first post found on the issues analyzed). Specifically, I studied 27 bloggers who identify themselves as Black women (see Table A.2 of the Appendix for the descriptions of the blogs and also for how they were selected for this study).[2] The time periods were selected to avoid peaks in terms of prevalence of issues and to reflect changes, over time, in response to social and political conditions and our knowledge advancements. I also selected this time period, primarily, as it coincides with the growth of Black female elected officials (see Bositis, 2001). I focus on the talk of these three groups as it is Black congresswomen and others with public visibility who are most saliently demonstrating the silences about HIV/AIDS, domestic abuse, and mental illness.

Combined, the 27 blogs yielded 176 data sources, inclusive of HIV/AIDS, domestic abuse, and mental illness. I do not include readers' responses to the bloggers' posts. *Essence* and *Ebony* contributed a total of 345 data sources for the time period 1997 to 2007. The search for Black female elected officials' speeches, for the same time period, yielded 528 data points among 18 women.

To unearth subjugated knowledge(s), I rely on a mixed-methods approach, which permits me to offer a deeper and more nuanced understanding of the complexity that is Black women's politics. I opted for a mixed-methods approach because it was better suited for uncovering the silences embedded in Black women's talk (Creswell and Plano Clark, 2007). If forced to "name" my approach I would use interpretive Black feminist phenomenological frame analysis. My approach fits within Black feminist research, which has common themes of visibility/invisibility and belonging/marginalization. Furthermore, it continues the tradition of analyzing Black women's "testifying" and story-telling practices (see Atwater, 2009; Broussard, 2004; Carey, 2016). This approach allows me to link theory and practice. Beyond this, it accomplishes the following: it situates Black women in their lived realities as expressed via their talk; thereby allowing us to look at their positionality; it allows for the recognition of context—history, economic, cultural, for example; it views Black women as key meaning makers.

To understand the intersection of the scripting of Black women's bodies and HIV/AIDS, domestic violence, and mental illness and the resulting silences, I employ an intersectional interpretive frame analysis, grounded in Black feminist epistemology and ontology. Intersectionality takes into account how multiple forms of oppression, race, class, gender, and sexuality inform the lived realities of Black women and women of color. Additionally, intersectionality seeks to understand and explain how these women respond—politically and culturally—to such oppression (Combahee River Collective, 1977). The approach merges intersectionality with frame analysis, a form of discourse analysis that is concerned with analyzing how an issue is defined and ultimately how the issue is addressed (or not). Gitlin's (1980, p. 7) definition of framing stresses two functions that are useful for unpacking the core ideology/ideologies and embedded meaning/meanings of the Black woman's body and the construction of social issues by Black women. The first is the function of presentation—"selecting emphasis and exclusion"—and the second is the function of interpretation—"persistent patterns of cognition, interpretation, and presentation. Symbol handlers routinely organize discourse, whether verbal or visual." This understanding of framing, integrated with interpretive phenomenological approach (IPA), allows me to describe and interpret the structure and power of a communicating text (Entman, 1993; Gitlin, 1980; Tuchman, 1978). In the case of this study, the Black woman's body serves as the communicating text. The body is used to communicate scripts ascribed to it. Jackson (2006) describes scripting in terms of writing, and theorizes the body as a canvas, which is written on or scripted by another. It is via the scripts written on the Black female body that I analyze the function of presentation and the function of interpretation. In this research, by showing the relationship between scripts and silences, I delineate how some Black women are made visible and others invisible in the Black woman's quest for equality and justice.

As intersectionality has traveled across disciplines and fields of study, it has been met with some critiques. Intersectionality has been critiqued as a theory that lacks specificity and as an approach that lacks a specified model for inquiry and analysis (see Carastathis, 2008; McCall, 2005; Nash, 2008). At the heart of these criticisms is how does one theorize, conceptualize, and measure the subjectivity of oppressed peoples. Carastathis (2008, p. 39) writes that the "intersectional model of identity fails in its two primary analytical aims: first, to render visible the experience of hyper-oppressed subjects; and second, to supplant the normative, race- and class-privileged subject of feminist theory and politics."

McCall (2005) opined that intersectionality research that relies on qualitative methodologies, such as narratives, cannot adequately capture the complexity of what she terms "intercategorical approaches to intersectionality."[3] McCall uses the typology of categories of intersectionality, especially her focus on the intercategorical approach, to make intersectionality available to social science researchers in a manner that requires minimum changes to their research methodologies. Specifically, McCall's project offers a quantitative methodological approach to "standardizing" intersectionality. This, she argues, allows the researcher to capture the complexity of identity. However, in her analysis of wage differentials, McCall's approach while explaining the gap between two groups does not fully inform us of how power relations work and how said power relations influence interactions between these two groups.

Much of the critiques of intersectionality seek to standardize it as a mode of analysis. The underlying assumption seems to be that if intersectionality is not standardized, and made somewhat static in nature, then it fails to adequately address the lived realities of minoritized and marginalized communities. What is often ignored in these critiques are that intersectionality is a standpoint theory, and that the primary concern of intersectionality is to challenge power structures. In response to the critiques of intersectionality it has been argued:

> The recasting of intersectionality as a theory primarily fascinated with the infinite combinations and implications of overlapping identities from an analytic initially concerned with structures of power and exclusion is curious given the explicit references to structures that appear in much of the early work. . . . Departing from this work, however, critiques of intersectionality's supposed reification of categories often reflect distorted understandings of identity politics. (Cho, Crenshaw, & McCall, 2013, p. 797)

If we consider the history of Black women's theorization on their lived experiences, I argue that it is apparent that Black women are not advocating for a "standardized" understanding of their experiences with power. Instead, they recognize how identity is fluid—especially vis-à-vis the state—and as such sought to theorize their experiences in a way that would challenge race-gender power structures and resulting oppressions as opposed to who or what people are (see Alexander-Floyd, 2012; Berger, 2004; Chun, Lipsitz, & Shin, 2013; Dill, 1983; Isoke, 2013; King, 1988).

Another aspect of the critique of intersectionality, levied by some empirical researchers, is that it lacks a method. Consequently it is argued that it remains unclear how intersectionality affords researchers the analytic tools for analyzing simultaneous oppressions without either reducing them to unitary categories or reverting to an additive model (Belkhir & Barnett, 2001; Bowleg, 2008). This is why I maintain that it is important to remember that intersectionality is a standpoint theory that seeks to unmask power relations. As a consequence, this suggests a methodology that privileges the experiences of the individual(s) being studied. For example, the intersecting identities of race and gender were centered in Crenshaw's initial work because they were germane to the population (and legal cases) she was analyzing. When undertaking an intersectional analysis, it is incumbent upon the researcher to determine how marginalized groups understand the structures they are confronting. To this end, Bowleg (2008, p. 323) asserts that "approaches grounded in the experiences of ordinary people, in stark contrast to traditional top-down approaches hold incredible promise for helping researchers address and respond to the many methodological challenges of intersectionality research."

My initial foray into this research journey caused much frustration. Part of my frustration stemmed from my subscription to "academic norms" and "practices" that were limiting how I could conceive and develop my argument. For example, I was initially wedded to a particular understanding of data—one has to show it for it to be valid. In essence, my approach to the study was heavily invested in what Black feminists have long challenged—the notion of knowledge production and truth (that there is only one truth which manifest in a particular understanding of data). Then one day I had a conversation with my over 80-year-old grandmother. She told me one story after another of her life. Some of these stories I had heard previously, but some were new. A few days later I had a conversation with my mother. In both instances I simply sat and listened to these two women tell their truths, speak of their challenges as Black women across time and space and their understandings of surviving and flourishing. They used songs, poetry, Biblical references, humor, and a series of discursive techniques to tell their stories. It was only after this process, inadvertent in nature, that the approach to this study emerged. Through stories Black women theorize their experiences. They bring together what seems disparate to make a way out of no way. This is exactly what I do in this work.

I start and end this analysis with stories of Black women. These stories do a type of methodological and data work that "standard" academic methods and data could not—primarily because they are not bounded by Western philosophic understandings of knowledge production. Consequently, such narratives allow me to speak to intersectionality in a way that transcends "categorical" analyses and in a manner that seems more aligned with Black feminism. Through the use of narratives I can expose the intragroup functioning of intersectionality in a manner that was not available to Black female politicians, bloggers, and *Essence* and *Ebony* magazines. I use these stories, as they offer "a way of reading inscriptions of race" (particularly but not exclusively blackness), "gender" (particularly but not exclusively womanhood), and "class in modes of cultural expressions" (Smith, 1989, p. 39). The narratives I use expose the silences that seem to be pervasive in Black women's public speech.

Given this analysis's focus on power and intragroup dynamics between Black women, I follow the understanding of intersectionality, as articulated by Black feminist and other critical scholars, that sees intersectionality as an analytic tool for understanding power dynamics in a manner that centers the lived experiences of the research subjects (see Collins, 1991; Dill & Zambrana, 2009; Lewis, 2013; Mohanty, 2003). I do this through my use of narratives, my own, my mother's, and those of the women who inspired this work. As a bridge to understanding how Black women frame and understand their experiences, I bring together these narratives, nonfiction writings, and music as a means of offering a cultural knowledge production that is grounded in Black lived experiences. I do what my grandmother and mother did to tell their stories. Narratives, told within their specific cultural context, can espouse values and beliefs, which in turn can influence the understanding and construction of individual identity and understandings of community. The approach taken in this study is grounded in the belief that reality is based on multiple perspectives and that truth is grounded in the everyday living of marginalized groups who are often muted by majority structures and processes; thus the use of songs, literature, and narratives. One implication of the study includes the "introduction" of a method/methodological approach to political science, and other disciplines, that allows for the capturing of the ambiguity, complexity, and dynamism of intersectionality.

THE BOOK'S ROADMAP

In this book, I outline a theory of black women's response to cross-cutting issues that disproportionately affect Black women. A central goal is to show how Black women confront and transform Crenshaw's understanding of political and structural intersectionality. To this end, chapter 1 situates the analysis in the larger context of Black women's political behavior. Additionally, I define what I mean by the term *silence* and why silence, in addition to speech, is worthy of analysis. Using Huckin's (2002) understanding of discreet silence, I show how Black women in their representation and interpretation of other Black women tactically deploy it. Additionally, I offer the theoretical foundation of the study, which is grounded in Black feminism, muted group theory, and body studies. The amalgamation of these theories allows me to identify scripts and explain how they function in the formation and maintenance of community, which ultimately influences representation. In chapter 2 I explore the process of scripting and investigate how the Black woman's body, individually and as a group, is scripted. I detail the characteristics of the scripts—the *Ass* script and the *Strong Black Woman* script—to show the relationship between scripting, the framing of issues, and ultimately the proposals offered to address these issues. Using scripts as an understanding of identity makers or narratives, via an interdisciplinary approach, I theorize how power is used to shape talk and silences among Black women. This theoretical approach shows how shadow bodies result from the intersection of silence and talk.

Chapter 3 serves three purposes. For one, it shows how silence, particularly discreet silence, fits into Black women's political practices. Second, the chapter seeks to offer my method for analyzing Black women's silence as part of their political praxis—it speaks to how and why I analyze the three sources of talk. The third purpose of this chapter is to show how discreet silences are analyzed. I use an intersectional interpretive frame analysis to analyze the talk and silences of these women to explain how shadow bodies are produced.

The three empirical chapters, 4–6, present the analysis of Black women's talk and silences. The central purpose of these chapters is to identify and analyze which categories of differences are employed in the talk. As such I focus on what is said as a means of showing the spaces of silence. This allows us to see how Black women make sense of HIV/AIDS, domestic abuse, and mental illness and their relationship to Black womanhood across a variety of identity markers, such as class and sexuality. Analysis of the frames enables us to determine which identities of Black womanhood become salient and which remain in the shadows. I focus on the discursive structures and rhetorical devices in these chapters, as they are an integral part of understanding how scripts influence and shape policy frames and suggestions. To this end, the analysis of the data asks the following questions:

- Do the frames employ an intersectional approach? More specifically, I ask how are constituting systems of race, gender, class, and sexuality, which produce marginal experiences and identities among those who are affected by HIV/AIDS, domestic violence and/or mental illness, recognized in the talk? And how are these systems integrated into the understanding of these social issues?
- Do Black women offer transformative suggestions on how to address the issues? Transformative approaches would critically address systemic inequalities and structural violence for example.

Combined, these questions reveal how identity intersects with representation to generate possibilities for social transformation in Black women's responses to HIV/AIDS, domestic violence, and mental illness.

In chapter 4 I analyze the talk on HIV/AIDS. I show how within the talk there exist three forms of discreet silence. These silences include: (a) who is left out, for example Black lesbians; (b) what issues are not discussed, for example structural violence and class; and (c) what types of actions are advocated for—personal responsibility versus public political action. Many of the discourses on HIV/AIDS and Black women use a language of crisis to discuss the impact of HIV/AIDS among Black women. This growing crisis threatens to take away Black women, often thought of as the backbone of the community, from the community. Yet, the Black community remains relatively silent about this epidemic.

Chapter 5 presents Black women's talk on domestic violence. I first consider how Black women's talk gives voice to Black women of different social locations. Specifically, I look at how they recognize Black women who occupy diverse social locations in terms of class and sexuality for example. Doing such allows me to excavate how the *Ass* and *Strong Black Woman* scripts influence the framing of domestic violence and its intersection with race and gender. The analysis shows that (a) there is limited talk on domestic violence, (b) the talk tends to be universal in nature, and (c) the actions suggested center on personal growth and development. These frames fail to challenge the structural violence experienced by Black women who are abused in their intimate relationships. I argue that reliance on the *Strong Black Woman* script—the protector of Black men and being able to overcome all challenges—and also failing to treat Black women as politically important—the *Ass* question subscript—results in our ability to challenge domestic violence at multiple levels. Consequently battered Black women are treated as shadows.

The taboo subject of mental illness, the central topic of chapter 6, is slowly being brought into the public sphere. First-person narratives and autobiographies (see Danquah, 1998; Taylor, 1995; T. M. Williams, 2008), and clinical and other academic treatments (Beauboeuf-Lafontant, 2009; Brown & Keith, 2003a; Cannon, Higginbotham, & Guy, 1989; Tomes, Brown, Semenya, & Simpson, 1990) have done much to address the issue of the intersection of race, class, gender, and mental illness. This chapter offers an analysis of Black women's talk to determine how they give voice to Black women of different social locations who face mental illness. In addition, I consider how this talk works to challenge normative aspects of race–gender power relations. Black women's talk, during the time period 1997–2007, on mental illness was scant. The analysis shows that the frames used by Black women were not particularly progressive and transformative. Again, I argue that this is the result of the normative behavior that results from the scripts written on the bodies of Black women. For example, Black women who suffer mental illness challenge the notion of the sacrificial/nurturing strong Black woman. These Black women are perceived as unable to function in this role and thus they are set aside in our larger conversations of justice and equality.

The purpose of chapter 7 is to show how the discreet silences discussed in chapters 4–6 manifest from the scripts ascribed to Black women's bodies. I first show how and why the scripts *Ass* and *Strong Black Woman* influence Black women's framing of HIV/AIDS, domestic violence, and mental illness. From there, I show how the *Ass* and *Strong Black Woman* scripts produce shadow bodies by demonstrating how they function (a) within groups of Black women, (b) between groups of Blacks in the larger Black community, and (c) in our practices and institutions, thereby limiting opportunities for a more democratic and inclusive Black women's politics. Focusing on how the scripts ascribed to Black women's bodies function at these various levels opens up and furthers our discussions of the intragroup performance of intersectionality. Finally, I craft an approach, grounded in intersectionality, for challenging muting and silencing among and between Black women. This allows for the movement of Black women's bodies out of the shadows, thereby allowing them to be seen and valued for who and what they are (Berger & Guidroz, 2009; Crenshaw, 1991; Hancock, 2007). By doing such, Black women are able to craft a more inclusive and democratic politics.

My goal in *Shadow Bodies* is to show how the scripts ascribed to the Black female body influence in-group politics in hopes that Black women's politics becomes more democratic. At this point, I pause to address what this book is not. For one, this book is not designed to lay blame. While I am interested in accountability for the purpose of informing our future politics, I am not interested in blaming any particular group for the fact that some bodies are not represented in our political projects. Second, this is not a project of victimhood. I recognize that Black women have been victims of multiple oppressive structures; however, I also recognize that Black women have consistently fought against these structures. Finally, this book is not a comprehensive exploration of all scripts that can be inscribed on the bodies of Black women.

Black women are "disappearing" from our political landscape. Policy makers seem minimally concerned with the experiences of Black women as they become subsumed under the universal category of "woman" (see Harris, 2010; Jordan-Zachery & Wilson, 2008). Beyond the political neglect and misuse of Black women, they are also rendered socially invisible. Indeed, a study conducted by Amanda Sesko and Monica Biernat (2010) on Black women's social visibility illustrates that Black women are often not seen. They conclude that Black women, in comparison to Black men and White men and women, overwhelmingly go unnoticed by others in a group or social setting. Given this apparent shadowing and muting of Black women (if they are not seen, then their speech cannot be heard), it is even more important that we ask: Who is speaking for Black women and how are they speaking?

1 · DIFFERENT STREAMS OF KNOWLEDGE

Theoretically Situating This Study

Anna Julia Cooper, in 1892, counseled Black women to critically articulate the complex and various ways that racism and sexism affected their lived realities. She argued:

> The colored woman of today occupies, one might say, a unique position in this country. In a period of itself transitional and unsettled, her status seems one of the ascertainable and definitive of all the forces which makes for our civilization. She is confronted by a woman question and a race problem, and is as yet an unknown or unacknowledged factor in both. (Cooper, 1995, p. 45)

Cooper's concerns remain a core theme of Black feminist thought. Central to Black feminist thought, through the ages (I am not suggesting that Black feminist thought is static) is the concern of the representation of Black women. From Cooper to Crenshaw to Alexander-Floyd and others, Black feminists have sought to render the invisible visible in an attempt to encourage a more democratic politics. These social activists and researchers examine how mutually interlocking systems of oppression—race, gender, class, and sexuality—construct and perpetuate marginal identities and experiences, and also foster opportunities for resistance within the Black community in general and Black women specifically.

This research joins a growing body of work that centers on Black women's political behavior—generally defined—that seeks to render what is invisible visible. Additionally, it represents my attempt to continue the political work of my mother—moving Black women who live at the intersection of mental illness, domestic abuse, and/or HIV/AIDS from the shadows. My mother's work was and is political. Consider Joy James's description of Black women's political behavior. According to her, "Black women have tended incredible, secluded gardens within the expansive wasteland of this dysfunctional democracy" (1999, p. 2). James, like other critical race and gender scholars, recognizes that Black women's political behavior must be contextualized and theorized in a nontraditional manner in order to capture their experiences. Literature that directly or indirectly focuses on the political behavior of the majority group tends to center traditional forms of political behavior, such as registering, voting, and monetary contributions. Traditional approaches to measure this behavior can privilege attitudinal factors such as socialization and socioeconomic factors including but not limited to education. This type of research is apt to leave Black women in the gap—where the wide spectrum of their political behaviors is not always analyzed and/or explained.

Additionally, James suggests that the American democratic process is not always accessible to, inclusive of, and representative of Black women. Even after winning the formal right to engage in the political process, Black women still find themselves marginalized. Given this, Black women have created alternative spaces within which to engage in politics (see Berger, 2004; Isoke, 2013). Traditional research can also fail to appreciate and theorize such spaces because these actions are not easily conceptualized and operationalized to fit into "standard" ways of knowing (see Christian, 1988). Consequently, traditional research can miss the political agency of Black women. So how do we begin to understand Black women's political behavior?

Extant research that centers Black women's relationship with formal politics informs us that Black women's political acts and attitudes are influenced by their social location. Gay and Tate (1998), Mansbridge and Tate (1992), Simien (2005), and Simien and Clawson (2004) speak to the influence of the intersection of gender and race on the political attitudes of Black women. Orey and Smooth (2006) show how intersectionality influences the political strategizing of elected Black women. Studies of this nature argue that interlocking identities of race, class, and gender influence Black women's political activities and behaviors.

Research that centers nontraditional political participation of Black women addresses, in part, how Black women use their voices and words to critique, challenge, and offer alternatives to their inequitable social position. Much of this scholarship focuses on African American women's literacy practices and is primarily historical in nature (focusing on women of the 19th and early 20th centuries). Most notably are Logan's *We Are Coming* (1999), McHenry's *Forgotten Readers* (2002), Peterson's *"Doers of the Word"* (1995), and Royster's *Traces of a Stream* (2000). Similar to studies on Black women's involvement with formal politics, these studies argue that although constrained by multiple oppressive structures, these women engaged literacy practices that critiqued the raced-gendered status quo. Black women rhetors such as Anna Julia Cooper, Frances Harper,

Harriet Jacobs, Ida B. Wells, Maria Stewart, Mary Church Terrell, Victoria Earle Matthews, and several others used their words as political acts.

> African American females' language and literacy practices reflect their socialization in a racialized, genderized, sexualized, and classed world in which they employ their language and literacy practices to protect and advance themselves. Working from this rhetorical situation, the Black female develops creative strategies to overcome her situation, to "make a way outa no way." (Richardson, 2003, p. 77)

Richardson (2003) further informs us that Black women employed multiple means such as storytelling and a number of verbal and nonverbal communication methods—including the manipulation of silence in their challenge to race and gender hierarchies.

The development of this knowledge of Black women's speech and silence as political is not evenly distributed across all disciplines. One discipline where growth of this type of scholarship continues to lag behind is political science. Michele Berger's (2004) *Workable Sisterhood* disrupts the more traditional studies of Black women and politics. Berger, using the concept of intersectional stigma, provides us with a different way of reading power, oppression, and speech. The women analyzed by Berger are stigmatized as a result of their experiences with HIV/AIDS and their histories as sex workers. Berger shows how they (re)construct themselves into activists and truth bearers. These modern-day women are very similar to the historical Black women who inform our analyses on Black women's discourses. They use their talk—written and oral—as radical political acts designed to challenge and replace existing inequitable positions.

Research on Black women's discourses frequently considers the social role and positioning of the physical Black female body in conjunction with the spoken/written word. We see this more often with analyses of women such as Sojourner Truth and Frances Ellen Watkins Harper (see Peterson, 1995). A norm in such analyses is to first consider how the majority (that is, Euro-Americans) reads and responds socially, culturally, politically, and economically to the Black female body, and second the response of Black women to such actions (Bennett & Dickerson, 2001; hooks, 2000; Orleck, 2005; Roberts 1997; R. Y. Williams, 2004). It has been argued that in response to such scrutiny, Black women engage in a politics of "silence" or a politics of "respectability" as a means of protecting Black female personhood (Higginbotham, 1992, 1993). In essence Black women have adopted a politics of strategic, discreet silences.

While the Black female body has been the topic of discussion of many scholarly treatises and cultural analyses, many have not explored how the Black female body functions in political representation, in the sense that it serves as a text in which power hierarchies are embedded and read and acted upon by Black women. Researchers tend to look at the female body as a recipient of actions—cultural, political, and social. To build on this body of research on the politics of Black women's talk, I focus on the intragroup reading of the Black woman's body and its relationship to their articulations/speech/discourses and silences. I explore the points of intersection between discourses of HIV/AIDS, domestic violence, and mental health and the socio-politicization of the Black female body. I focus on how social power—articulated via the body—enables subject positions that marginalize or exclude some members of the community and determines which experiences are worth talking about, how they should be talked about, and how resources should be distributed among community members.

I this chapter I offer the theoretical approach that I employ to understand the intragroup use of silence. I start by offering a brief review of what I mean by *silence*. This is followed by the presentation of the concept of intersectionality, muted group theory, and body studies—which combined, offer the theoretical framework for the study. While often treated as separate concepts and theories, I bring them together in an attempt to offer a more comprehensive understanding of silences and the resulting shadow bodies for understanding the intragroup performance of intersectionality among Black women.

UNDERSTANDING SILENCE

This analysis explores the "meaning making practices" (Halliday, 1994) of the talk on HIV/AIDS, domestic violence, and mental illness and the ways this talk is used to represent reality as well as the positioning and social roles of various Black women in the Black body politic. Existing research on meaning making among Black women tends to focus on verbal or visual language, often ignoring the silences (see Henderson, 2010; Hobson, 2012). To understand how some bodies become shadow bodies requires that I analyze the deployment of silence within the context of (a) who is speaking, (b) what is being said/talked about, and (c) what is also not being said in the discourses. Silence, like talk, is a way of managing meaning and subjectivities. As I argue, shadow bodies emerge in that space between talk and silence.

Huckin (2002) argues that the public does not always notice silence. However, the failure to notice silence does not render it powerless. Indeed rhetorical silence does ideological work by either reinforcing bias and/or prejudice in those who are reading, writing, or even listening. There exists a substantial amount of research on the general topic of silence where silence tends to be treated as metaphorical, ambiguous, or as a negative (see Bruneau, 1973; Jensen, 1973; R. L. Scott, 1972). While silence has been the subject of study in communication literature, for example, there remains an area that, while growing, is undertheorized and understudied. There is very little written on how silence can serve to communicate messages. Furthermore, research in this area tends to focus more on conversational silences, often leaving uncovered the ideological work done by textual silences. As such the methods/methodological approaches for "showing" silences, textually, is underdeveloped—after all how does one show something that does not exist particularly when there appears to be lots of words (talk) present?

As defined by Huckin (2002, p. 348) textual silence is "the omission of some piece of information that is pertinent to the topic at hand." To date, research on textual silence tends to focus on how the media omits information (see Chomsky, 1987; Jackson, 1999; van Dijk, 1986). I extend this by looking at political and cultural text to show how silence is manifest. Within communicative structures there exists (and it is much needed) that which is made explicit and what is not. Consequently, silence should not be viewed as a pause or absence of communication. Silence, instead, should be understood as serving a functional role and thus as embodying its own meaning and interpretive value (see Jaworski, 1993; Tannen & Saville-Troike, 1985). Silences become evident when the reader, as in the case of this study, (re)constructs what is said by focusing on who is speaking and the context within which the speech is occurring. Thus, silences have to be culturally and situationally read in the sense that the person (re)constructing the silence has the templates (the scripts, discussed in chapter 3, are the templates) for understanding not only what is spoken but that which goes unspoken.

In my attempt to bring to light what might not be easily seen, I rely on Huckin's (2002) typology of "textual silences." This typology offers the following understandings of silence: (1) *speech act silences* are used as a form of communicative import, but only if the reader or listener, because there is a shared set of expectations, is able to arrive at the intended understanding; (2) *presuppositional silences* involve the speaker or writer not stating what is assumed to be common knowledge, but is instead easily recoverable from context; (3) *discreet silences* are used as a means for avoiding the mention of sensitive subject, resulting from issues of tactfulness, confidentiality, or taboo topics; (4) *genre-based silences* result from the norms and conventions of a particular genre; and (5) *manipulative silences* involve the deliberate actions to conceal relevant information from the reader/listener. I focus primarily on discreet silences in this research and argue that this form of silence is the result of the taboo nature of HIV/AIDS, domestic violence, and mental illness and their perceived negative reflection on Black womanhood.

THEORETICAL ORIENTATION

Silence in relation to the scripts ascribed to Black women's bodies and their articulations of policy issues is not extensively studied in political science. Literature on agenda setting, the process by which social issues are brought to the public and the policy agenda, suggest that there are a number of factors that influence this process (Bachrach and Baratz, 1963; Baumgartner and Jones, 2002; Gaventa,

1980; Fischer, 2003; Kingdon, 1984; Lukes, 1974; Schneider and Ingram, 1993, 1997; Stone, 1988; Strolovitch, 2007). These researchers, among others, suggest that the movement of an issue to the public and policy agenda is influenced by factors such as resource differentials and power imbalances for example. Crenson (1971, pp. 177–178) posits that "'victims' of political power may remain politically invisible—indeed, invisibility may constitute their response to the power of non-decisionmaking." Crenson, like E. E. Schattschneider (1960, 1975), argues that there is a "mobilization bias" that results in the policy concerns of the weak being left out or ignored in politics and policy deliberations. While this well-respected body of literature helps us to understand the non-decision making and the faces of power, it does not allow us to fully understand how multiple-identity marginalized groups, as opposed to "singly marginalized" groups (Baird, 2010) are treated in politics and policy decision making. Given this limit, Karen Baird (2010, p. 10) asks, "what about black women?" She then claims that "complex population constructions for intersectionally marginalized groups and the influence of such construction on the policymaking process need further research and specification." She suggests using intersectionality, as a means of enhancing the above theorizing, to better understand how issues affecting multiple-identity marginalized groups make it onto public and policy agendas.

Theories tend to be general and do not consider multiple identities and roles, thereby making their applicability to Black women a challenge (Howard-Hamilton, 2003). Additionally, the empirical literature on Black women's intragroup talk and silence is scant. The difficulty of "measuring" silence and its relationship to demobilization and representation may, in part, account for this dearth of analysis. Given this, I offer a framework that amalgamates a number of theories to understand the silences around HIV/AIDS, domestic violence, and mental health (all cross-cutting issues). My theoretical orientation, while drawing, in general, on the above-referenced literatures on agenda setting and the exercise of power, is grounded in Black feminist studies (particularly intersectionality), muted group theory, and body studies. While these theories have been developed across various disciplines and might not have a single unified theoretical understanding, they are particularly well suited for this analysis. While developed in fields such as Black women's studies, anthropology, philosophy, and feminist studies, these theories have achieved interdisciplinary appeal. These various theories are complimentary as at the core of each is a concern with the exercise of power. Individually and collectively the theories are concerned with how power is used to subjugate, silence, marginalize, and control some groups while privileging others. This interdisciplinary approach to the study of the intragroup performance of inter-sectionality allows for the identification of how talk and silences are employed "to negotiate [raced and] gendered cultural identities, affirm sisterhood, build community, and confront, demystify and overcome oppression" (Houston &

Davis, 2002, p. 12). As such they are well positioned to explain how some Black women become shadow bodies.

I start with a singular exploration and review of the theories and highlight their interrelatedness. However, I recognize that none of these theories are "settled." For example, there is much debate on how to approach an intersectional study (see Dahmoon, 2008; McCall, 2005). Theorizing on the body and its role in politics, social policy, and the body politic is not free of contention. I do not, for example, address the mind/body duality proposed by Cartesian thought or Judith Butler's (1990, 1993) challenge to this duality. My goal is not to settle these debates but to use the various theoretical developments to explore how Black women's bodies influence their talk and silence on specific social issues. Instead, I recognize the fluidity and interrelationship between the mind and body (see Sklar, 1994). Furthermore, the social and cultural environments influence what is done to the body and how the body responds to these actions.

The Black feminist contribution to my theoretical orientation stems from two interlocking components that characterize Black feminist thought: Black feminist standpoint theory and the recognition of the diversity of Black women's experiences. First, there is the notion that Black women share a common experience of being Black and female that affords them a peculiar view, or standpoint, of the world and a similar experience of oppression. Since the early 1800s (if not earlier), Black women have recognized and eventually named their experiences with race, class, and gender as an intersectional identity. The Combahee River Collective again articulated this identity and its impact on the bodies of Black women in 1977. In 1989, Kimberle Crenshaw named Black women's experiences with multiple systems of oppression as "intersectionality" (Crenshaw, 1989).

Crenshaw's theoretical understanding, in part, speaks to political and structural intersectionality. Political intersectionality reflects the different (and sometimes conflicting) political agendas of the various groups to which an individual may belong, or within which they "define" their identity. Scholars most often note the challenges Black women face, having been left out of the women's movement and ignored in the modern Black freedom struggle. I think of political intersectionality in terms of how Black women craft their political responses to being rendered invisible and silenced. Such political strategizing is in response to the Euro-American oppression of Black women and is also a function of the Black community's internal structuring. I recognize that these two processes are distinct, but intimately connected.

Structural intersectionality centers the operation of systems and structures in society that result in the marginalization of individuals—in terms of their social needs and legal status. Crenshaw (1991, p. 358) offers the following claim to demonstrate the functioning of structural inequality: "Intervention strategies based solely on the experiences of women who do not share the same class or race will be of limited help," because individuals operate from (and are treated differently in) different social locations that are influenced by race, gender, class, and sexuality identities. Additionally, Crenshaw envisions Black women as acting upon and against what Collins (1991) refers to as interlocking systems of domination. Barbara Smith (1995, p. 260) states, "The concept of the simultaneity of oppression is the crux of a black feminist understanding of political reality." For Crenshaw, both forms of intersectionality influence the lived realities of Black women in multiple and diverse ways.

The second component of intersectionality asserts that Black women have different and divergent experiences with multiple systems of oppression (Collins, 1986; Combahee River Collective, 1977; Lorde, 1984). Toni Cade Bambara (1970) poignantly describes Black women as

> A college graduate. A drop-out. A student. A wife. A divorcee. A mother. A lover. A child of the ghetto. A product of the bourgeoisie. A professional writer. A person who never dreamed of publication. A solitary individual. A member of the Movement. A gentle humanist. A violent revolutionary. She is angry and tender, loving and hating. She is all these things—and more. (p. xviii)

As suggested by Bambara, there is indeed no one understanding of Black womanhood. Consequently, one would expect a divergence in needs and possibly different expressions of these needs.

Intersectionality in theory recognizes the heterogeneity of Black womanhood and that there is no universal Black woman politics. Theorists such as Angela Davis and bell hooks realize that there is a danger in essentializing differences within Black womanhood. Yet, in some of our analyses on Black womanhood, there is a tendency to treat Black women in a monolithic manner, thereby failing to recognize the nuances of intersectionality. This is due, in part, to the types of issues that are analyzed when seeking to determine how, for example, elected Black women engage in politics. Our analyses tend to focus on issues such as affirmative action, and not cross-cutting issues such as AIDS that tend to disproportionately and directly affect some Black women who "are the least empowered" (Cohen, 1999, p. 9).

Furthermore, our analyses tend to focus on out-groups' use of oppressive structures while ignoring in-groups' use of oppressive structures. Audre Lorde (1984, p. 187) encourages us to deal not only with "the external manifestations of racism and sexism," but also "with the results of those distortions internalized within our consciousness of ourselves and one another." Our overreliance on consensus issues and failing to see the heterogeneity within Black womanhood in our analyses of Black women suggest that Black women see themselves as speaking for the voiceless (Carroll, 2002; Fenno, 2003). While these analyses are invaluable in demarginalizing the lives of Black women, they leave us in a theoretical vacuum. Unfortunately, we know very little about how Black women, when faced with cross-cutting issues, represent other Black women. This is where muted group theory can prove useful.

Muted group theory is helpful as a starting place for "theorizing from the margins" (Orbe, 2005, pp. 65–66). The theory is designed to critically analyze the experiences of marginalized groups, particularly women, whose voices and experiences often are silenced. However, being muted should not be conflated with silence. Instead, muting should be seen as the hindrance of a marginalized group's communicative outlets and abilities at the hands of those in power. In the process of muting, some groups are denied representation, as they are limited in their ability to speak and to choose how they want to speak (see Berger, 2004; R. N. Brown, 2008). Muted groups, through the process of socialization, learn to follow the communication norms and engage in actions that perpetuate their own muting.

Central to muted group theory is the assumption that marginalized groups, using the language of Black feminists, have a different standpoint relative to dominant groups. These marginalized groups tend to see the world differently because of the inequitable distribution of access, goods, and services (Berger, 2004; Dates & Barlow, 1990; Isoke, 2013). This is reminiscent of Crenshaw's understanding of structural intersectionality (if we were to apply muted group theory to the Black woman's experience). Like intersectionality, muted group theory suggests that marginalized groups' perceptions and interpretations of reality are influenced by the dominant groups' constructions. This influence works, as argued by Kramarae (1981), because each society constructs "template structures," which are a series of beliefs, values, and opinions that collectively define a particular worldview. In turn, these template structures provide members of society with the "language," images, and symbols that are then used to construct and understand reality (see E. Ardener, 1975). The body serves as one site on which these templates are written and recorded.

In body studies, a Foucauldian approach to understanding the body in society suggests that discipline and social regulation are inscribed on the body. These inscriptions are then used to produce the "norm"—a norm that can be used to mute marginalized groups vis-à-vis the scripts ascribed to the body. Foucault (1977) considered how biopower, employed and deployed through institutions such as the prison, is exerted on the bodies of individuals. Biopower is used for categorization purposes to demarcate notions of belongingness and otherness. Scripts often are used to facilitate this process. Bodies are used to classify individuals along categories of sane/insane, diseased/nondiseased, and deserving/ undeserving, and are subjected to evaluative regimes. Categorization becomes a part of the state's apparatus for the monitoring and surveillance of individuals. While Foucault focuses on the use of biopower at the state level, I utilize his theorizing to explain how this process occurs within groups. It is applicable because some groups' members, using scripts, directly or indirectly, can exert power over other members of their own group (see Feagin & Sikes, 1994; Guy-Sheftall, 1995; Harper, 1996) and "imprison" them as a result of identity markers of belongingness. Their talk and silences, which are outgrowths of the scripts and other factors, is but one means used to deny some members representation within the larger group.

Building on Foucault's analysis of the relationship between power and the human body, critical feminist and Black feminist scholars such as Collins (1991) and Gatens (1996) and others such as Carey (2016) and Spillers (2003) argue that the body is important not only as a site of knowing—in the sense of understanding power dynamics, but also as a site of resistance—in terms of resisting the same power that is exercised against it. Furthermore, these scholars argue that social policy and politics recognize and treat bodies differently. So, for example, disabled bodies are treated differently relative to able bodies. Black female bodies are treated differently in comparison to White female bodies and Black male bodies.

Identities are inscribed on bodies and can be read from bodies. Inscriptions hold gender, race, class, and sexuality scripts. As articulated by Judith Butler (1993), the matter of bodies is mediated by discourse and is therefore comprehensible only through that mediation. An analysis of scripts can make visible the extent to which socioeconomic and political processes are predicated on the dichotomy of the "norm" and the "other." The scripts, as they serve as template structures, become useful in normalizing practices in relation to race, gender, class, and sexuality. Scripts are used to determine the distributions of benefits as they influence how issues are talked about, if at all. Additionally, scripts can serve a disciplinary role. With regard to social policy, it has been argued that sexuality, for example, is used as a form of discipline (see Carabine, 1998; Pharr, 2000).

Black women's bodies are sites through which knowledge about race, class, sexuality, and gender and their intersections are structured. Dorothy Roberts (1997) articulates how knowledge about race and gender are inscribed on Black women's bodies when she argued,

> America has always viewed unregulated Black reproduction as dangerous. For three centuries, Black mothers have been thought to pass down to their offspring the traits that marked them as inferior to any white person. Along with this biological impairment, it is believed that Black mothers transfer a deviant lifestyle to their children that dooms each succeeding generation to a life of poverty, delinquency, and despair. A persistent objective of American social policy has been to monitor and restrain this corrupting tendency of Black motherhood. (p. 8)

Black women's bodies are used to determine the distribution of goods and services and to determine categories of worth. Consequently, the Black female body, per scripts ascribed to it, is key to understanding the performance of intersectionality—in terms of how community is constructed both between and within groups.

Black feminist theorizing, muted group theory, and body studies are useful for exploring Black women's intragroup practices, vis-à-vis the body, of intersectionality. Muted group theory, although originating in anthropological studies of women (E. Ardener, 1978) and later applied to communication studies (Kramarae, 1981; Orbe, 1998), allows for further exploration of Black feminists' articulations on differences among Black women. Furthermore, it allows us to analyze how cross-cutting issues may result in the muting of some Black women's voices because "the struggle over which differences matter and which do not is neither an abstract, nor an insignificant debate among women" (Crenshaw, 1991, p. 11).

The amalgamation of body studies and muted group theory with Black feminist theory allows for a more nuanced understanding of the production of shadow bodies. In a Foucauldian sense, Crenshaw and other critical Black feminists demonstrate the relationship between intersectionality and the processes of inclusion and exclusion. The use of power to include or exclude those from the community is exercised even among the marginalized. The exercise of this power centers the negotiation of gender, race, class, and sexuality. Again, linking this to the body, I show how the *Ass* and *Strong Black Woman* scripts play a role in this dynamic process of negotiating inclusion and exclusion. The scripts, once read from Black women's bodies, serve as the templates for the talk or silences on HIV/AIDS, domestic abuse, and mental illness. It is through this process of reading these scripts that shadow bodies are created and represented. This process can be seen in how Black women talk (both the silences and the spoken word) about some issues in terms of who is privileged and how. These scripts influence interactions within the group of Black women and within the Black community at both an individual and structural level. This is not to suggest that these scripts are always read in the same way over time, or that there is only one way for them to be read.

2 · INSCRIBING AND THE BLACK (FEMALE) BODY POLITIC

The scripting of the Black female body is a relational, dynamic process. It is relational in the sense that the Black female body is scripted relative to Whites, Black men, and other Black women. Yancy (2008a) asserts that

> the meaning of Blackness is constituted and configured (relationally) within a semiotic field of axiological difference, one that is structured vis-à-vis the construction of whiteness as the transcendental norm. To say that whiteness is deemed the transcendental norm is to say that whiteness takes itself to be that which remains the same across a field of difference. (p. 3)

Historically, Black women's bodies have been scripted by Europeans' gaze on "the dark continent" (see Morgan, 1997). Europeans scripted Black women's bodies as different, highly sexual, and the "other." Their early gazes laid the discursive groundwork for more current scripting and readings of Black women's bodies, which signifies a particular notion of gendered Whiteness. Blackness relative to Whiteness is often viewed as "other," as negative, and as subhuman. The Black body is racialized in a manner that upholds and perpetuates a specific racial and gender ideology. Therefore, the scripts inscribed on the Black male body and White male body can differ, as is the case with scripts inscribed on the Black male and Black female bodies.

Black women's positionality, via the body, is not only scripted relative to Whites, but also relative to Black men and other Black women. Black female identity is also a result of the construction of Black patriarchal norms and practices. Additionally, the Black female body is scripted in relation to other Black women—this offers intrascripting and reading processes. Both processes can produce silences around some issues and self-censorship. While I recognize that out-group and in-group scripting processes are not always neatly separated, my analysis centers the in-group scripting and reading processes. Since scripts also reflect a Black–Black dialectic, it is equally important to offer a critical analysis of this scripting and reading process from an in-group perspective (see Lorde, 1984). The internalization of scripts can result in the creation of "other" vis-à-vis Blackness, or what Cohen (1999) refers to as secondary marginalization. Consequently, intragroup scripting and reading processes can result in some Black women becoming shadow bodies relative to other Blacks.

Such relational scripting reflects power structures that are deployed to situate what on the surface appears to be the "same" body—the Black woman. Because scripting is ideologically driven and is embedded in hegemonic discourses, the process contributes to the claim that the Black woman's body is a highly contested site on which various meanings are projected and interpreted. As noted by Jacqueline Bobo (1995, p. 36), "fictionalized creations of black women are not innocent; they do not lack the effect of ideological force in the lives of those represented in that black women are rendered as objects and useful commodities in a very serious power struggle" (emphasis in original). These creations of Black women, what I refer to as scripts, determine who can talk and set the rules for how issues are discussed and what actions can be taken. In the context of Black women, scripts allow for the creation and maintenance of racialized-gendered boundaries.

As such, the scripts ascribed to Black women's bodies exposes what Yeatman (1990) terms the "politics of discourse"—a fight over definitions of social issues and notions of belonging. By recognizing the politics of discourse, we are better able to "explore the linkages between discourse, ideology, and power" (Fairclough, 1993, p. 135). Using Black feminist theory, and Spillers, Foucault, and Barthes's understanding of the functioning of text, signs, and power, I consider the relationship between discursive texts, ideology, and representation. I present two dominant scripts ascribed on Black women's bodies that employ the politics of discourse. First, there is the metanarrative script of the *Ass*. This script is actually a compilation of three subscripts—the *physical ass*, a *piece of ass* (sexual relations), and, borrowing from Ralph Ellison (1995), the *ass question*—which focuses on issues of democracy and belongingness. The second script is one of the *Strong Black Woman*—this is both externally and internally inscribed onto Black women's bodies, and over time has resulted in the muting and silencing of Black women. Similar to the *Ass* script, there are three (at least) subscripts that constitute this larger *Strong Black Woman* script: *physical strength, sacrificial/ nurturing,* and *spiritual/supernatural*. These metascripts are used to show how Black women, via the discourses used by Black women, become shadow bodies.

This chapter lays out the understanding of the *Ass* and *Strong Black Woman* scripts. I start by presenting a brief review of the process of scripting and Black-gendered corporeal inscription. This is followed by the description of the two metascripts. My analysis at times calls upon cultural representations—both literature and music—to explore how the scripts function. The selected works provide fertile ground upon which to grapple with the central question explored in this analysis: How do discursive practices, both speech and silence, support and maintain, hegemonic understandings of Black womanhood, thereby rendering some Black women as shadow bodies? Although I rely on these various works, I also recognize that they are not necessarily representative of their genres.

THE PROCESS OF SCRIPTING

Scripting involves inscribing a set of meanings onto the body (see Foucault, 1984; Jackson, 2006). As Jackson argued (2006, p. 12), "It should also be understood that scripting, as a paradigm, is not just about stereotypes and negative images, it is about how the treatment of Black bodies as commodities has persisted for hundreds of years and continues today." Although Jackson focuses on the Black masculine body, his understanding of scripting is relevant to my analysis. I build on his work by using Black feminist theory, muted group theory, and body studies to analyze and explain the scripting of the Black feminine body. In this study, scripting is understood as the process of the transformation of the body into discursive text, to which signs and stereotypes can then be applied for the purpose of assigning meaning.

As Grosz (1994, p. 46) explains, "The body functions almost as a 'black box' in this account: it is acted upon, inscribed, peered into, information is extracted from it and disciplinary regimes are imposed on it." The body serves as a discursive text and the scripts (what I refer to as the *Ass* script and the *Strong Black Woman* script) evoke particular modes of narrative framing by the public—that is, they offer identity narratives. It is worth noting that I am not necessarily concerned with the sources/origins of these scripts—that requires a different project. Both the *Ass* and the *Strong Black Woman* scripts are influenced by racial and gender ideologies, and they exert influence on social and political relations. These scripts provide the template structures that inform how Black women talk about HIV/AIDS, domestic violence, and mental illness. Scripts allow us to ask and explore what types of actions are likely to be promoted.

BLACK-GENDERED CORPOREAL INSCRIPTION

Scripting is a complex, dynamic, cultural, political, and social process, and individuals and/or institutions can employ different scripts depending on their purpose (Jackson, 2006). The scripts and the meanings they assign to the Black female body have a long and multifaceted history. Europeans' early gaze on Black women's bodies resulted in particular scripts of not only her total body, but also its individual parts. The Black woman's lips, nose, buttocks, and other body parts were scripted to result in the narrative of the Black woman as "other" and "non-woman." Early discursive texts of the Black woman's body suggested that she was "ugly," "exotic," "different," "sexualized," "deviant," and "dangerous" (Collins, 1991; Wallace-Sanders, 2002a). In her analysis of early European explorers' writings on Africa, Jennifer Morgan (1997, p. 191) posits that the writers "turned to black women as evidence of a cultural inferiority that ultimately became encoded as racial difference." Guy-Sheftall (2002, p. 24) further supports Morgan's claim in her assertion that "within the penetration of Europeans into sub-Saharan Africa during the fifteenth century, memories of travelers characterized African women as grotesque, dangerous creatures who engaged in 'deviant' sexual behavior." The gazes of these early European travelers, on the uncovered body of the African woman, resulted in a script of difference—difference in terms of sexuality, human belongingness (i.e., the notion that Africans were animalistic), and level of civility (see Jewell, 1993 for an in-depth discussion on the sexualization of the Black woman). The early scripts of Black women's bodies were "legitimized" through "scientific" evidence (see Gilman, 1985) and continue to be used in current interactions—social and political—in modern times (Jordan-Zachery, 2009). As I mentioned earlier, Blacks can internalize this process and they can then use these scripts to organize their "internal" communities and decide who is included and excluded. Additionally, because the scripts can be inverted and challenged by African Americans, it is possible for scripts to be (re)imagined and used differently.

SCRIPTING AND READING THE BLACK FEMALE BODY

My approach borrows from Black feminist theory and politics, from Foucault's (1972) understandings of discursive formations, from Barthes's (1972) conceptualization of popular ideology, and from Spillers's (2003) concept of pornotroping. Black feminists seek to theorize and address the various manifestations of intersecting oppressive structures and ideologies. Consequently, Black feminists have concentrated much of their efforts on exposing, challenging, and dismantling dominant structures and ideologies that result in the marginalization of Black women (Combahee River Collective, 1977). Some Black feminists and critical scholars argue that social power is negotiated through the use of language, narratives, and representations; that is, images, myths, and icons (see Alexander-Floyd, 2007; Collins, 1991; Morrison, 1992). Scripting, which provides a means for understanding, projecting meanings, and categorizing, is an integral part of the marginalization of Black women, as it influences how groups (both in- and out-groups) interact with Black women.

The scripting of Black women's bodies embodies both Foucault's and Barthes's understanding of the functioning of text, signs, and power. As argued by both Foucault and Barthes, there is a relationship between language and signs, and ideology and power. Foucault suggests there is a network of statements that work to create what is meaningful. In an analysis of the network of statements, one considers the organization of the collection of texts with respect to each other. Statements, as described by Foucault (1972), are usually unspoken theories about the nature of things and function as the necessary and implicit starting points for framing and constructing an issue. Over time, statements—that is, the background assumptions used to interpret and react to situations and others—become part of an established and naturalized way of speaking. According to Barthes (1972), texts are not simply a representation of the world. Instead, texts are a system of signs in which meanings are generated by the interplay of these signs. Barthes proposed that language cannot be separated from the structures of ideology and power. He suggested that signs can express a number of connotations, which are dependent on the processes, conventions, and expectations of the society within which the sign and image are generated. In other words, signs are ideologically driven. Ideology serves to normalize and naturalize what are human constructions. Additionally, ideology can limit challenges to what is perceived as normal. Consequently, power relations in society are obscured and often hidden (see Eagleton, 1991).

Hortense Spillers's notion of pornotroping shows how signs and symbols function in relation to the Black woman's body. As used by Spillers (2003), *pornotroping* refers to the "othering" of Black women and girls' bodies. This "othering" is the result of the production, reproduction, circulation, and maintenance of myths that are superimposed on Black women's bodies through signs, symbols, significations, and representations. These myths, as Spillers argues, as they are transported via a variety of messages and representational codes, can become "reality," thereby producing structures of meaning that maintain and perpetuate Black women and girls' oppression. However, Spillers informs us that while pornotropia is powerful, it is not completely and fully determining as individuals can exercise their response(s) to such.

Using Black feminist theory, muted group theory, body studies, Foucault's understanding of text, Barthes's theory on signs and Spillers's concept of pornotroping, I suggest that the Black woman's body is written on, figuratively, in a way that represents a dominant ideology of its value and functioning in society. The body, in this analysis, is considered a text, thereby allowing for a reading. Scripts are inscribed on individual bodies and on the collective community. The Black female body functions as "a site of rhetorical wealth" that "inhabits a social and discursive universe within which she is constantly named, always already interpellated" (Yancy, 2008b, p. 9). As discussed here, my primary focus is on the scripting of the community of collective Black female bodies. I now turn my attention to the two metascripts: the *Ass* script and the *Strong Black Woman* script.

THE *ASS* SCRIPT: THE METANARRATIVE

While it isn't humongous, per se, it is a solid, round, black, class-A boo-tay. Try as Michelle [Obama] might to cover it with those Mamie Eisenhower skirts and sheath dresses meant to reassure mainstream voters, the butt would not be denied. . . . Here was one clear signifier of blackness that couldn't be tamed, muted or otherwise made invisible. (Kaplan, 2008)

The butt, the buttocks, boo-tay, ass, derrière, or whatever name it is given, often serves as a metaphor, indicating what or who is valued or rejected by society. The value given to the derrière can vary between cultures and among ethnic groups and over time. For example, First Lady Michelle Obama's behind is used to suggest a form of racial pride and authenticity. For Kaplan, a Black woman, the size of Michelle Obama's behind is viewed and valued as a challenge to standard (White) beauty norms—it is something to celebrate. This, in part, is a result of the relative absence of Black women from mainstream media and Black women's intragroup valuing of body types that do not fit the mainstream understanding of "beauty" and "normalcy" (see Gentles and Harrison, 2006; Harrison 2003)

The Black woman is reduced to her buttocks—a singular part of her body—that is used for selling, viewing, and, as I argue below, to determine her belongingness. The *Ass* script is multidimensional. It involves the physical—the derrière, the private—sexual relations, and the public—notions of citizenship, community, and belonging.[1] From Saartjie Baartman, the so-called Hottentot Venus, to tennis phenomenon Serena Williams, the Black woman's derrière has been part of the European gaze. From 1810 to well after her death in 1816, Baartman, of South African descent, was displayed in London and later Paris for what was considered her "freakish" buttocks and genitalia. Although separated by the passage of time, Serena Williams's buttocks also serve as a sign of difference among the tennis elite (see Douglas, 2002, n.p.). "The attention to and criticisms of Serena Williams's body . . . call unabashed attention to her generously-sized backside, thus inviting comments such that sexiness was "lewd" and "obscene" (Hobson, 2003, p. 88). Both Saartjie and Serena signify the fascination with and obsession over the Black woman's derrière—in the physical sense. They also signify the relationship between gender, race, and sexuality. Saartjie Baartman became a symbol of debased Black sexuality and a marker of racial differences among Europeans. The Black woman's buttock for Europeans, is not necessarily a sign of beauty and femininity. Notions and representations of femininity are the result of the dominant culture's values and convey "powerful, if subtle, racist messages that confirm not only cultural difference, but also cultural superiority" (Ware, 1992, p. 14).

Within the Black community, Hobson (2003) and Springer (2008) suggest that Black women's derrières are viewed as a site of contestation, a protest against

European notions of beauty and femininity. The Black woman's buttock is often celebrated in popular culture in songs such as "Baby Got Back" (by Sir Mix-a-Lot), "Da Butt" (performed by E.U. as a part of the sound track to the movie *School Daze*), and Alison Hind's "Roll It Gal" (a Barbadian calypso song). In the song "Da Butt," E.U. suggests that (Black) women's behinds are amazing, in a positive sense, and are indeed sexy. In the words of the all-female singing group, Destiny's Child, the Black woman's derrière is "Bootylicious." Alison Hinds encourages women to roll it (a type of dance) in an effort to show strength and resilience. Durham (2012, p. 43) writes that the booty "represents racial and class differences for Black women." This is the case because the "hip hop booty has been reassigned to working class Black women specifically." (Durham, 2012, p. 41) Durham's analysis shows how the booty fractures the Black community as it serves to not only demark class boundaries but also morality boundaries. Such demarcations occur since "lower-class" or "ghetto" women associated with a particular type of booty are also simultaneously linked to a particular type of sexuality that does not align with middle-class Black respectability Thus, while recognizing the subversion of this sign in Black culture, Collins (2004, p. 129) asserts it is important to recognize how "objectifying Black women's bodies turns them into canvases that can be interchanged for a variety of purposes." Human beings, when they are reduced to body parts, are then devoid of a mind, of emotions, and of feelings. Thus, the individual is not necessarily viewed for their humanity. Below, I explore three subscripts that make up the larger meta-narrative of the *Ass* script. These subscripts—the *physical ass*, the *piece of ass*, and the *ass question*—work to dehumanize Black women both within and outside of the Black community.

Subscript 1: The Physical Ass

In various cultural productions, the Black female body is often reduced to the sum of its parts. As needed, her lips, breasts, hips, and derrière have been used to market diamonds and other commodities. In the magazine *Complex* (December 2006/January 2007), there is a six-page pictorial titled "Black Diamond" that features the model Jessica White. The pictorial depicts this Black woman "wearing" diamond-encrusted jewelry. In the majority of the pictures, she is clad in a two-piece swimsuit with her breasts exposed and typically, her legs spread open. The final picture partially depicts the model's body. On display are her lower back, buttocks, and the top part of her thighs. She is posed in what Durham (2012) refers to the "backwards gaze." Accordingly, the backwards gaze is pornographic as it "frames the backside as an erogenous zone of racial difference complementing the breast as a signifier of gender difference for Black women" (Durham, 2012, p. 38).

Furthermore, White is clad in a pair of black thongs and lying on rocks; strategically placed on her buttocks is a diamond-encrusted snake. Once again, the

Black woman is reduced to her derrière, which is displayed for the viewers' pleasure. The shot of White's butt is center stage, displayed for consumption in and of itself. The symbolism of this picture is astounding. It brings to memory the public display of Saartjie Baartman (the "Hottentot Venus") whose buttocks and genitalia, as mentioned earlier, were paraded for the amusement of European audiences. It also brings to mind images of tennis player Serena Williams. While Serena is engaged in a tennis match, the cameraperson often presents rather tight shots of her derrière. This is in contrast to her White counterparts who are usually captured in full-body shots or the public is given a view of a close shot of their faces. The face shot, I assume, is to provide the audience with the opportunity to gaze at the intense concentration and focus of the White tennis player. Like her sister, Venus's derrière is also incorporated into the spectatorship process of tennis. For example, in the 2010 French Open, "When Venus Williams served Sunday in the first round of the French Open, photographers were down on the ground, getting as low as possible to get pictures up her dress . . . and plenty of people sitting behind her when she served and her dress flew up, were giggling and gasping" (Couch, 2010). It should be noted that Venus Williams was wearing flesh-toned shorts. In this gaze of Black women's behinds, there is an implicit and sometimes explicit notion of an alien body—something to be stared at and giggled over. While viewed as an alien body, primarily by Whites, it is simultaneously used to evoke erotic pleasure—a chance to look at the "forbidden fruit" of Black flesh. These women, across time and space, are reserved for male erotic pleasure. Consequently, there is a form of visual objectification of Black women.

Beyond the use of the public display of the Black woman's buttocks to sell goods and for entertainment purposes, the use of the Black woman's derrière, covered in a snake, signifies a particular type of sexuality (Black Diamond 2006–2007). There are biblical undertones to such a pose as it brings to mind the story of Eve and the Garden of Eden. So, this woman is portrayed as a temptress and as sinful (she is working with the snake, the "devil"). Thus, this pictorial reifies the belief of the debased, sexualized Black woman as it brings together a particular ideology of race, gender, morality, and sexuality. One sees this notion of debased Black female sexuality displayed in music videos with Black performers. Critics of such cultural productions suggest that the various discourses evident in hip-hop culture work to reproduce dominant and distorted ideologies of Black women's sexuality (hooks, 1992; Morgan, 1997; Perkins, 1996). For example, women are told to "drop it like it's hot" and women are shown shaking their derrières, usually for the pleasure of the males depicted in music videos featuring what Perkins (1996) refers to as "booty rap." As defined by Perkins (1996, p. 24), booty rap is "characterized by an obsession with sex and perverted eroticism, visually backed by scantily clothed women mimicking sex and sometimes actually performing it on stage." For some artists the deployment of a debased, hypersexual

Black woman is used to represent these women as "bitches" and "hoes" ready to get their "freak on."

Black women, through their behinds, are being used as a part of a larger voyeuristic exploit that commodifies Black women's bodies and devalues their humanity. I wholeheartedly recognize that there exist, simultaneously, a number of discourses on the issue of sexuality, race, and gender. However, while it is celebrated, there is a danger in reducing a Black woman's body to her ass for the amusement of others. The buttock, while used for entertainment, erotic fantasies, and selling goods, has been simultaneously employed to pathologize and denigrate Black women.

Subscript 2: A Piece of Ass—Sexuality, Power, and Private Matters

The Black woman, through the *Ass* script, is read as a sexual object. She becomes a simple possession to create desire, entertain, and serve as a source of pleasure and as a means of managing/exerting racialized patriarchy. Accordingly, "For far too many Black men, all that seems to be left to them is access to the booty, and they can become depressed or dangerous if that access is denied. In this scenario, Black women become reduced to the sexual spoils of war, with Black men defining masculinity in terms of their powers in conquering the booty" (Collins, 2004, p. 151). What Collins suggests is that the Black woman is viewed as a commodity, a commodity that is readily accessible and available to Black men to use at their will and as a means of dealing with the external challenges they face. Read as objects to be used, as signified in terms like "booty call," the Black woman has been reduced to a "piece of ass." A booty call (also referred to as "friends with benefits") is used to denote a sexual relation sans commitment. It is usually characterized by a late night phone call that leads (hopefully) to either the male or female "visiting" the other for a sexual encounter. The notion of a booty call is not peculiar to men; however, it tends to be masculinized and is often treated in a heterosexual manner (see Collins, 2004, chapter 5).

Sexual power relations are embedded in the construction of the Black woman as a piece of ass or as a booty call. The *piece of ass* subscript is discursively constructed in a heterosexual manner and is often couched in discourses of privacy and family. Ralph Ellison's (1995) novel, *Invisible Man*, and particularly the battle royal scene, shows how this sexual power relation is depicted in the cultural realm. The story of the battle royal highlights the composition and production of women as sex objects who exist solely for the pleasure of men. The scene is set in the Golden Day, a brothel visited by the Invisible Man (the protagonist). The prostitutes, who are all Black women, are given little to no voice except to speak to the customer. For these prostitutes, their value occurs in relation to the other—they are there as part of the background, to provide context for a deeper understanding of Invisible Man. They are constructed as shadow bodies whose purpose is designed to reflect men's desires and wants. Ellison's use of the Black female prostitutes embodies alterity and difference reflecting and normalizing patriarchy and the use of the Black female body. Such a composition and production that runs throughout the novel drives Invisible Man to conflate the "woman question" with the "ass" question; thereby moving issues of gender equity from the public into the private sphere.

Ellison speaks to the socio-sexual aspects of Black–White and even Black–Black relations in ways that challenge facile notions of equality and democracy. Sylvander (1975, p. 77), in her gendered analysis of *Invisible Man*, states that the narrator "loses what slight recognition he has of woman-as-human . . . as he becomes more closely allied with manhood, the Brotherhood, and his own personhood." It is next to impossible to recognize women as human when they are scripted as a "piece of ass"—readily available for sexual conquest. These power relations operate at both the microstructure and the macrostructure levels of the family.

The dominant sexual ideology renders Black women shadow bodies in the construction and use of the family, thereby allowing Black men to engage the patriarchal standards that have become normalized in U.S. society. I am aware that Black men cannot engage patriarchy in the same manner as White men; however, at the microstructural level of the family, the *piece of ass* subscript is used to suggest that the issues of Black women are relegated to the private domain because sex is often constructed as a private matter between a man and a woman. At the microstructural level, Black women are expected to protect Black men from the various ills of the larger society. They protect their men via multiple actions, of which providing sex is one. Thus, Black men are allowed to have their manhood. One means through which Black men can have their "manhood" is via the family, which Collins (1998, p. 78) argued is an "ideological construction and principle of social organization." The family as an ideological construction and principle of social organization works to demark the private and public realms. Black women, through sexual intercourse, then become important to the functioning of the family in the private realm as it allows Black men to engage in patriarchal pursuits.

The use of the *piece of ass* subscript at the macrostrucural level is linked to a rather masculinist understanding of Black liberation. Similar to the microstructural use of this script, the family is invoked through the use of the *Ass* script at this level. Family, in this instance, is read as a racial family. As Nikol Alexander-Floyd (2007) argues, this notion of the racial family can be used to support the theses of the Black man as endangered and the Black woman as a traitor. Combined, the endangered Black man and the traitorous Black woman suggest that gender issues be treated as secondary in the quest for Black liberation. This racial family often requires that some groups and issues be excluded from discussion in the public domain. So ensconced in the *piece of ass* subscript are particular raced/gendered ideologies that results in Black women being used to support Black men while marginalizing Black women's issues.

Subscript 3: The Ass Question: The Question of Gender, Authenticity, and Belongingness

A male colleague once said to me that I was not a "real" Black woman. According to him, I was not authentically Black because my "ass was flat" (personal communication, 2007). He then chuckled as though he had made an amusing comment. This reading of my body captures a dominant script used within the Black community, where the Black woman's derrière is a sign of racial authenticity. It is sometimes revered if you have "junk in your trunk," that is, a large buttocks. Although revered and admired, the ass poses a problem for Black politics. On the one hand, the physical ass is accepted; however, the complete being—physical, emotional, etc.—to which this "ass" belongs is often marginalized. This subscript, the *ass question*, deals with the issue of the public voice and representation of Black women. The script touches on issues of both physical authenticity and political authenticity as it relates to Black politics and the Black community.

Once again, I turn to *Invisible Man* to discuss one cultural production of this script. Invisible Man's relationship and involvement with the Brotherhood movement provides a glimpse into the forces that produce the invisibility and shadowing of Black women and the exclusion of women's issues, in general, from serious consideration within the Black community. In his first introduction to the Brotherhood, the protagonist was asked by a "plain" (according to the text) woman, "What is your opinion to the state of women's rights?" Before he could offer a response, he was quickly hurried away "to a group of men," signaling the exclusion of women's issues from the "larger" concerns of the "movement" of the Brotherhood (Ellison, 1995, p. 311). As his stature as a "leader" in Harlem grows, Invisible Man is sent downtown to lecture on the "Woman Question." Invisible Man is not particularly enthused by this opportunity. He responds by wondering, "Why, god-damit, why did they insist upon confusing the class struggle with the ass struggle, debasing both us and them—all human motives?" (Ellison, 1995, p. 311). The woman question was reduced to the *ass question*.

I cannot speak to what Ralph Ellison was trying to convey when he wrote this; however, I can interpret (within context) the meaning being conveyed. First, this statement suggests that issues pertaining to women are not worthy of being discussed in a public setting. At one level the statement "confusing the class struggle with the ass struggle" connotes that this is a private issue between men and women (the text reads in a very heterosexual manner). Private issues between men and women are culturally defined as relating to intimate issues, of which sexual relations are a part. Invisible Man's response brings to mind the subscript of Black womanhood that suggests they are a *piece of ass* (see above). Second, this response suggests that women have no issues beyond their duties to satisfy their man (provide a piece of ass or "booty call"). Doing such limits Black women's concerns to the private realm. It also suggests that their issues are not worth fighting for. In fact, to do so would be to detract from the larger

(Black) freedom struggle. Third, Invisible Man suggests that the "community's" agenda is full and to stray from its particular agenda items, which appear devoid of women's issues, would be futile. Black women who challenge this masculinized approach are often deemed as threats to the community—they are considered the enemy within (Alexander-Floyd, 2007; Cole & Guy-Sheftall, 2003).

To illustrate further how this subscript is read and used, I turn to another personal experience. After a paper presentation on the Black political and politics response to fatherhood and marriage promotion, a second male colleague informed me that while he enjoyed my presentation, he found it problematic. He told me that my focus on the invisibility of Black women in the (Black) response to these policy proposals was problematic. According to my colleague, this was not an authentic and organic Black issue. He also suggested that I had misconstrued the problem, which in his mind was a private issue—between a man and "his" woman. My colleague suggested that patriarchy was not a problem that was internal to the Black community. Instead, any tension within the Black family was a result of external forces such as racism. He went on to tell me that I was being used as a tool for White women in that I was introducing a nonissue and detracting from the larger issue at hand—the fight against racism. My (Black feminist) politics, like my physical ass, was used to remind me of my "inauthentic" Blackness. My politics, grounded in Black feminism, was deemed inauthentic to the Black community and to the larger Black freedom struggle. These two experiences reminded me that in order to gain access to Black politics, I had to make a choice. My belongingness was conditioned on me not raising the "ass question" in a public forum. Such issues could only be dealt with in a private, interpersonal setting. This meant that I could not be viewed as an entire human being—one who is both raced and gendered. My colleague, like Invisible Man, reduced the woman question (one of democratic practices and inclusion) into an ass question. As I suggested, the three subscripts that make up the larger metanarrative *Ass* script makes the "woman question" an ongoing problematic for Black politics. I now turn my attention to the *Strong Black Woman* script.

THE *STRONG BLACK WOMAN*: THE METANARRATIVE

The Black woman's body is often scripted as strong—both physically and mentally. Then, this *Strong Black Woman* script is used to suggest that the Black woman is not really a woman. Strength has been required of Black women for a number of reasons. For Euro-Americans, strength was required to justify Black women's exploitation as a source of labor. The notion of the strong Black woman operated to exclude Black women from the "Cult of True Womanhood" (Welter, 1966). The script of the *Strong Black Woman* was and continues to be exercised to suggest that she was the antithesis of a "real" woman—soft, delicate, and weak. Europeans, juxtaposing the script of the *Strong Black Woman* against the Cult of True Womanhood, were able to rationalize using Black women's bodies for the production of crops, goods, services, and additional laborers (Carby, 1987; hooks, 1981).

Both Europeans and other Blacks have used the script to justify some Black women's punishment and subjugation. The *Strong Black Woman* script is problematic for Black women not only as a result of the external usage by those in power, but because it can be internalized and consequently shape how we see ourselves. The internalization of this script can lead to a perpetual state of sacrifices and mental illness among Black women (see T. Harris, 1995). Similar to the *Ass* script, this script permits the commodification of Black women in a manner that allows her to be used for hard physical labor and as cultural bearers of the community. Because of the existence of multiple axes of oppression (Collins, 1991), Black women find themselves as "mules" who are expected to be the "beast of burden" (Hurston 1991 [1937]). As they are commodified as workers and are expected to support and uplift others, Black women are not seen as individuals in need of support and uplift. They easily become shadows in others' quest for advancement.

Michele Wallace, in detailing what she terms the "Black superwoman," captures the essence of the *Strong Black Woman* script that is ascribed to Black women. As she argued (1990 [1978]),

> Through the intricate web of mythology which surrounds the black woman, a fundamental image emerges. It is of a woman of inordinate strength, with an ability for tolerating an unusual amount of misery and heavy, distasteful work. This woman does not have the same fears, weaknesses, and insecurities as other women, but believes herself to be and is, in fact, stronger emotionally than most men. Less of a woman in that she is less "feminine" and helpless, she is really more of a woman in that she is the embodiment of Mother Earth, the quintessential mother with infinite sexual, life-giving, and nurturing reserves. In other words, she is a superwoman. (p. 107)

Strength claims define Black women's goodness as a combination of invulnerability, fortitude, and compassion, as well as the possibility to destroy (think of the image of the "welfare queen"—originally attributed to Ronald Reagan—who emasculates the Black man because of her misplaced sense of strength and independence). For some Black folk, strength is required for survival of not only the microstructural family, but also for the macrostructural racial family. Like the *Ass* script, this metanarrative of strength is composed of a number of subscripts. These subscripts—*physical strength, sacrificial/nurturing,* and *spiritual/ supernatural*—are explored below. In an attempt to explain the functioning of the *Strong Black Woman* script, I rely on its cultural literary productions by Blacks.

Subscript 1: Physical Strength

Hurston (1991 [1937]), in *Their Eyes Were Watching God*, declares, "De nigger woman is de mule uh de world so fur as Ah can see. Ah been prayin' fuh it tuh be different wid you. Lawd, Lawd, Lawd!" (p. 14). The notion of Black women as mules, to be used for other people's purposes, captures much of the *physical strength* subscript ascribed to Black women's bodies. She is used for labor and to allow others to achieve their dreams. Consider Celie (the protagonist in Alice Walker's *The Color Purple* (1982). Celie is habitually and relentlessly told that not only is she skinny, Black, and ugly, but also that her only value is in her ability to perform duties for others. She is expected and required to serve her husband and his children by cleaning his house, tending his fields, and caring for his children. Black women, real and fictional, are read as having "an ability for tolerating an unusual amount of misery and heavy, distasteful work" (M. Wallace, 1990 [1978], p. 107). Celie, like real Black women whose bodies are scripted as physically strong, becomes a "mule of the earth" as discussed by Hurston and the "super-woman" as discussed by Wallace as a result of the inscription of *physical strength* onto their bodies.

The scripting of the Black female body as physically strong manifests itself in the stereotypic image of Mammy. Part of Mammy's strength, who worked primarily as a domestic worker, stemmed from her ability and willingness to work long hours often with little to no compensation. In her role, Mammy was expected to be subordinate, nurturing, and self-sacrificing (see Jewell, 1993). The welfare mother, in the more modern era, supplanted the Mammy symbolic icon (Jordan-Zachery, 2009). As a result of the 1996 legislative changes to what is commonly referred to as welfare, poor welfare-reliant Black women were expected to work in exchange for benefits. The Personal Responsibility and Work Reconciliation Act of 1996 (PRWORA) mandates work requirements for beneficiaries. It also imposes a time limit of two years at any one time and a five-year lifetime limit for the receipt of benefits. Katha Pollitt (2010), in her article "What Ever Happened to Welfare Mothers?," wrote

> Millions of welfare mothers found work, albeit often casual, low-wage jobs that did not lift them out of poverty. How much of a triumph is it that in the late 1990s, 65 percent of former recipients in South Carolina were working, earning an average hourly wage of $6? Or that in Maryland, in one quarter, about half of former recipients had found work at pay that annualized to roughly $9,500—way below the poverty line for an average family? (n.p.)

The post-1996 welfare era "welfare mother" and her earlier version "Mammy" embody the notion of the strong Black woman; they are expected to work often with little to no compensation and with little to no complaining. There is a belief that these women are more suited to be in the labor force, as opposed to staying at home to care for their families. For these women to "play" the role of the stay-at-home mother violates a particular race/gender/class hierarchy. This is related to the scripting of the Black woman's body. As this woman's body is scripted as strong and suitable for labor (hard labor), it has become acceptable (particularly among those in power) to expect these women to work outside the home.

Because of her physical strength, it is assumed that the Black woman is able to play a number of roles at both the microstructural and macrostructural levels. The notion of the strong Black woman as "happily" assuming these multiple roles, often simultaneously, ignores the question of why. Discourses of the strong Black woman ignore the realties that force Black women to assume these multiple roles and the impact of doing such on their well-being (see Dumas, 1980). Consequently, we are not afforded the opportunity to critically analyze how structural violence often forces Black women to engage in harmful behavior, such as trying to live up to the iconic notion of strength.

Subscript 2: Sacrificial/Nurturing

This subscript tends to cast Black women in the role of mother—biological, communal, and/or cultural. It often requires women to "tame" or "control" their anger (at least, delay to a more appropriate time), as a means of survival. Consider the actions of the character Baby Suggs (in Toni Morrison's *Beloved*). Even after losing her eight children to the institution and practices of slavery, she served as a comforter to others such as Sethe. In her autobiography, Harriet Jacobs ([1860]1987) describes this iconic image of the sacrificial strong woman. Jacobs wanted to escape slavery; however, because of her role of mother, she felt constrained:

> I could have made my escape alone; but it was more of my helpless children than for myself that I longed for freedom. Though the boon would have been precious to me, above all price, I would not have taken it at the expense of leaving them in slavery. Every trial I endured, every sacrifice I made for their sakes, drew them closer to my heart, and gave me fresh courage. (1860/1987, p. 59)

In 1959 Lorraine Hansberry described the character Mamma Lena Younger, of *A Raisin in the Sun*, as

> The Black matriarch incarnate: the bulwark of the Negro family since slavery; the embodiment of the Negro will to transcendence. It is she who, in the mind of the Black poet, scrubs the floors of a nation in order to create Black diplomats and university professors. It is she who, while seeming to cling to traditional restraints, drives the young on into the fire hoses and one day simply refuses to move to the back of the bus in Montgomery. (quoted in S. Carter, 1991, pp. 52–53)

The Black woman as the "uplifter," the one who is willing to sacrifice her needs so that others might advance, is also captured in Ellison's *Invisible Man*. The protagonist, Invisible Man, muses about his relationship with Mary, stating: "Nor do I think of Mary as a 'friend'; she was something more—a force, a stable, familiar force like something out of my past which kept me from whirling off into some unknown which I dared not face" (p. 258). Mary (one of the few women in the novel with a name) is described as having a "heavy, composed figure" (p. 255). In essence, it appears that Mary plays somewhat of the "Mammy" role in the life of the Invisible Man. With little attention to the oppressive nature of the role, Ellison consigns Black women to the gendered demands of racial uplift. Excluded from the erotic imaginary by racist constructions of desire, Black women are expected to serve selflessly as a stabilizing force, protectors of the community who devote themselves to the well-being of Black men and Black children while taking little time for concerns about their own well-being (the alternative, at least in the case of *Invisible Man*, is to cast them as prostitutes). Mary plays the role of the strong Black woman. Although Invisible Man wonders, *"What were Mary's problems anyway; who articulated her grievances"* (p. 297; emphasis added), he does not devote any serious consideration to such issues. As a result of the *Strong Black Woman* script, "the idea that [Black] mothers should live lives of sacrifice has come to be seen as the norm" (Christian, 1985, p. 234). The normalization of the functioning of the Black woman as mother (biological and/or cultural) leads to the expectation that she will sacrifice so that others can make progress while simultaneously denying her needs and dreams.

Subscript 3: Spiritual/Supernatural Strength

According to Thomas (2001), Black women, as a result of multiple oppressions, endured over centuries, developed spiritual coping mechanisms and strength. The *spiritual/supernatural strength* subscript serves as a source of transformation. It has been charged that African American women's spirituality serves as a coping mechanism, as a way to give meaning to the hardships they and their community face, and as a conduit for growth (Banks-Wallace & Parks, 2004; Mattis, 2002). One sees representations of the strong spiritual woman, who often serves as a champion/guide for the oppressed, in works such as *The Secret Life of Bees* (Kidd, 2003) and *The Help* (Stockett, 2009), among others.

The script of the spiritually/supernaturally *Strong Black Woman* appears to permeate the Black Diaspora. Marlon James (2009), in *The Book of Night Women*, wrote:

When the time come for the whipping she don't even need nobody to get her. She go to the tree early and raise her hands up. She stop cry and only wince when the lash too hard . . . When they cut the rope, she drop to the ground and pick herself up. She stand and stagger a little, but still stand. Lilith raise her chin and walk over to her bundle of clothes. . . . Every three of four steps she limp, and one time she nearly drop, but her chin still raise. (p. 168)

James is describing the ongoing beatings suffered by Lilith (an enslaved girl about age 15) on a Jamaican plantation. This child/woman is characterized as the embodiment of strength, a type of transcendent strength. Such strength is not only necessary for her survival, but for the survival of the other enslaved individuals on the plantation. Lilith showed the possibility of survival, particularly survival with dignity.

In their essay, "Black Women and Survival: A Maroon Case," anthropologists Kenneth Bilby and Filomena Chioma Steady (1981) recount the history of Grandy Nanny, female leader of the revolutionary group in Jamaica known as the Windward Maroons. They stress in particular the supernatural aspect of Nanny's power in leadership:

In the various Maroon legends recounting Nanny's great deeds of the past, there is one dominant theme: the supernatural. . . . Her great mystical power was derived from her close contact with and intimate knowledge of the spirit world, the realm of departed ancestors. In this role, as mediator between the living and the dead, Nanny symbolizes the continuity of Maroon society through time and space. . . . Maroon storytellers overwhelmingly attribute the great historical victories of the Maroons to Grandy Nanny's phenomenal supernatural powers. The tales they recite underscore the importance of Nanny, and by . . . extension, the female contribution, to the survival of the Maroons. . . . There is no doubt that an important personage named Nanny really existed. It is believed that her ethnic background was Akan and that she was born in Africa. There are references to her in the contemporary British literature as a powerful obeah-woman. . . . There is no doubt that she wielded great authority, military and otherwise. . . . Although Nanny was clearly an exceptional woman, there are indications that she was not the only woman of influence among the Maroons. . . . Other powerful women are remembered in oral tradition, such as Mama Juba, like Nanny a great "Science-woman"—as Maroons refer to those well-versed in the supernatural arts. (pp. 458–460)

This type of transcending strength is often used to depict a history and connection of peoples of the African Diaspora. So in this case Nanny is strong, in part, as a result of her ability to communicate with the ancestors of an African past. This type of communication becomes important in the creation of an identity, which serves as a site of protest and contestation to the identity imposed by Eurocentric understandings of Black folk. It also provides them with a sense of control of their destiny in a world where structures, such as the slave driver, are used to take control (often through brutal means) away from enslaved and colonized bodies.

Beyond their personal transcendence into the spiritual realm, Black women, through ritualistic healing baths and the laying of hands, are also constructed as strong. Such baths and laying of hands are depicted in *The Women of Brewster Place* (Naylor, 1982), *Praisesong for the Widow* (Marshall, 1983), and *The Book of Night Women* (M. James, 2009). James, in detailing the events after the rape of the protagonist, captures this healing strength of Black women. Accordingly he depicts the following:

> HOMER SQUEEZE BLOOD OUT OF THE RAG AND DIP HER HAND in the bucket. She squeeze some of the warm water out and rub Lilith face careful. She touch Lilith neck, then forehead. She wipe the dirt and dry blood from Lilith. Now Lilith on the bed as Homer washing her. . . . Homer cut some sinkle-bible plant stalk and scrape the clear jelly out of the middle. . . . First she rub some on Lilith face, then neck. Gorgon rub down her breast . . . Gorgon scrape some jelly out of a stalk and rub her belly." (M. James, 2009, pp. 159–160; emphasis in original)

These women "laid hands" on Lilith in a way that suggest their supernatural strength. They brought her back from the "dead" in the sense that she had been brutally raped by several men, and as one character, Gorgon says, "it like dey was tryin' skin de gal neck" (M. James, 2009, p. 159). Through their ministrations, they were able to expunge the men from Lilith's body. In essence, they cast out the "demons."

In Toni Morrison's novel *Beloved* there is a similar laying of the hands. Baby Suggs cleans Sethe's body. "She cleaned between Sethe's legs with two separate pans of hot water and then tied her stomach and vagina with sheets. . . . Roses of blood blossomed in the blanket covering Sethe's shoulders . . . wordlessly the older woman greased the flowering back" (Morrison, 1987, p. 93). These women, who are a part of a "league of women," all suffered the brutalities of slavery; however, they were able to transcend the injustices extolled on their bodies and tend to other (younger) women. In essence, they engage in a restorative transitional process, if only temporary, from the horrors of slavery. The process of laying hands and the use of healing baths offer a safe haven and a spiritual space where the mind and body can have a reprieve from the brutalities of slavery and other oppressive structures; they offer survival.

The *spiritually/supernaturally strong* Black woman is also used to transcend worlds—present and past. At times, the women who transcend spiritually become gods themselves and serve as an affirmation of feminine power and as a source of feminine solidarity. Audre Lorde (1978, p. 6), in the poem from the house of Yemanja calls on Yemanja (in Yoruba mythology she is the mother of all other gods) to come and rescue other women: "Mother I need your blackness now/as the August earth needs rain." In describing the revolt that Homer plotted and led, James (2009) stated, "Homer step to the window and raise her hand. The sunset hit her body and she change to black. She wave the rifle in the air. The redcoats fire and riddle her body with bullets. She dance from the rifle fire and her whole body shoot blood. She make a yell, then fall, with half her body hanging off the balcony" (p. 410). However, the book suggests that this woman, after being tortured and severely beaten prior to the event described above, somehow survived. Lilith's daughter Lovely Quinn says, "even the blind niggerwoman who live in the bush, who thin like stick, who hair white like cloud and who smell of mint and lemongrass, going sing it too" (p. 427). This is the same manner in which Homer was described earlier in the novel, suggesting that not only has Homer survived, but also she will sing the song(s) to celebrate the league of women. She serves almost in the same manner as does Yemanja in Audre Lorde's poem. She is not only some force that allows women to celebrate, but also is a guide because "the blind niggerwoman in the bush, she tell me everything" (M. James, 2009, p. 426). Mary, from *Invisible Man*, is also cast in a similar vein as the strength of the past. In their godlike state(s), these women serve as cultural bearers, as protectors, and as guides. They are there to support the racial family regardless of their needs.

Given the usage of the "strong Black woman" there is a type of seduction associated with it that can lead some Black women to internalize the *Strong Black Woman* script and use it to organize their responses to a number of issues. However, there is a danger in internalizing the *Strong Black Woman* script. Wallace-Sanders (2002a, p. 4), in discussing the danger of the mythology of Black womanhood, stated, "Black women are trapped by this externally imposed second skin of misconception and misrepresentation. This shell is both *skin deep*, as it emphasizes the most superficial versions of Black women, and *skin tight*, as it has proved to be nearly inescapable, even in Black women's self-conception and self-representation" (emphasis in original). We do this because we are striving to maintain the image of the "strong" Black woman as a means of coping and as a sign of survival. As such, "individual and group responsibilities are distorted, personal and political boundaries are blurred, and personal and community priorities are unbalanced" (Scott, 1991, p. 11). Many Black women find themselves donning the strong warrior approach that helps to perpetuate their invisibility and subsequently their construction as shadow bodies.

The *Strong Black Woman* script can be a wellspring for social action and a site of resistance. This script, in its various forms, ascribed to the Black woman's body can indeed promote/encourage her survival and the survival of the community. However, it can also hurt Black women because it leads to denial—the denial that Black women have issues that are worthy of attention. As such, "individual and group responsibilities are distorted, personal and political boundaries are blurred, and personal and community priorities are unbalanced" (Scott,

1991, p. 11). Denial of Black women's issues can occur at the intrapersonal and interpersonal level. Consequently, Black women who are impacted by HIV/AIDS, domestic violence, and mental illness are treated with a code of silence. Why? Because of the script that the strong Black woman can transcend or escape it all.

CONCLUSION

This chapter explores the scripts ascribed to Black women's bodies and how they are presented and represented. In this work, my focus is on the Black intra-group use of the *Ass* and *Strong Black Woman* scripts. However, these scripts can also be used by those external to the Black community. While the scripts are particularly gendered—in a masculinist manner—they can be internalized by Black women. Furthermore, the deployment of the *Ass* and *Strong Black Woman* scripts can be contested. Take for example Karyn White and Alicia Keys's individual representation of strength. In 1988, Karyn White (Edmonds, Reid, & Simons, 1988, track 4) sang

> I'm not your superwoman (Oh, no, no)
> I'm not the kind of girl that you can let down
> And think that everything's okay
> Boy, I am only human (I'm only human)
> This girl needs more than occasional
> Hugs as a token of love from you to me

Some nine years later, Alicia Keys (Augello Cook, Perry, & Mostyn, 2007, track 3) sang,

> Even when I'm a mess, I still put on a vest
> With an S on my chest
> Oh yes, I'm a superwoman.

These two songs embody much of the more recent social science research that focuses on the iconic figure of the strong Black woman. Particularly, they invoke much of Beauboeuf-Lafontant (2005) critical analysis of this image. Her critique recognizes the legacy of the images, one that is often displayed as a badge of honor and that signifies belongingness to the Black racial family. However, she argues that there are times when Black women embrace this understanding of Black womanhood often to their detriment.

White rejects the script of strength and centers her needs/desires. Alicia Keys celebrates strength and the fortitude of (Black) women to persevere regardless of what is going on. These tensions around this script exist through time and space and can often influence our understandings of the Black community and subsequently who is represented. Simultaneously there exist the possibility of the celebration and even reverence of the iconic strong Black woman (as in the case of Keys) while using it to limit the options of some Black women. The notion of the strong Black woman leaves little room for that Black woman who is perceived as failing to embody strength. Ipso facto, she can be vilified and expelled from the community.

Consequently, the strong Black woman is simultaneously revered and vilified in the Black community. Her work of racial uplift is reverenced. While at other times, she is vilified as her strength is constructed as harmful to Black men and as a liability to the Black community. M. Wallace (1990 [1978]) said, "The black woman's act needed intensive cleaning up. She was too domineering, too strong, too aggressive, too outspoken, too castrating, too masculine. She was one of the main reasons the black man had never been properly able to take hold of his situation in this country" (p. 91). Wallace's statement captures the troubling aspect of the *Strong Black Woman* script. In this assertion Wallace shows the contradictions of the cultural iconic figure—the strong Black woman who is viewed as needed for the uplift of the community and also as a danger to the community.

While I recognize that the *Ass* and *Strong Black Woman* scripts can be used and inverted by Black women in a way that is celebratory, they are generally harmful. I make this claim because of the ability of the scripts to make Black women shadow images. Scripts create a particular identity of Black womanhood. In the words of Storrs (1999, p. 200), these identities are racialized and gendered and are "not simply imposed on individuals, but are achieved through interaction, presentation, and manipulation." Scripting the Black woman as an *Ass*, that is, reducing her to her *physical ass*, as *a piece of ass*, and as a troubling *ass question* and/or strong embodies her value to society. Such scripts influence how her body is treated and affected, particularly by those in power.

In this study the *Ass* and *Strong Black Woman* scripts are recognized as the mechanisms (the templates) that influence and shape identity makers such as the intersection of gender and sexuality. Scripts are the mechanisms that produce shadow bodies. The scripts allow me to ask: (a) what is being discussed in the talk on HIV/AIDS, domestic violence, and mental illness; (b) who is being discussed in this talk; and (c) given the framing of the issue (a and b) how do Black women construct policy proposals?

As I argue, scripts work to normalize practices and can encourage or produce fragmentation or moments of solidarity. In the context of HIV/AIDS, domestic violence, and mental illness, the two scripts are more likely to encourage and produce fragmentation within the community of Black women. I argue such because these two scripts inscribed on the Black woman's body suggest the following:

- Black women are devoid of humanity, feelings, and emotions;
- The Black woman's body is to bring sexual pleasure;
- The Black woman exists for the purposes of others;
- While the Black woman's body can be viewed publically, its primary use and value is contained to the private realm; and
- Nonprototypical Black women will be responded to with nontransformative policy suggestions. That is, policy is not designed to challenge the multiple systems of oppression that make Black women susceptible to HIV/AIDS, domestic violence, and mental illness.

Combined, these scripts do not always allow for the reading of Black women's bodies as a site that can be victimized, hurt, or damaged. As such, the Black woman's body, and consequently the Black woman in totality, can never truly be a victim of HIV/AIDS, domestic abuse, or suffer mental illness.

In the following chapters (4–6), I bring to the forefront the discreet silences in the talk on HIV/AIDS, domestic violence, and mental illness. As a reminder, these chapters are designed to analyze and identify which categories of differences are employed in the talk. To this end, I focus on what is said as a means of showing the spaces of silence. In chapter 7 I show how the discreet silences result in Black women being shadow bodies—they exist in a space in-between, a space of both proximity and separation. They are there but never really seen, as a result of the scripts inscribed on Black women's bodies.

3 · UNCOVERING TALK ACROSS TIME AND SPACE

Black Women Elected Officials, *Essence* and *Ebony*, and Black Female Bloggers

My research has not yielded political science scholarly works exploring Black women's textual silence as a rhetorical political tool. In an attempt to analyze Black women's political behavior, as a means of understanding their use of silence, I find myself once again fusing together separate literatures. In my attempt to situate silence as a part of their political praxis, in this chapter I bring together various understandings of Black women's political behavior. This chapter serves three purposes. For one, it shows how silence, particularly discreet silence, fits into Black women's political practices. Second, the chapter seeks to offer my method for analyzing Black women's silence as part of their political praxis—it speaks to how and why I analyze the three sources of talk. To this end, I use the theory of intersectionality (Collins 1998, 1999; N. E. Brown, 2014b; Giddings, 1984; Smooth, 2013), which suggests that Black women recognize how they operate within structures and systems of multiple oppressive structures, including race and gender, and as such organize their politics within this context. Although Black women recognize intersectionality, this is not to suggest that they operate from the assumption that all Black women experience intersectionality in the same manner. Second, I rely on the argument that there is a tension between resisting and reinscribing raced-gendered differences. According to this argument, while attempting to challenge negative constructions of Black womanhood, Black women can engage in practices that reinscribe scripts and stereotypes; thereby resulting in the perpetuation of the unequal treatment of Black women (Collins, 1991). Finally, I utilize research that suggests that activism is constrained by Black women's social location and the structural factors unique to their context. I argue that these factors cut across all spaces of talk (see Combahee River Collective, 1977; Robnett, 1997; Springer, 2005). The third purpose of this chapter is to show how discreet silences are analyzed. Frame analysis and interpretive phenomenological analysis (IPA) are used to analyze the talk and silences of these women to explain how shadow bodies are produced.

Merging the various understandings of Black women's political praxis serves as a means of understanding if and how the talk, through the engagement of discreet silences, creates shadow bodies that become evident in the framing of the intersection of Black womanhood, HIV/AIDS, domestic violence, and mental illness. By bringing together the theoretical foundation detailed in chapter 1, the scripting of the Black female body (see chapter 2), and research on Black women's political behavior, I am able to better answer the following questions: Who speaks for Black women and how are Black women represented in public discourses, by other Black women, around issue of equality and justice, particularly as they relate to HIV/AIDS, domestic violence, and mental illness? I start with a theoretical review of Black female elected officials; this is followed by a review of existing research on *Essence* and *Ebony* and Black female bloggers. In doing such, I explain not only the data used in the analysis, but also how I uncover and interpret the silences.

ON THE FLOOR: BLACK FEMALE ELECTED OFFICIALS

The Joint Center for the Political and Economic Studies declared "2001 the Year of the Woman." In this report, Bositis (2001) informs us:

> This modest increase in the number of BEOs [Black elected officials] masks a significant trend that has been seen since the early 1970s, but which has accelerated since 1998—the growth in the number of black women holding elected office. . . . This pattern has been seen in every BEO survey since 1998—that is, a decline in the number of male BEOs from the previous year, and all the gains in the total number of BEOs being credited to Black women. (n.p.)

This is why, in part, I include Black congresswomen in this study (see Table A.1, Appendix). Additionally, I include this group as it is often claimed that they conceptualize themselves as speaking for marginalized communities. The steady increase of Black female elected officials has given rise to the number of research efforts designed to explain how these women function in their legislative capacities. Much of this research concentrates on determining the openness of the American democratic process to what is often constructed as a marginalized group (see Hawkesworth, 2003). Within this strand of research, intersectionality has been deployed to analyze and explain how these women legislate.

Using intersectionality theory, Orey and Smooth (2006) stated that, regarding the policy-making process, Black women perform differently in comparison to other groups such as White women and Black men. Orey and Smooth, like many others, spotlight how these women's positionality influences their political strategizing, the types of issues they are likely to champion, and how they represent their constituents. The various attempts at explaining women's legislative behavior, and particularly Black women's behavior, are apt to focus on what is referred to as "women's issues" and/or what I term "integration" issues affecting African Americans in particular and people of color generally (Barrett, 1995; Bratton, 2005; N. E. Brown, 2010; Reingold, 2000; Swers, 2001; Thomas, 1994). Thus, analyses concentrate on issues of welfare, education, and health care when discussing women in general. Research that centers African American women include the above-referenced issues, affirmative action, and other policies deemed as targeting the Black community (Bratton & Haynie, 1999; Wolbrecht, 2000). However, when we consider the policy issues analyzed across these bodies of research, there tends to be a convergence of the types of policy issues studied. Most studies analyze what Cathy Cohen (1999) terms consensus as opposed to cross-cutting political issues. This leads to results that suggest that these women serve as advocates for the marginalized.

Scholars suggest that African American legislators, regardless of party identification or district demographics, tend to support and advocate a more liberal policy frame in comparison to their White counterparts (Dowe, 2016; Gamble, 2007, 2011; Haynie, 2001; Tate, 2004). Additionally, it is posited that Black elected officials are more likely to introduce legislation deemed as relevant to the African American community (Bratton & Haynie, 1999; Canon, 1999; Reingold, 2000). Historically, it has been argued that "linked fate" explains the behaviors of Black elected officials. The notion of linked fate suggests that while there exists varying experiences and backgrounds among Black Americans, there also exists a shared memory and understanding of discrimination and continued social and economic disparities among this group (Dawson, 1994). Although not employing the notion of linked fate, Snow (2001) suggests that embedded in collective identity is an emancipatory spirit or collective agent that can result in collective movement action. Furthermore, it has been argued, by Hunt and Benford (2004, p. 433) that incorporated into collective identity are "kindred concepts such as solidarity and commitment."

Consequently, it is opined that even in the face of differences, African Americans believe that their individual interests are tied to the group. In terms of legislative behavior, linked fate manifests itself in Black legislators being more likely to mention Blacks and other marginalized groups in policy deliberations. More recently, Nadia Brown, among others, has brought into question the functioning of linked fate. Brown asserts that one cannot simply view Blacks through the theoretical lens of linked fate, as it "fails to clarify the reasons for agreement and disagreement within the Black community and among African American women as a distinct race/gender group or its link to Black women's legislative behavior" (2014b, 14–15). Whether it is linked fate or a commitment to championing the "interest of Blacks and underrepresented population" (Smooth, 2006) that influences Black women's political behavior is not necessarily settled in the literature on Black women's political behavior. This suggests that we need additional research on Black women's political behavior. Although not necessarily focused only on Black women elected officials, the collected essays in *Black Women in Politics: Identity, Power, and Justice in the New Millennium* (Alexander-Floyd and Jordan-Zachery, 2014) show that Black women political actors' behaviors are influenced by the intersectionality of oppressive structures and that their efforts are designed to achieve equality for members of their collective group and other oppressed groups. In this analysis, I do argue that there is some form of "linked fate" or group identity and recognition of intersectionality that informs the behaviors of the Black elected officials (see N. E. Brown, 2014b; Dowe, 2016; Smooth, 2006, 2014).

In terms of gender identification, a number of researchers argue that gender influences the policy making process (Bratton & Haynie, 1999; Thomas, 1994) and impacts how legislators define their constituency (Carroll, 2002; Swers, 2002). In comparison to men, women are more likely to support feminist positions on "women's issues" (for a non-U.S. analysis see Chattopadhyay and Duflo, 2004). Women's issues are typically defined as those addressing health care, welfare, and education (see Carroll, 1994; Flammang, 1997). Additionally, according to female members of Congress who were interviewed by the Center for American Women in Politics, they feel a "responsibility to represent women" regardless of whether the women were members of their district (Carroll, 2002, p. 53). Furthermore, analyses suggest that female elected officials at the state and local level claim that they are more responsive to their constituents. They also believe that in comparison to men, they tend to be more approachable, trusted, and committed to community relations (Beck, 1991; Diamond, 1977; Flammang, 1985; Johnson & Carroll, 1978; Merritt, 1980; Mezey, 1978).

Research that simultaneously considers the impact of race and gender on legislative behavior informs us that women of color "talked in somewhat different ways" about their responsibilities to minority and other marginalized groups (Carroll, 2002, p. 57). Some of these women "expressed the inseparability of their identities as, and their responsibility to, people of color and women." Furthermore, others articulated a strong sense of responsibility to poor and working-class women and/or to women globally. This suggests that these women of color see themselves as representing what we might term the "voiceless." They construct themselves as a surrogate for these individuals who are marginalized from the political process (Fenno, 2003; Simien 2006; Smooth 2006).

What these various literatures suggest is that Black congresswomen's policy deliberations are influenced by (a) their sense of belonging to a larger community that is influenced by and influences intersectional structures and processes that work to oppress them and members of the their constructed communities—which crosses social locations and geographic boundaries, and (b) their desire to serve as a voice for the voiceless regardless of boundaries. One gets the sense that there is, at least in principle (or maybe just theoretically), a commitment to inclusiveness among Black female elected officials. As such, I would expect them to speak on behalf of the women who serve as a backbone of this study. I would also expect the officials to speak on their behalf, especially if others are not speaking for the women and if, for various reasons, they cannot speak for themselves. This is where an analysis of the intragroup performance of intersectionality, integrated with muted group theory and body studies, becomes useful. Such an analysis can provide us with insights into how these women speak for the voiceless. In chapters 4–6 I take a look at how Black female elected officials frame Black womanhood; systems of inequality; and HIV/AIDS, domestic violence, and mental illness.

This study considers the talk, floor speeches in particular, offered by 18 Black congresswomen. The congresswomen are all Democrats and have a range of years of service, with the earliest being elected in 1991 and the most recent elected in 2005 (see Table A.2, Appendix). To find their talk, I searched the online congressional record (the Library of Congress Thomas website) using various key words including *HIV* and *AIDS*, *domestic abuse*, *domestic violence*, *inter-partner violence*, *mental health*, *mental illness*, and *depression*. For each congresswoman, I downloaded their speeches and followed the protocol discussed below to find themes.

In this analysis, I move away from determining if Black female legislators tend to support more liberal policies in comparison to their male and White counterparts. Additionally, I move away from exploring how these women conceptualize themselves as policymakers and how they respond to various institutional structures and processes. Such research endeavors are worthwhile; however, there is a part of this puzzle that warrants further exploration. From various research efforts, we are led to believe that Black female legislators operate from a point of intersectionality and they often view themselves as surrogates for the invisible and the voiceless. I recognize that Black female elected officials must negotiate a number of processes and structures that can impose limits on their behavior in congress. They operate in a race-gendered institution (Hawkesworth, 2003) that can sometimes constrain their options in terms of the framing of issues and the policy suggestions offered. As a result, their articulation of intersectionality can be constrained. However, these women claim that they serve as a voice for the voiceless. As such, women of color legislators construct themselves as a surrogate for these individuals who are marginalized from the political process. This suggests that they recognize their "unique" place and their responsibilities to act on behalf of those with limited representation. My question is: How? How do they speak of these individuals? How do they conceptualize the groups that they work on behalf of and how does this conceptualization help to fight the oppressive structures often experienced by these marginalized communities?

THINGS WE'RE TALKING ABOUT:
ESSENCE AND *EBONY* MAGAZINES

According to Rhodes (1993, p. 25) "women of color often fall through the cracks, unless a deliberate effort is made to study them as subjects, audiences, and producers of mass communication." Several years later since Rhodes' declaration, women of color, and specifically Black women, continue to fall through the cracks in our analyses on power and mass communication. While some progress has been made, Black women's journals are now discussed in a full-length monograph (Rooks, 2004) and there is increasing discussion on how the media treats Black women as "subjects" (see Baker, 2005; Shepherd, 1980), there is a dearth of analyses in terms of our understanding of how Black women are portrayed (not simply a focus on how they are depicted in advertisements) within the pages of "Black" magazines. More specifically, given the dearth of analyses we are left with little understanding of how intersectionality is performed in the pages of Black magazines that directly target Black women. As such, it has proven difficult to theorize the findings throughout this analysis.

In an attempt to explore how intersectionality is performed in print media (or what might now be considered "old" media in comparison to computer-mediated media such as blogs), I selected *Essence* and *Ebony* magazines.[1] Both magazines seek to rehabilitate and offer alternative understandings and depictions of Black folk (primarily in the U.S. context); therefore, one could read *Essence* and *Ebony* in terms of a project of racial pride. *Essence* and *Ebony* position themselves as concurrently addressing the White media's often negative depictions or omission of Blacks and as offering a space where Black folk can take pride in their heritage, their history, and their future. The space-making project of *Essence* and *Ebony* is accomplished by presenting African Americans in general, and Black women more specifically, with an opportunity to define themselves; the magazines offer them the ability to develop and grow wealth and present alternative understandings of what it means to be a Black woman in the United States.

Essence magazine, founded in 1968, says that it has a "monthly circulation of 1,050,000 and a readership of 8.3 million" (www.essence.com, 2010). The 2015 Media kit says that *Essence* has a readership of 7,721,000 and that 46.5 percent of this readership has a household income of $50,000+ (www.essence.com, 2015). According to the magazine, "ESSENCE occupies a special place in the hearts of millions of Black women—it's not just a magazine but her most trusted confidante, a brand that has revolutionized the magazine industry and has become a cultural institution in the African-American community" (www.essence.com, 2010). *Ebony* magazine, founded in 1945, while not geared directly towards Black women specifically, suggests that it was "founded to project all dimensions of Black personality in a world saturated with stereotypes" (*Ebony*, 1995, p. 80). It is worth noting that while *Essence* constructs itself as the preeminent lifestyle magazine for Black women (*Essence*, 2015), in 2005 Edward Lewis (one of the magazine's co-founders) sold the publication to Time, Inc. While there are still Black editors and staff, *Essence* is currently under White ownership (Gaynor, 2013). The founders of both *Ebony* and *Essence* constructed the publications as speaking to the diversity of Blackness—as inclusive. In 1945 and in 1970, a discourse of racial uplift, rehabilitation, and affirmation began.

Given the longevity of both *Essence* and *Ebony*, I am amazed at the limited research conducted on these magazines. The scarcity of analysis limits our understanding of the cultural production of issues germane to Black communities. There is limited attention paid to how these publications frame a variety of issues, and also there is limited information on how, if at all, they speak to the diversity of Black womanhood. Rooks (2004, p. 6) states, "Black women's magazines' importance lies in their asking us to think more deeply about, or, in some instances, rethink what we are sure we know about Black women, and to draw attention to the split image of Black women produced by both white and black media makers." This leaves us with the question: Who is included in the pages of *Essence* and *Ebony*?

I seek to continue the work of Rooks (2004) by focusing on how *Essence* and *Ebony* magazines produce Black women. The first part of the analysis presents a brief history of both publications and lays out the missions of both *Essence* and *Ebony*. From there, I develop a theoretical approach that is useful in explaining how intersectionality is performed in the stories on HIV/AIDS, domestic violence, and mental illness within their pages.

Essence and *Ebony*: A Brief Look at the Publications

Essence magazine, the brainchild of Edward Lewis, Clarence O. Smith, Cecil Hollingsworth, and Denise M. Clark, was founded in 1968. It is worth mentioning that *Essence*, although founded by men, has maintained a number of women in its editorial positions. The magazine positions itself as speaking to the specific and diverse interests of Black women. In fact, *Essence* declares (in its masthead) that it is the magazine "for and about Black women." The magazine seeks to offer features and articles "from a Black perspective—that would necessarily include the full spectrum of Black women" (quoted in Rooks, 2004, p. 143).

The articles in *Essence* rely on a so-called intimate, girlfriend-to-girlfriend tone to discuss issues pertaining to dating, fashion, beauty, lifestyle, family, and career. The lifestyles of various celebrities are also covered in the magazine. *Essence* claims a readership base of "nearly 70 percent of African American women (www.essence.com, 2010). Given its readership base, the magazine is positioned as a potentially "powerful site for voicing and redefining who Black women are in an arena that includes a large and various population of Black women" (Woodward & Mastin, 2005, p. 266).

From its inception through current times, the nature of the publication has changed. Rooks (2004) sums up this change in the assertion, "no longer would African American women be placed firmly in the midlist of a radical political narrative. No, by the middle of the 1970s, they would be shown to have a far greater interest in clothes, travel, and cosmetics than in political struggle" (p. 146). She further argues, "Today, its significance lies less in its editorial policies, fashion pages, or political content than in its success as a gateway through which mainstream advertisers are able to reach a lucrative group of African American consumers of both genders" (Rooks, 2004, p. 141). *Essence* recognizes its potential to be a gateway to the African American consumer and actually boast of itself as being the "leading authority on African-American women" in its marketing to advertisers (www.essence.com, 2010).

While recognized and celebrated as being a key and central publication that specifically targets Black women and their communities, *Essence* is also critiqued for occupying a rather complex space. Woodward and Mastin (2005) argue, "*Essence* possesses a dual contextuality," because "It is part of a capitalist consumer and patriarchal system that enables it to be a successful money-making venture for the Black men who publish it, while its editorial content is controlled by Black women editors who refuse to be defined by mainstream stereotypes" (p. 267).

Before I explore and discuss this dual contextuality, I should mention that *Essence* is owned by Time Warner Communications. In 2000, two of the founders sold 49 percent of the publication to Time Warner, which then, in 2005, acquired the remaining 51 percent. Now back to the issue of dual contextuality. It is this dual contextuality that influences not only the types of articles and features covered in *Essence*, but also how they are covered—that is, how they are framed. The scripts ascribed to Black women's bodies further influence this dual contextuality. Scripts influence the nature of the articles and how they are presented (I explore this in more detail in the remaining chapters).

Ebony, relative to *Essence*, has one of the longest publication histories among Black magazines. It was first published in 1945. According to John H. Johnson, *Ebony*

> was founded to project all dimension of the Black personality in a world saturated with stereotypes. We wanted to give Blacks a new sense of somebodiness, a new sense of self-respect. *We wanted to tell them who they were and what they could do.* We believed then—and we believe now—that Blacks needed positive images to fulfill their potentialities. (*Ebony*, 1995, p. 80, emphasis added)

Mr. Johnson's statement indicates some similarities between the two publications. Similarly to *Essence* magazine, *Ebony* seeks to present an alternative understanding of Black folk. The publication offers a range of articles on topics such as careers, money management, celebrity lifestyles, entertainment, and the arts. *Ebony*, unlike *Essence*, is not geared specifically towards Black women, but is designed to speak across genders to both men and women. In its 2010 Media Kit, *Ebony* says that it has a readership of 12 million. Of this readership, women represent 62.5 percent and men represent 37.5 percent. It is because of its substantial female readership that I include *Ebony* in this analysis.

I suspect that *Ebony* also confronts a type of dual contextuality, and is also constrained by a "capitalist consumer and patriarchal system." The Johnson Publishing Company, which publishes *Ebony*, declares that its "brands resonate credibility and showcase an aspirational lifestyle. In short, we are your passport into the African-American and multicultural communities." The magazine sets itself up as a gateway to Black consumers, which in part shows a commitment to capitalist structures. *Ebony*'s production, distribution, and consumption also take place within a larger culture of patriarchy. Although *Ebony*, at the writing of this book, has a woman serving as editor, I make this claim for the same reasons that Woodward and Mastin (2005) make the claim against *Essence* magazine. *Ebony*, like *Essence*, finds itself trying to present a different understanding of Black womanhood within the context of capitalism and patriarchy.

A Framework for Analyzing *Essence* and *Ebony*

As previously discussed, research on *Essence* and *Ebony*, particularly Black feminist analyses, are not vast. There is research that focuses on how the magazines present issues such as HIV/AIDS (Krishnan, 1997; Willis, 2010), depression (Clarke, 2010), women's bodies in advertisements (Spates & Davis, 2010), and how *Essence* and *Ebony* confront negative portrayals of Black women (DeLoach, 2007). While these articles are particularly useful in helping us understand the work done by *Essence* and *Ebony* on behalf of the Black community, for the most part they are informed by an underlying assumption of a monolithic Black woman. Such works do not systematically investigate how, and if at all, different Black women are treated in the pages of these magazines. This forced me to bring together a number of theoretical approaches in my attempt to understand how *Essence* and *Ebony* might engage in such political behavior on their pages.

To do this, I fuse insights from Black feminist theory and media framing theory. Combined, the theoretical insights lead me to suggest that while *Essence* and *Ebony* are useful in challenging some of the more controlling dominant constructions of Black womanhood, such as Mammy and Jezebel, they are generally constrained in their talk of women who might be constructed as "troubling" to the Black community. There are capitalist and patriarchal constraints as suggested by Woodard and Mastin (2005); however, there are also constraints resulting from the racial system of the United States and particularly the racialized-gendered scripts ascribed to Black women's bodies. The media, in its various forms, serve to perpetuate these racialized-gender scripts in its framing of issues—even among those that position themselves as challenging racialized norms.

Several scholars have explored media depictions of African Americans. Such studies have looked at Black women and television (Bogle, 2001; Smith-Shomade, 2002), the depiction of Black women in hip-hop (see Armstrong, 2001; I. Perry, 2004; Rose, 1991), and body size/image of Black women (Kean, Prividera, Howard, & Gates 2014). Critical analyses of the media show how mainstream media and Black producers perpetuate typically negative stereotypes of Black women (hooks, 1993a; M. Wallace, 1990). Beyond critiquing the depiction of Black women in the media, scholarship also strives to rehabilitate the Black female image via their discussions of stereotypical characteristics, themes, and tropes that permeate the media.

According to hooks (1992, p. 5), media's representation of Black women "determines how blackness and people are seen and how other groups will respond to us based on their relation to these constructed images." Furthering hooks' analysis, Simone Cottle (2000), in her analysis of minorities in the media, said:

> The media occupy a key sight and perform a crucial role in the pubic representation of unequal social relations in the play of cultural power. It is in and through representations, for example, that members of the media audience are variously invited to construct a sense of who "we" are in relation to who "we" are not, whether as "us" and "them," "insider" and "outsider," "colonizer" and "colonized," "citizen" and "foreigner," "normal" and "deviant," "friend" and "foe," "the west" and "the rest." By such means, the social interest mobilized across society are marked out from each other, differentiated and often rendered vulnerable to discrimination. At the same time, however, the media can also serve to affirm social and cultural diversity and, moreover, provide crucial spaces in and through which imposed identities for the interests of others can be resisted, challenged, and changed. (p. 2)

Media images of African Americans in general result from dominant ideologies of race, class, gender, and sexuality (see Collins, 2004; Hudson, 1998). These ideologies, as I argue in chapter 2, inform the scripts ascribed to Black women's bodies. Scripts, such as the *Ass* and *Strong Black Woman*, are employed to produce images and stereotypes of the nature of Black womanhood. Furthermore, these scripts can be internalized by Black women, thereby "simultaneously reflect[ing] and distort[ing] both the ways in which black women view themselves (individually and collectively) and the ways in which they are viewed by others" (Hudson, 1998, p. 249). Although some in the media strive to challenge the negative portrayal of Black women, they can indeed perpetuate such depictions. Brooks and Hébert (2004), in their analysis of Spike Lee's movie *Bamboozled*, showed how this is accomplished in their claim that Lee perpetuates sexist norms of Black womanhood. Other scholars have systematically charted and theorized about the functioning of the Black female body, particularly its sexualization in the media (Collins, 2004; Gaunt, 1995; hooks, 1994; L. Jones, 1994; I. Perry, 2003; Rose, 1994).

> How individuals construct their social identities, how they come to understand what it means to be male, female, black, white, Asian, Latino, Native American— even rural or urban—is shaped by commodified texts produced by media for au- diences that are increasingly segmented by the social constructions of race and gender. Media, in short, are central to what ultimately come to represent our so- cial realities. (Brooks & Hébert, 2006, p. 297)

The media help create a framework through which the negotiation and renego- tiation of Blackness and belongingness is enacted. The discourses that appear on the pages of *Essence* and *Ebony* magazines, over time and space, present a view of the "authentic" Black woman that becomes idealized and culturally encoded. The Black woman becomes the subject produced through discourse, and "cannot be outside discourse, because it must be subjected to discourse. [Consequently,] it must submit to its rules and conventions, to its dispositions of power/knowledge" (Hall, 1997, p. 55). *Ebony* and *Essence* magazines inform their readers as to what is considered appropriate behavior not only by covering and highlighting certain issues, but also via the manner in which the issues are talked about—in terms of who is included in the talk and what solutions are offered to address the issues.

Media studies suggest that the media focuses attention on certain events and issues, which they then present within a particular meaning—that is, they frame the issue. Choices are made as to what issues to highlight and how and what issues to neglect, and what bodies to represent via the frames that are used—in other words there is a strategic use of silence in news reporting. According to Cappella and Jamieson (1997, p. 47), frames not only activate knowledge, but also stimulate "stocks of cultural morals and values, and create contexts" for understanding public problems and issues. While these studies focus on the media in general and tend to ignore issues of race, one could extrapolate to Black-centered or -generated media.

Woodward and Mastin's analysis (2005, p. 277) helps to merge Black femi- nism and media studies. According to the authors, *Essence* is "a feminist-oriented magazine . . . [that] adheres to some of the basic tenets of Black feminism" (Woodward & Mastin, 2005, p. 277). These authors seek to show how *Essence*, through its coverage, challenges various myths and stereotypes usually projected onto Black women by offering alternative frames. In addition to discussing how *Essence* supports Black feminism, Woodward and Mastin also show how it fails to adequately address the diversity of Black womanhood, as suggested by their finding that *"Essence* is a very middle-class-oriented magazine" (Woodward & Mastin, 2005, p. 277). Despite *Ebony's* attempt to relate to diverse groups of

African Americans, Myers and Margavio (1983) argue that the focus on "achievement, recognition, and respectability clearly reflects a middle-class value system." *Ebony's* readers tend to be relatively high in socioeconomic status, highly educated, and women (Digby-Junger, 2005). This, too, hints at the possibility that *Ebony* might not represent the diversity of Black womanhood.

This focus on the middle class can be expected to influence how issues are talked about, how Black womanhood is represented, and who is represented in the pages of *Essence* and *Ebony* magazines. I would expect both magazines to employ representational strategies that align with a particular understanding of Black (female) respectability (Higginbotham, 1992). By presenting particular understandings of Black womanhood (which is dependent on scripts that serve as the template structures) and with consistent repetition, the magazines establish normativity, often with little space offered to challenge it.

Using the key words, *HIV* and *AIDS, domestic abuse, domestic violence, interpartner violence, mental health, mental illness,* and *depression,* I searched the historical records of the magazines to locate talk. The decision was made not to include letters to the editor in the analysis. Other than that any use of the above-mentioned terms was analyzed.

HAVING THEIR SAY: BLACK WOMEN IN THE BLOGOSPHERE

Winer (2003) characterizes blogs as the "unedited, published voice of the people." Additionally, "Blogging produces an unregulated narrative, which counters hegemonic norms without directly confronting the state, as do other traditional forms of political or social activism" (Rifaat, 2008, p. 53). It is for these reasons that I include blogs written by Black women in this study. I recognize that all discourse shared with the public is "censored" is some manner; therefore, blogs are not completely "free" of internal scrutiny performed by the writer and that identities are mediated (see Boylorn, 2013; A. Johnson, 2013). However, unlike the editors and writers of *Essence* and *Ebony* magazines and unlike Black female elected officials, I argue that there is a different type of freedom of expression experienced by bloggers (see Table A.2, Appendix, for the list of blogs used in this study). Some, especially those who are not linked into advertisers and who are not paid—monetarily or otherwise—are not necessarily constrained by having to write in a way that satisfies the needs of these external forces. Consequently, blogs, unlike *Essence* and *Ebony* magazines and Black female elected officials, offer us a relatively unscripted and unedited voice of the people.

There are very few research projects that look at the act of blogging via an intersectional approach. Emerging research that centers race specifically, appears to be privileging analyses of Twitter (Black Twitter, for example) and Instagram with an emphasis of the use of hashtags (see Clark, 2014; Edwards Tassie and Brown Givens, 2015; Florini, 2013; Sharma, 2013). Blogging, as a site of research on Black women identity and representation, seems to have taken second place in this emerging body of scholarship on "digital Blackness." This might be the case since according to A. Smith (2014), relative to other demographic groups, Black women dominate Twitter. Thus, we are left with research efforts that tend to take a singular approach and focus on gender and blogging, or race and blogging. Overwhelmingly most research engages in race- and gender-neutral analyses. Those bloggers who are simultaneously gendered and raced are often rendered invisible, not because they are not blogging, but because they have not been seen as credible research subjects. As such, my theorizing on Black female bloggers borrows from multiple research strands. I rely on the work of theorists (such as Giddings, 1984; Robnett, 1997; Springer, 1999, 2005) who analyze Black female activism; theorists who focus on race and blogging (Brock, 2007; Kvasny and Igwe, 2008; Poole, 2007); and communication literature that addresses how and why individuals maintain blogs (Hookway, 2008; Jones & Alony, 2008) to generate a better understanding of Black female bloggers.

Blogs, as a form of computer-mediated communication, emerged in force in the late 1990s. According to Blood (2000), in 1999, there were 23 blogs. By July 2007, Pedersen (2007) asserted that there were 90 million blogs. The ever-increasing blogosphere has fueled a number of research interests that seek to better understand why people blog, the types of blogs they write, and the impact of blogs on the political and social spheres. Schmidt (2007), among others, focuses on categorizing the nature of blogs. He offers a typology that includes, for example: political blogs, corporate blogs, expert blogs, and personal knowledge blogs. Beyond this categorization, blogs are also thought of in terms of whether or not they are filter blogs. Within a filter blog, commentary is typically constructed around selected hyperlinks in a way that allows for the filtering of information from various other sources (see Blood, 2002). While there are various types of blogs, Blood's description captures the general essence of what a blog is. Blood (2002) describes blogs in this manner:

> Some provide succinct descriptions of judiciously selected links. Some contain wide swaths of commentary dotted sparingly with links to the news of the day. Others consist of an endless stream of blurts about the writer's day; links if they exist, are to other, similar, personal sites. Some are political. Some are intellectual. Some are hilarious. Some are topic driven. Some are off the wall. Most are noncommercial and all are impassioned about their subjects. They are weblogs. What they have in common is a format: a webpage with new entries placed at the top, updated frequently . . . sometimes several times a day . . . Weblogs are hard to describe but easy to recognize. (p. 1)

Many of these blogs are written by individuals and are typically characterized as online journals designed to share the individual's view on a range of issues, from reflections on day-to-day activities and events, to star gazing, to commentary about socio-political structures. Blogs provide a space for individuals to express, challenge, or support constructed identities. Among the bloggers' comments is a range of reflexivity on current events, including reflection on what might be considered cross-cutting issues (Cohen, 1999). This in part is due to how they construct and mediate their online identity.

Individuals blog for a number of different reasons and they represent various social locations/identities. Herring, et al. (2005), Huffaker and Calvert (2005), and Lenhart and Fox (2006) offer a number of insights into the socio-demographics of bloggers, their motivations, and their habits. What we have learned is that among the personal journal type of bloggers (this form of blog constitutes the majority of blogs analyzed in this study), females and teenagers tend to dominate. When we consider the intersection of gender and blogging, we learn that "55% of current bloggers are female" (Watt, 2006). Additionally, Watt informs us that women, in comparison to men, start more blogs and are more likely to sustain them over a longer period of time. Women and people of color, in 2006, were among the fastest-growing population of bloggers (In These Times, 2006). However, there is a gender disparity, and I would include a race disparity, in the visibility of women and people of color's blogs. According to Watt (2006), among the top 10 most visited blogs, only two were hosted by women. The invisibility of women's blogs, as articulated by Herring, Kouper, Scheidt, and Wright (2004), is the result of news media and researchers not paying attention to female bloggers because their work is perceived as being about personal experiences. Chen (2013) explains this phenomenon as resulting from an ideology that perceives content along gender lines; thus seeing female content as not conforming to societal norms of "online success." It is possible to construct a similar argument concerning the relative invisibility of blogs maintained by African Americans in general and by Black women more specifically—they are made invisible in our studies of blogs as a result of intersecting identities.

The type of blogger that I analyze in this project often does not rely on linking other blogs and might not be registered among the list of "top bloggers." However, among these bloggers, and those who read and comment on their posts, there is a sustained, often evolving, and dynamic community that is fostered and nourished based on shared interest(s) and identity/identities (Hodkinson, 2006; Wei, 2004). Black (2006, p. 171) asserts "computer-mediated communication (CMC) and the Internet provide new opportunities for using discourse and text to discursively construct and enact achieved identities in online environments." Through nourishing shared interests and identities, CMC offers these individuals a safe space to discuss issues that might not typically be discussed in mainstream media.

While CMC is recognized for its ability to foster a space where individuals who share interests or identity can come together in a manner that might not be afforded via other means, its value is sometimes questioned. Feminists have questioned how and if the constructed identities used in CMC can challenge existing social inequalities. Scholars, particularly feminist scholars, have questioned whether or not the emerging technologies can offer a new space for feminism, cyberfeminism, and feminist work. Cyberfeminism is not a settled term and is indeed a contested framing of the presence of women in cyberspace. Orgad (2005), among others, has suggested that CMC can serve as an effective means for women to resist and challenge gender hierarchies. Others such as Gajjala (2003) and McCaughey and Ayers (2003) challenge this "liberating" conceptualization of the use of the Internet. In addition to the contestation as to whether or not cyberfeminism can exist, also contested is how to define the concept. I do not get involved in this rather interesting debate here. Instead, I concentrate on how one might begin to think about the manifestation of cyberactivism and how it might be useful in understanding Black female bloggers. To this end, I rely on Vegh's categorization of cyberactivism. Vegh (2003, pp. 72–73) suggests that activism can be thought of as employing either Internet-enhanced or Internet-based activism strategies. *Internet-enhanced* strategies "are only used to enhance the traditional advocacy techniques, for example, as an additional communication channel, by raising awareness beyond the scope possible before the Internet, or by coordinating action more efficiently." *Internet-based* strategies, on the other hand, are "only possible online, like a virtual sit-in or hacking into target web sites." Additionally, Vegh argues that cyberactivism can be categorized into three general areas: awareness/advocacy, organization/mobilization, and action/reaction. Such an understanding of cyberactivism can prove fruitful in understanding the blogging activities of Black women.

Black bloggers, commonly referred to as the "Blackosphere" are described in the following manner:

> These blogs are by and principally for Black people, focusing not only upon Black people but upon people and issues deemed relevant to the Black people who write these blogs and post comments. At Black blogs, we comment on the issues of the day raised in white newspapers and blogs, but we also highlight issues that whites mostly ignore, such as the unfair criminal prosecution of individual humble and unknown Blacks. Our commentary and the relative importance that we give news are informed by our unique historical perspective on and position in America. From our vantage point, we share with each other a distinct perspective and critique that white people, including progressives, cannot have and generally do not want. (Holland, 2007)

African Americans, like women in general, are increasingly using blogs and social media to draw attention to their concerns. Poole (2005), in one of the few research-length articles on race and blogging that speaks specifically to African

Americans, suggests that Black bloggers are using this space to engage in political activity—such as to encourage voting among their readers and to provide race-centered analyses of social and political phenomena. "As African Americans increasingly use social media, such as blogs and social networks, to produce their own content and foster virtual communities that serve their collective interests, there is potential for new modes of social activism to materialize" argue Kvasny, Payton, and Hales (2010, p. 19). As such, some blogs can be read as a continuation, using new media and formats, of the larger ongoing African American struggle for freedom and equality.

Blogs, while relatively new in relation to *Essence* and *Ebony* for example, are seen as an additional means of facilitating a long tradition of activism in the Black community. Kvasny, et al. (2010) show how the Internet, and the Blackosphere in particular, was instrumental in the Jena 6 protest.[2] They argue that Internet activism, through information sharing, organizing, fundraising, and communication, played a key role in organizing the protest. This online activism is often credited for generating and encouraging the on-the-ground activism. Additionally, it has been argued that it was Internet activism, as opposed to mainstream media, that generated the attention which ultimate led to the resignation of then Senator Trent Lott (see McKenna & Pole, 2006).[3] Increasingly, social media has been credited for generating a number of protests occurring globally among Africans, such as the protest that occurred in Egypt. In the case of Egypt, it is argued that social media influenced the protest movement in the following three areas: organizing protests, shaping the narrative of the protest, and pressuring political structures locally and globally (see Boyd, 2011; Crovitz, 2011).

Similar to the research on African Americans and blogging, we are offered a few analyses that begin to explain Black women's use of the blogosphere. In describing Black female bloggers, Washington (2010) writes,

> Representing a full spectrum of backgrounds, perspectives, and lifestyles, blogs written or hosted by black women cover most aspects of adult life—careers, family, romance, self-discovery and development—with a particular eye to the varied concerns and interests of black women and their allies. The best of these blogs weave their readers into an informed and activated community, capable of educating their online and offline neighbors on social, political, and personal issues encompassing race, gender, and sexuality.

Black female bloggers seem to fit, in terms of subject areas, with the general trends among bloggers. Washington (2010) does highlight one aspect that might differentiate Black female bloggers from others, which is their integration of intersectionality in their blogging activities. While Washington provides an intervention that helps us better understand Black female bloggers, a number of questions still remain, resulting in an information void. What we do not have are socioeconomic demographics of these bloggers. Who are they? What have their experiences been with the modern civil rights movement and/or with the women's movement? While these are all interesting questions, they are outside the purview of this current study.

What we do know, according to Rapp, Button, Fleury-Steiner, and Fleury-Steiner (2010), is that African American women's blogs can indeed serve as a site for social protest against inequalities and injustices. In this article, the authors show how Black women used the Internet to challenge a response to the rape and beating of a Black woman and her son in "a housing project known as Dunbar Village." Black women used the Internet to protest a "traditional" civil rights approach to this issue where Al Sharpton and the National Association for the Advancement of Colored People (NAACP) rallied around the young men who allegedly committed the crimes. Sharpton and the members of the NAACP rallied around what they saw as the primary injustice—the inequitable treatment of these four young men in comparison to a group of White young men of comparable age who had also committed a similar crime. Rapp et al. (2010) show how Black women took to the web to challenge the protest of Al Sharpton and the NAACP. The Black women strategized and used the Internet to bring attention to the mistreatment of Black women in race-centered civil rights protest. As they argued, a "'viral e-mail' entitled "Stop Al Sharpton and the NAACP from Endangering Black Women" initiated much of the "thousands of angry phone calls and emails" received by the offices of NAN and the national and Florida chapters of the NAACP (p. 252). This was a start of an online protest that "challenge[d] the longstanding failures of mainstream racial justice groups to take the victimization of Black women seriously" (Rapp et al., 2010, p. 255). This exploration of Black women's use of the Internet to challenge their oppression is part of a long tradition of Black women's activism. African American female abolitionists, as described by Yee (1992, p. 151) "campaigned for equal rights within the context of organized black abolitionism." This signifies a long-standing concern among Black women for the intersection of race and gender, and the impact of this intersection on their lives.

The Internet hints at the possibility of another crack, or space, within which Black women can engage their politics. The Internet, and blogs in particular, can afford Black women with a new and different manifestation of space. Consider that, according to Macías, "many Black women who engage in conversations with one another find that it enables them to cross boundaries to share stories about similar oppression, create supportive networks and redefine themselves for themselves. To that end, they wholeheartedly believe that it is indeed a very legitimate form of activism, agency and empowerment" (n.d., p. 14). Given the current theorizing on cyberactivism and race, and gender and blogging, combined with information on Black women and activism, I make the following assertions about how one might understand Black female bloggers. First, there is the notion of constructed online identities—I would expect Black female bloggers to construct an intersectional identity. Additionally, I expect that they will engage in actions to define themselves and reject definitions of Black women that they find problematic—such as the dangerous/bad Black woman. Patricia Hill Collins (1991) asserts that these various images of Black womanhood serve as controlling images and that Black feminists have long sought to debunk and often replace these controlling images. I also expect that Black female bloggers will express self-love and appreciation for other Black women. However, I do expect that the construction of the online identities might be constrained and as such might lead to their silences around some issues and/or influence the nature of the discourse. Severin and Tankard (1988) suggest that on controversial issues, individuals will first determine if their framing fits with the majority's framing of the issue. In the event that their framing of the issue is outside the "mainstream" then they tend to remain silent on the issue, which then causes others to remain silent. Black women's silence around certain issues is the result of the "politics of respectability," which seeks to present Black women in the most positive light by normalizing their behaviors (Higginbotham, 1993). Under the guise of respectability, there is an existence of a power structure that determines who is a part of the Black community and who is not. Consequently, those who cannot be normalized, or who are perceived as rejecting being normalized, are often not considered a part of the Black community (see Cohen, 1999). Black female bloggers, I suspect, are not immune from this process. Blogs can serve as a site for discussion and dissent. However, bloggers do desire some interactivity with their readers. As such, readers can directly or indirectly mediate the behavior of bloggers; thereby influencing not only their online constructed identities, but also what issues are discussed and how the issues are discussed.

Second, I expect that Black female bloggers will engage in some form of activism and agency designed to present alternative constructions of Black womanhood. Du Cille (1994), Phillips and McCaskill (1995), Townes (2006), and other womanist scholars argue that central to womanist thought and action is the deconstruction and critique of the forces that are designed to marginalize and oppress Black women. Additionally, womanists strive to present alternative constructions of Black womanhood as part of the larger goal of empowering and asserting the Black woman's voice. With this understanding of the nature of activism, I further expect Black women bloggers' cyberactivism to follow what Vegh (2003) refers to as *Internet-enhanced* strategies designed to spread the word and to coordinate activities among various groups of women and other supporters in an attempt to engage in Black feminist/womanist practices.

To get a sense of how Black female bloggers are framing the intersection of Black womanhood and HIV/AIDS, domestic violence, and mental illness, I analyze the posts of 27 bloggers. It should be noted that I only analyze the posts of the authors (or guest authors) of the blog sites and not the comments offered in response. This was done in an effort to ensure that I was using similar data for the bloggers, as was the case with the other two sites of data. Simply put, I wanted to understand what I conceptualize as "first order" (not mediated directly by someone's response) frames of the understanding of HIV/AIDS, domestic violence, and mental illness. Similarly to my search for congressional women's talk, I also use the key words *HIV* and *AIDS, domestic abuse, domestic violence, inter-partner violence, mental health, mental illness,* and *depression* to identify blog posts. See Table A.1, Appendix, for more details on the criteria for blog selection. "In many ways, social media platforms like Twitter and blogs have served to translocate 'safe spaces' which previously enabled Black women's storytelling and oral history to take place in churches, salons and cotton fields to now take place in Twitterverse and other online, virtual spaces" (Macías, n.d., p. 14).

The increasing use of blogs by African Americans and women has caused researchers to expand our understanding of race and gender, activism, and how their intersections unfold in the context of increasing technological advancements. The emerging field of digital Blackness suggest that on line spaces offer a virtual homeplace in the sense that they offer sites of support, sites of resistance, sites of networking, and sites for healing (Lee, 2015). But how are these homeplaces fueling activism and particularly a type of activism that does not essentialize differences? There are a number of issues surrounding what constitutes activism: How do researchers analyze these new modes of expression, and whether this form of activism is actually able to influence politics and policy? In other words, does it result in social change? We have to look at how bloggers, for example, are shaping and reshaping our discourse of freedom and equality in the 21st century. As we seek to understand these new spaces, we should analyze the discourse used by bloggers and how they conceptualize the issues that, according to Holland (2007), mainstream White America is ignoring. Janell Hobson's (2016, n.p.) analysis of Black-women-centered online projects (around the theme of beauty) led her to conclude, "A black beauty project must now grapple with a more complex examination of the intersections of race, gender, class, sexuality, and disability that can reframe black embodiment beyond commercialized spectacles and toward more diverse representations of liberated bodies." The level of inclusivity of the community, in terms of what issues are taken up by Black bloggers and how these issues are framed, should also be analyzed. While recognizing that the dynamic and transient nature of the Internet presents some research challenges, it is relevant and important for researchers to analyze it as a potential space for engaging in civic engagement and social change (Elin, 2003).

VOICING SILENCE: HOW THE SILENCES ARE ANALYZED

I employ an interpretive Black feminist phenomenological frame analysis to analyze and explain the textual silences used in the construction of HIV/AIDS, domestic violence, and mental illness. I choose this approach to gain a more detailed and nuanced understanding of the complex phenomena of Black womanhood's intersection with HIV/AIDS, domestic violence, and mental illness and to identify not only themes but theoretical understandings that inform the talk and silence of Black women. This approach permits me to identify the modalities of Black womanhood (hooks, 2009; E. P. Johnson 2003) and responses to such— that is, this approach allows me to analyze identity and its interaction with multiple forms of oppression and Black women's responses to such.

The intersectional interpretive frame analysis approach permits me to move beyond counting explicit words or phrases and instead focus on identifying and describing the ideas that are both implicitly and explicitly articulated within the talk and those that are not. Given that my focus is in how black women mobilize and deploy identity and the embedded ideologies, "counting responses" seemed inappropriate as a method (Pyett, 2003, p. 1174). My approach offers an analysis of "the participants [who] are trying to make sense of their world" and I the researcher who is "trying to make sense of the participants trying to make sense of their world" (J. A. Smith, 2008, p. 53). In this analysis I employ meaning-based rather than statistical forms of data analysis. As argued by Yardley (1997), and others, qualitative research, such as that performed here, seeks to produce one of many possible ways of analyzing and interpreting data. Brocki and Wearden (2006) posit, given IPA's requirements for the researcher to be both interactive and dynamic, that the goal is not to produce a singular truth of the data, but instead, the research should be concerned with ensuring credibility of the themes produced. Given that this is an interpretive analysis, it is very much possible for another reader to organize the frames differently and/or to possibly uncover additional frames and also to interpret them differently (see Schwartz-Shea and Yanow, 2012 for a discussion on why issues for replicability are not applicable to interpretive analyses).

The approach taken in this study is part of a tradition of evidence within progressive scholarship in political science, Black politics, and new political science. More importantly, this approach is well aligned with relatively recent research designed to center the lived realities of Black women. Black feminist scholars and Black critical scholars such as Nikol Alexander-Floyd (2010), Michele Berger (2004), Ruth Nicole Brown (2008, 2013), Nadia Brown (2014a, 2014b), Duchess Harris (2011), Zenzele Isoke (2013) Julia Jordan-Zachery (2009, 2013), and Adryan Wallace (2014) utilize postpositivist approaches and nonquantitative methodologies as a means of describing and analyzing Black women's politics and meaning making.

Frame analysis provides me with the tools to identify the silences, and IPA offers me the tools to explain the meaning making of these silences. I use IPA because "Phenomenology, like poetry, intends to be silent as it speaks. It wants to be implicit as it explicates. So, to read or write phenomenologically requires that we be sensitively attentive to the silence around the words by means of which we attempt to disclose the deep meaning of our world" (van Manen, 1990, p. 131).

Van Manen (1990) argues that the silences around the words can be just as powerful as the words themselves, as the silences also inform how we see and understand our reality. Dauenhauer (1980) similarly speaks to the value of silence in communication. Accordingly, he argues that there is an interconnectedness between discourse and silence, and it is the "interpretation of discourse, silence, action, and desire" that need to be explored (Dauenhauer, 1980, p. 138). He, too, recommends a phenomenological approach for understanding the relationship between discourse, silence, and action. I choose IPA as the methodology of this study to gain detailed information about complex phenomena of Black women's representation of "nonprototypical" Black women who experience HIV/AIDS, domestic abuse, and/or mental illness.

Central to IPA is the belief that individuals seek to make sense of their experiences. Consequently, an analysis of Black women's talk and silences of HIV/AIDS, domestic violence, and mental illness can shed light, even if partially, on how Black women make sense of their experiences—at both micro and macro levels. Beyond this, IPA recognizes an interaction between the participants' accounts of their experiences and the researcher's interpretive framework(s); hence, the analysis is both phenomenological and interpretive (Smith, Flowers, & Larkin, 2009). I employ an interpretive approach as my objective was to gain an "understanding of how individuals interpret events and experiences, rather than assessing whether or not their interpretations correspond to or mirror the researcher's interpretive construct or 'objective' reality" (Mishler, 1990, p. 427).

According to Smith, Flowers, and Larkin (2009, p. 3), "IPA studies usually have a small number of participants and the aim is to reveal something of the experience of each of those individuals." Considering this, I provide an in-depth analysis of diverse Black women's talk and silence in different contexts: Congress, in magazines, and through blogs. I employ theoretical sampling, which focuses on the saturation of information—meaning, there is a redundancy of information and no new frames, that is, ways of constructing the issues and the women, emerge, to determine that the frames are adequate and "complete" across the three platforms of talk.

Frames, as imagined by Goffman, offer a basic cognitive structure that provides a guide for understanding and constructing our reality. There is some debate as to whether frames are consciously or unconsciously manufactured and used (see Entman, 1993). I assume that frames can be both consciously and unconsciously produced. Goffman (1974, p. 24) asserts, "We tend to perceive events in terms of primary frameworks, and the type of framework we employ provides a way of describing the event to which it is applied." These primary frameworks—"the natural" and "the social"—inform how members of society understand daily living (Goffman, 1974, p. 26). Natural frameworks "identify occurrences seen as undirected, unoriented, unanimated, unguided, 'purely physical.'" Social frameworks "provide background understanding for events that incorporate the will, aim, and controlling effort of intelligence, a live agency, the chief one being the human being" (Goffman, 1974, p. 22). The scripts ascribed to Black women's bodies merge the "natural" and "social" frameworks to suggest how "good" Black women should behave not only among Black women, but also in the larger Black community. Borrowing from frame studies, I argue that the scripts ascribed to Black women's bodies are a system that organizes signifying elements which simultaneously specifies the promotion of a particular set of ideas. The body, which can be read as a text, also offers to the receiving audience the code necessary to process and understand the information.

I rely on Taylor and Bogdan's (1989) understanding of themes to identify the frames used in the talk on HIV/AIDS, domestic violence, and mental illness. Accordingly, themes are defined as units derived from patterns such as "conversation topics, vocabulary, recurring activities, meanings, feelings, or folk sayings and proverbs." (Taylor & Bogdan, 1989, p. 131) Themes can be thought of as the repetition of ideas or articulations that are evident across the individual platforms of Black women's talk (see Auerbach & Silverstein, 2003). Once the frames were identified, I used an emergent protocol to develop a categorization process. This protocol involved interactive readings of the transcripts. The transcripts were then analyzed and coded for common frames. My approach to understanding the talk of these various women first involved a simple reading of the text to get a sense of the issues they were discussing. My second and third readings determined what frames were employed in the talk. To guide the analysis, I asked the following questions: What is emphasized about the issues? How do these women engage multiple systems of oppression in their framing of the issues? And what is the nature of the responses offered to confront HIV/AIDS, domestic violence, and mental illness? Additionally, as part of the analysis, I considered the frames in relation to each other (Willis, 2010). In identifying the frames I also looked for convergence and divergence around issues. Finally, it should be noted that the frames were identified independent of theory.

The thematic elements that form the basis of the analysis show the manifestation of discreet silences and as such, how shadow bodies are produced. In the presentation of the themes (chapters 4–6) I look for connections and patterns across the time period 1997–2007 and across the various platform of talk. The grouping of themes follows more of a conceptual approach where I consider broad themes, while recognizing that these broad themes might also incorporate a number of smaller, but related themes. Accordingly, these themes reflect the part of the analysis where I attempt to make meaning of what was said and not said. At the stage of presenting the themes, I do rely on my theoretical knowledge. However, I was conscious in "titling" the metathemes in a manner that did not flatten out differences across the various platforms of talk. More importantly, in grouping the themes I was conscious of not allowing my voice to dominate the voices of the women who inform the study. The central question underlying the organization of the themes and my titling was: Did the title authentically capture the talk of Black female elected officials, in *Essence* and *Ebony*, and as used by bloggers? Themes also reflect the focus of the research and the central questions of the analysis. In the analysis of Black women's talk (chapters 4–6), I include long quotes "to allow the reader to learn something about both the important generic themes in the analysis, but also about the life world of the particular participants who have told their stories" (J. A. Smith, 2004, p. 42). This process is used to privilege the speech and to show the discreet silences of the various women.

In short, the analysis of Black women's talk on the intersection of Black womanhood and HIV/AIDS, domestic violence, and mental illness involved three primary "steps." The analysis involved:

1. Identifying prominent thematic concerns and parameters (the frames) used by Black women in their talk on HIV/AIDS, domestic violence, and mental illness—that is, Black women's meaning making of the three issues;
2. Identifying the discreet silences—that is, which Black women are talked about and which group is not mentioned in the talk; and
3. Interpreting the talk and silences—that is, my identification of the implicit ways issues are being discussed and how the scripting of the Black female body serves as a mechanism for such meaning making.

While I make this study as transparent as possible, I would be remiss if I did not recognize its limitations. Similarly to some analyses that employ IPA, this study is subject to concerns around its subjectivity and empirical applicability.[4] Throughout the analysis, I am mindful of these concerns by ensuring that I am transparent. As such, I provide detailed quotes (in the spirit of an interpretive analysis) from the women's three platforms to offer the reader an opportunity to critically assess the logic of my interpretations. Empirical applicability is addressed not necessarily through the findings, but more so in terms of the approach to the study. Furthermore, I do not offer a "comparison" group in an attempt to show how these women's talk differ and/or is similar to other types of talk, neither do I attempt to quantify the silence and/or talk. These are approaches that are often used more in positivist social science research as opposed to the interpretive in-depth qualitative research. Finally, as mentioned earlier, I make no claim that the two metascripts underlying this study are the only scripts ascribed to Black women's bodies. Indeed, I hope that others will continue to build on this study by exploring, via a similar method, other scripts ascribed to the Black female body. Frame analysis and IPA are effective analytical and interpretive means for making present that which appears absent as they allow me a means for explaining differentiation and power relationships. Together, the approaches are efficient and effective for developing theories and explanations to enhance researchers' ability to better understand human experience.

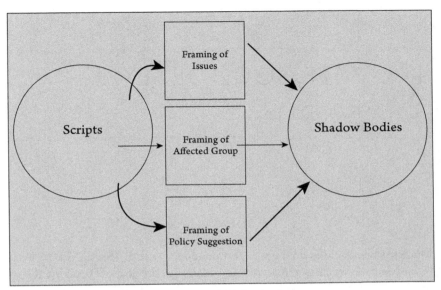

FIGURE 3.1 Relationship between scripts and shadow bodies

MAPPING THEORY, PRAXIS, AND REPRESENTATION

Existing studies on Black women's political behavior chronicle and identify the manifestations of collective actions and democratizing potential. However, there are gaps in this body of research as Black women continue to be understudied in terms of their wide spectrum of political behavior. Nevertheless, such theorization offers a springboard for considering how shared narratives, for example scripts, are important for examining the discursive performance of some aspects of Black female identity.

Using these various scholarly contributions, discussed in this chapter and chapters 1 and 2, I assemble an approach to understanding how shadow bodies are produced and integrated into Black women's political praxis. The interwoven theories show the link between scripts, silence, and power. I have put together a coherent, even if incomplete, perspective as a way of understanding Black women's lived reality. As I argue, scripts (as understood vis-à-vis body studies) are used to interpret and also express Black women's lived reality. These scripts hold beliefs, values, and opinions that influence and that are influenced by rhetoric, both talk and silence. This in turn influences, directly or indirectly, the categorization of individuals, which then affects how individuals are represented in the public sphere (see Figure 3.1). Black feminist standpoint theory merged with muted group theory affords me a means of interpreting the framing of the issues and Black women's political behavior as it relates to representing diverse Black women.

4 · "SAFE, SOULFUL SEX"[1]
HIV/AIDS Talk

Much has been written on the silence around HIV/AIDS. This silence has been discussed by journalists and academics alike, with the goal of "breaking the silence" to facilitate the necessary steps to stem the spread of the disease. It is implied that although we are now more than 30 years into the disease, the initial framing still dominates our current thinking. Some of the theorizing suggests that the silence results from the fact that AIDS is still considered a "gay man's disease" (see Hammonds, 1992). Others propose that Black folk and the Black church in particular are silent around HIV/AIDS because of its intimate relationship to morality (see Cohen, 1999). While we discuss the silences, what is often not discussed is who among Black women are produced as shadow bodies and what this means for Black gender justice.

In the first three chapters I argued that the scripts ascribed to Black women's bodies are the templates used to define and understand an issue and that such definitions embody power structures within the Black women's community (see Figure 3.1). In this chapter I begin to show how such power structures are represented in the talk and silence related to HIV/AIDS and its intersection with Black womanhood to show how shadow bodies are produced. At this point of the analysis, the central point of this chapter is not necessarily to link the *Ass* and *Strong Black Woman* scripts to the silences, as this is done in chapter 7. Instead, my focus is on the following:

- Understanding and analyzing the framing employed by Black congresswomen, Black female bloggers, and *Essence* and *Ebony* magazines. Specifically, I ask: how is intersectionality integrated into the HIV/AIDS frames?
- Understanding the suggestions made by these women for addressing these issues. I ask: how and if the talk is contextualized by Black women's social location and the relationship between structural violence and the spread of HIV/AIDS?

The analysis of the talk brought to the forefront the following frames (a) celebratory/recognition and (b) human disaster. The frames used to offer suggestions on how to address HIV/AIDS include: (a) take care of yourself and (b) education. These general frames incorporate subthemes used by Black female elected officials, *Essence* and *Ebony,* and by Black female bloggers. However, the overarching themes capture the general essence of their understanding of HIV/AIDS although they are informed by the central focus of the research project, which is to uncover how some Black bodies are produced as shadows (see Table A.1, Appendix). By centering the above, I am able to then identify and analyze which categories of difference are employed in the talk and if there are silences. As such, I am able to better understand how Black women make sense of HIV/AIDS and its intersection with Black womanhood. By focusing on who is included and excluded in the talk, on what types of actions are advocated for, and what types of actions are excluded from the talk, I am better able to understand intragroup Black women's politics.

The silences in Black congresswomen's, *Essence* and *Ebony,* and Black female bloggers' talk is evident in (a) who is left out, for example Black lesbians; (b) what issues are not discussed, for example structural violence and class; and (c) what types of actions are advocated for—personal responsibility versus public political action. To explain Black women's susceptibility to HIV and later AIDS, researchers argue that Black women's experiences with structural violence brings to the forefront the barriers they confront that increase not only their vulnerability and exposure to the virus, but also the barriers and challenges they face in seeking treatment and recognition. The intersectionality of racial discrimination, poverty, racial segregation, high incarceration rates, low-sex ratios, fractured gender-identity, gender roles, stigma, and high levels of illicit drug use results in Black women's disproportionate exposure to HIV and later AIDS (see Adimora & Schoenbach, 2002, 2005; Connors, 1996; Feist-Price & Wright, 2003; Krieger, 1999; Logan, Cole, & Leukefeld, 2002; Pequegnat & Stover, 1999; Whitehead, 1997; E. M. Wright, 2003; E. R. Wright & Martin, 2003). Yet Black women in their talk on HIV and AIDS do not talk about these issues. To show how these are indeed discreet silences, I analyze the frames used in the talk. It is only by seeing what is talked about that one can better see the absence of some frames and bodies.

WHO AND WHAT DO WE SEE? FRAMING HIV/AIDS AND ITS INTERSECTION WITH BLACK WOMANHOOD

Of the three issues analyzed, HIV/AIDS was the most talked about. Among Black elected officials, HIV/AIDS was discussed on the floor 396 times (see Table A.1, Appendix). Within the pages of *Essence* and *Ebony* magazines there were a total 128 stories (52 and 76, respectively) on HIV/AIDS, and Black female bloggers had 113 blog posts on the topic. There are two main frames, explored below, used in the talk on HIV/AIDS: celebratory/recognition and human disaster. These frames show how discreet silences are used, consciously or unconsciously, within Black women's talk.

Celebratory/Recognition Frame

Among Black female elected officials, *Essence* and *Ebony* magazines, and Black female bloggers the celebratory frame was the most deployed frame in their talk on HIV/AIDS. As I explored this dominantly used frame, I asked what type of cultural and political productions result from such framing. I present three typical celebratory/recognition subframes from elected officials, *Essence* and *Ebony* magazines, and bloggers. What cuts across this overarching frame, regardless of its structure, in these public spaces of talk is the deflection of attention from social-structural factors that are critical in understanding the spread of the virus among Blacks in general and Black women specifically.

A typical celebratory/recognition frame used among congressional members looks like this, from Representative Meek:

> We must never forget the contributions of those who have gone before us. Today as we recognize the 20th Anniversary of the discovery of AIDS. I commend the 12 National Organizations from across the country, who have come together to launch a national campaign to provide health care, treatment, and prevention education and information to millions of Americans impacted by this epidemic . . . AIDS Action Committee of Massachusetts, AIDS Project Los Angeles, The Balm in Gilead, Broadway Cares, Gay Men's Health Crisis, The National Association of People with AIDS, National Minority AIDS Council, The NAMES Project Foundation, San Francisco AIDS Foundation, and the Whitman-Walker Clinic are all to be commended for coming together in this unique partnership to launch a national public affairs campaign to provide health care, treatment, and prevention education and information to millions of Americans. (AIDS Epidemic, 147 Cong. Rec. E1035, 2001, p. E1035).

Given their social standing as elected officials, the information provided by Meek and other congresswomen serves as legitimized discourse that can impose meaning upon and orient attention to particular experiences. Meek's statement of support not only recognizes the organizations, but also draws attention to a number of issues in an attempt to address the epidemic. Primarily, her talk centers on awareness and treatment. Embedded in this frame is the silence of how to prevent HIV/AIDS by addressing poverty, incarceration, and housing segregation, for example. In essence, Meek does not offer transformational talk (this is the silence) that challenges HIV/AIDS beyond the personal responsibility approach.

Black women bloggers also center the work of celebrities within the recognition frame. A post by Brown Sista offers an example of the celebrity/recognition frame used by bloggers. Brown Sista (August 16, 2006) informs us about the activities of biker babes when she wrote,

> Actresses Gabrielle Union (Bad Boys 2) and Essence Atkins (Half and Half) will join the all-star celebrity line up for the NABB's Miami International Bikefest 2006 to be held Labor Day weekend in Miami, Florida. Presented by the National Association of Black Bikers (NABB), the Miami International Bikefest will be hosted by BET and radio personality Big Tigger and will bring together Hollywood celebrities, entertainers and athletes for the must-attend charity event August 31—September 3, 2006 in Miami. Joined by TV host Melyssa Ford and R&B Artist Tank, Union and Atkins will support the Miami International Bikefest and the Miami International AIDS Ride; the premier charity event for motorcycle enthusiasts and those attracted to the biking lifestyle. . . . A portion of the event proceeds will go towards donations to Big Tigger's Street Corner Foundation for their work in building public awareness of HIV/AIDS and New Horizons Community Mental Health Center for their work in mental health and substance abuse care.

The work of Sheryl Lee Ralph (Brown Sista), Alicia Keys (Black Girl Gives Back), among other celebrities, and their organizations were also prominent in bloggers' recognition frames. In these blog posts it appears that the celebrity is the primary subject in the story and HIV/AIDS is secondary—this can also be read as a form of discreet silence. As such, these posts might be considered more as "gossip" posts. This is an example of what I discussed in the introduction. On the surface there seems to be quite a bit of talk on HIV and AIDS; however, the talk fails to critically address AIDS.

Among bloggers, another recognition frame focused on World AIDS Day and National Women & Girls HIV/AIDS Awareness Day, and the resulting campaigns/activities of this day. Consider posts by Afrobella whose posts were titled, for example, "Are you Rocking Red Pumps Today?" (March 10, 2010). Afrobella tells her readers:

> Bellas, I can't even really *wear* heels, but today on Afrobella I'm proud to represent and rock these fly Alexander McQueen red pumps online all day! Today is National Women & Girls HIV/AIDS Awareness Day. One year ago, Karyn and Luvvie founded The Red Pump Project—an enthusiastic non profit organization which has tirelessly worked to raise awareness both online, and with a series of awesome events around the country. Today marks the celebration of the 500 in 50: Rock the Red Pump campaign—where fellow bloggers are encouraged to be part of the movement and show solidarity by featuring a Red Pump badge on their blog. And to write about what National Women & Girls HIV/AIDS Awareness Day means to them.

Posts such as the examples shared above prioritize concerns and normalize some behaviors—charity becomes the norm. Consequently, this talk can make invisible other concerns and alternate forms of action. Activities or programs such as "Rock the Red Pumps" represent a rather abstract and depersonalized way of addressing the issue of HIV/AIDS. Such an approach is similar to the "pinking" of products used in campaigns designed to raise breast cancer awareness. It is suggested that such campaigns are simply marketing ploys (see Singer, 2011). Pinking, similar to Rock the Red and other such campaigns, tend to focus on buying products (as a means of helping those in need). Furthermore, as V. Taylor and Van Willigen (1996) argue, the self-help movement that characterized the breast cancer movement of the 1990s fostered a movement that promotes internal reflection and personal transformation as opposed to external or structural change. Like pinking, rocking the red pump seems suitable for encouraging a volunteer citizen while making HIV/AIDS "chic" as it is linked more to celebrities than "regular" people. It promotes the status quo of our approach to HIV/AIDS, which encourages charity and not politics. What this suggests is a form of silence where HIV and AIDS are not linked to structural factors that require political action to foster and demand change. The personal approach, specifically the consumer approach, renders silent the role of government policy in addressing AIDS. Consequently, the U.S. federal government can continue its longstanding policy of no national AIDS policy outside of the Ryan White Act.

Similarly, *Essence* and *Ebony* magazines recognized the actions of celebrities in their talk on HIV/AIDS. In 2001, Murray saluted "20 of the most outstanding sisters leading the war on HIV/AIDS" (p. 82). Included in the list of women who were recognized were legislators, community pillars, facilitators, and the fact keeper. Also recognized was Nella P. Mupier (Miss Prairie View A&M University Queen) for her HIV/AIDS activism ("Black College Queens 2003," 2003, p. 138). Sports figures and celebrities, such as Magic Johnson and Montel Williams ("Champions for a cause," 2003, p. 92) and Alicia Keys (Cole, 2007, p. 68) were also recognized for their HIV/AIDS activism. Such frames more often than not took the following form: "In the last few years, the Jamie Foxx Foundation has supported causes related to orphanages in Haiti, HIV/AIDS in Africa through Save Africa's Children, and victims of Hurricane Katrina" (Gordy et al., 2006, p. 141). Again we see that charity as opposed to activism is promoted within this type of framing.

The deployment of a celebratory frame as a means of discussing HIV/AIDS can be inspiring and can encourage others to become involved in the fight against HIV/AIDS even if only in the form of charitable giving. However, while Black women are talking about HIV/AIDS, there is a silence. A celebratory frame fails to highlight how women live daily with AIDS and puts some distance between non-HIV-positive and HIV-positive women. These women become invisible, a form of discreet silence, as society never has to "see" them and as such never has to see their struggles as real. The result of this silence, in part, is reflected in how the Black community specifically and the wider society in general makes demands for the protection of this segment of the body politic. While the work of celebrities is highlighted in the talk, the HIV/AIDS status of these individuals remains private. In comparison, the talk on celebrity and mental illness and to some extent domestic violence speaks directly to celebrity experiences. This contributes to the silence. While HIV/AIDS appears to be in the public arena, the disease itself remains in the private realm. Consequently, Black women who are HIV positive and those living with AIDS become shadows when this celebratory frame is used because of the limited talk. Additionally, such a frame does very little to center the relationship between structural factors such as poverty, oppressive structures such as sexism, and the spread of HIV/AIDS among Black women.

Human Disaster Frame

Beyond the celebratory frame, Black women also employ the human disaster frame in their talk on HIV/AIDS. A human disaster frame is one that includes discussion on the number of victims, the impact on the individual and their family and society, and the prevalence of the illness. I borrow this frame, in part, from prior research that coded HIV/AIDS discourses (see Bardhan, 2001 and Princeton Survey Research Associates, 1996). As we analyze this frame, we must ask: How does it work to encourage social action, an inclusive social action? Below I offer three representative examples of this frame. These examples highlight the similarity in the talk of this issue among congresswomen, *Essence* and *Ebony*, and bloggers.

Congresswoman Maxine Waters, in discussing the spread of the disease and the changing face of HIV/AIDS, opined:

> What do we find when we look at the African American community? We find, of course, that it is the leading cause of death for African Americans between the ages of 25 and 44. What do we find when we look at African-American women? We find that in the new AIDS cases, we are 30 percent of that population. We also find that we are infected 16 times more than white women. (Combating HIV/AIDS in the Black Community, 145 Cong. Rec. H9180, 1999, p. H9180)

In *Essence* and *Ebony* magazines, the human disaster frame assumed the format of the following example: "Black females are diagnosed with HIV at 20 times the rate of White females and more than four times the rate of Hispanic females. Among Black females, roughly 78 percent of the HIV diagnoses were attributed to high-risk heterosexual contact. Intravenous drug use accounted for 19 percent" (Monroe, 2006, p. 154).

Brown Girl Gumbo's post is illustrative of the human disaster frame used among bloggers. She wrote: "According to the Centers for Disease Control, we African-Americans face the most severe burden of HIV in the United States. At the end of 2007, we accounted for almost half (46 percent) of people living with a diagnosis of HIV infection in the 37 states and 5 US dependent areas with long-term, confidential, name-based HIV reporting" (Brown Girl Gumbo, December 1, 2010). Beyond such reporting, Black women were often not explicitly discussed among bloggers.

The human disaster frame is often presented in a neutral and value-free manner. A human disaster frame, which relies on statistics, is frequently thought of as reflecting objective reality. The notion of an objective reality is used to offer the recipients of this frame a "realistic" depiction of HIV/AIDS and infected individuals. However, what remains hidden is the subjective decision of frame selection. Such a frame, while speaking to Black women's susceptibility, does not address risk factors—including those at the micro and macro level. As such, it might be easier for some to dismiss this frame, as they do not see themselves as being susceptible to the virus. Additionally, this seemingly neutral and value-free frame can hide the realities of the women behind these statistics. Consequently, alternative framing that might make HIV and AIDS real and visible is ignored—therein lies another form of silence.

While the human disaster frame is used in Black women's talk on HIV/AIDS to inform the listener/reader of the spread of HIV/AIDS, it is employed in a rather restricted manner. Such framing tends not to include talk of the realities of women living with HIV/AIDS and the impact on their families. For example, there are no stories in *Essence* and *Ebony* that profile women who are living daily with HIV/AIDS. However, there exist stories of women who have "triumphed" over domestic violence (see chapter 5). In AIDS stories we tend not to see Black women portrayed as either "patients" or "survivors." Thus, HIV/AIDS remains in the abstract realm. We have to ask: How does this human disaster frame work to transform HIV/AIDS from a personal problem into a social issue with consequences for the larger Black community?

Manifest in the framing of HIV/AIDS and its intersection with Black womanhood as a social problem are both the *Ass* and *Strong Black Woman* scripts. The use of these scripts, often implicitly, leads to a type of misrecognition and possibly a denial of the intersecting factors that contribute to the spread of the disease among Black women. Consequently, to borrow from E. E. Schattschneider (1960, 1975), many of the controversial factors, such as sexism, are organized out of politics. This is evident in the two frames discussed above. Neither the "celebratory" frame nor the "human disaster" frame, in terms of their content, speaks to the multiplicity of identities of Black women who are affected by the disease. Melucci (1995, p. 44) argues that "collective identity is an interactive and shared definition produced by several individuals (or groups as a more complex level) and concerned with the orientation of action and fields of opportunities and constraints in which the action take place." The *Ass* and *Strong Black Woman* scripts prescribe opportunities and constructions for actions. In the case of HIV/AIDS, these scripts do not permit Black women to engage, in a substantive manner, with the multiplicity of Black womanhood as they serve to delimit the understanding of community by determining who is talked about and why.

MISSING IN THE STORIES ON HIV/AIDS: BLACK WOMEN AND THEIR LIVED REALITIES

In this section, I consider how diverse Black women are represented in the HIV/AIDS talk. More specifically, I analyze how gender, class, and sexual identity, in the vein of Black feminism, are utilized in the talk. The tension between making visible the Black woman's experience with HIV/AIDS and also making them invisible becomes apparent in the structuring of the talk. Although the women spoke of Black women and HIV/AIDS, generally the talk did not address the structural factors often cited as contributing to the spread of the disease among Black women.

Consider this response that appeared in *Ebony* magazine. A letter writer asked, "Why have African-American women become the fastest-growing group of new HIV/AIDS cases?" Dr. Lorraine Cole responded:

> It is a result of unprotected sex with an infected partner. Biologically, women are more susceptible to contracting the virus than men and, subsequently, contract the disease at twice the rate as men. Women often believe they are in a monogamous relationship when they are not. A further complication is that many infected individuals do not know their HIV status and don't get early treatment or take precautions when engaging in sexual behavior. Also, one out of every three Black women does not have health insurance to access routine care, that means health problems that place some women at greater risk for contracting HIV are undetected. ("5 questions for Dr. Lorraine Cole," 2005, p. 26)

A primary focus on the response is on intimate relationships and as such her focus remains in the private realm and at the individual level. In her response, Dr. Cole speaks fleetingly of the issue of Black women's access to health care. However, she does not address gender roles and a host of other factors that contribute to the spread of the virus among Black women—this is a form of discreet silence, the unwillingness to discuss Black gender politics. These factors, cited by researchers such Adimora & Schoenbach (2002, 2005) and Wright & Martin (2003), are often left out in the talk by Black women. Although some Black women make HIV/AIDS visible in their talk, they are also making some Black women's experiences with the disease invisible—those who are susceptible to the disease as a result of gender politics, those who are lesbian and/or bisexual for example, and those for whom poverty enhances their susceptibility to the virus—thus casting them as shadows at best in the public understanding of the disease. It is important to consider what is left out of the talk as it helps us to analyze and explain how some Black women become shadow bodies. Below, I present examples of how this type of shadowing occurs. I start with the issue of gender.

One might argue that Black women's talk on HIV/AIDS does center gender. In their use of the human disaster frame, Black women do rely on statistics that speak to the rate of infection among Black women and other groups. While statistics are useful in telling stories of the extent of the disease among Black women, they do not speak to the relationship between the spread of HIV/AIDS and gender. Gender—roles, practices, and the resulting sexual scripts—is also a part of the contextual factors that influence Black women's exposure to HIV and AIDS. In terms of the gendering of AIDS, Weeks, Singer, Grier, and Schensul (1996) inform us that "Gender definitions and relations embody multidimensional ideals and interactions among women and men, including those associated with desires, preferences, and practices. They also express and embody relationships of power and dominance, assign value to kinds of sexual behaviors and relationships, and impose codes for "traditional," acceptable and forbidden roles and behaviors" (p. 341).

Gender norms and the resulting sexual scripts further perpetuate women's inequitable position, relative to men's, but such a frame is absent in the talk among Black women. There is a value of including such a frame in the talk on HIV/AIDS. Sexual scripts, as argued by Simon and Gagnon (1986), include cultural, interpersonal, and intrapersonal scripts that are used to inform and influence the individual's sexual decisions. The relative permanence of these scripts transcends time. Black women's reliance on existing gender norms and the ensuing sexual scripts can result in them being sexually passive, engaging in unprotected sex, and their inconsistent or nonuse of condoms because they see such behavior as normative or outside of the domain of the "good" woman (Bowleg, Lucas, & Tschann, 2004; Hynie, 1998; Jones, 2006; Maticka-Tyndale, 1991; Pulerwitz, Amaro, DeJong, Gortmaker, & Rudd, 2002). Black women did little to address and/or challenge gender roles, practices, and sexual scripts in their HIV/AIDS talk, and therefore failed to address gender equity and justice for Black women. Such failure is but one manifestation of discreet silences and reflects on how the subscript of the *ass question*, which looks at Black gender politics, influences collective action or inaction in this case. Given the failure of the larger Black community to critically engage in gender politics (see Alexander-Floyd, 2007; Wallace, 1990 [1978]) the Black women who inform this study focus on the act of sex and not gender inequality which influences how women engage in sex acts. Furthermore, in their understanding of the spread of HIV/AIDS they render silent a potential cultural approach to addressing and understanding this public health crisis.

In *Essence* magazine there was one article that explicitly discussed the issue of gender bias and its impact on Black women. It states:

> Men get more attention and more intensive treatment. At my clinic, I see women go into the doctor's office and come out in five minutes; men go in and come out in an hour. I think the doctors pay more attention to men because it was originally considered a man's disease. And they don't listen to Black women. They put us in a box—either you're a prostitute or a drug addict. Once they put you in a box, they stop listening to what your needs are, prescribe some drugs and send you on your way. I'm lucky I have a female doctor who listens. She understands that I'm a woman and that I have different needs. Still, it's real scary. I see Black women getting pushed against the wall and not being taken care of. (M. Perry, 1997, p. 130)

Perry utilizes a Black feminist stance, particularly in her treatment of the intersection of race and gender and the lived realities of Black women. In her piece, Perry seeks to empower readers by addressing the powerless position of women, relative to men, and how such a position complicates their treatment in general. Perry actively engages the limiting quality of the *ass question* subscript (see chapter 2). However, in her talk there is an implicit assumption that this is a universal experience among women, and so, for example, class does not influence the nature of treatment received by Black women (I discuss this form of silence below)

The silence on the relationship between gender and the spread of HIV/AIDS continues even among the "new" media (i.e., blog posts). Bloggers did not address Black sexual politics, gender roles and expectations, and the relationship to the spread of the virus among Black women. There were minimum posts that challenge the notion that Black women are the "new face" of AIDS. As argued by Brown Sista:

> As a Black woman, I'm so sick and tired of every time there is a media story about HIV/AIDS, a Black woman is featured predominately front and center. For example, Black In America, which was watched by nearly 5 million people in CNN's two-day airing, dedicated nearly the entire HIV/AIDS segment enforcing the poster person to be a Black female, but there are numerous other examples. Making a Black female the face of HIV/AIDS is a radical form of racism at its highest level and more proof that there is a conspiracy to keep Black women without love. This image of Black women creates more negative stereotypes that Black women are diseased and along with being loud, fat, bitches and hos, who are overbearing, booty-bouncing, undesirable she-men, no wonder Black women are the least married; sadly unbeknown, Black Women Need Love, Too! The trickery to take the stigma of HIV/AIDS from being a White male homosexual disease to

being a Black female heterosexual disease is consistent with racism in America. I cannot allow this type of deliberate prejudice to continue, especially since this is a big fallacy and here's why . . . : HIV/AIDS is NOT a female disease! Black women have NEVER encompassed the highest number of HIV/AIDS cases—the quote was "Black women are the FASTEST growing group of HIV/AIDS," which is no longer true, meaning Black women were growing in numbers fastest, but are not the most. Then why are Black women positioned predominately everywhere when this virus is discussed? The answer is RACISM and MISOGYNY at its finest. (August 13, 2008)

The Blogmother (August 5, 2008), in her blog post continues this critique with her assertion, "AIDS is NOT a 'Black Disease.'" She tells the readers that she "questions his [Phil Wilson founder and CEO of Black AIDS Institute] marketing methods" in terms of linking HIV/AIDS to Black folk. This marketing approach, she posited, was shortsighted because of "the damage that will likely follow if people are able to write off AIDS as a problem for 'that other group of people.'" She sees the problems as encompassing "a loss of funding, compassion and drug research." Why? Because, to paraphrase, Black folk are treated as second-class citizens.

It is worth mentioning that another challenge (again, minimally employed) focused on the mainstream media's depiction of Black women and HIV/AIDS. The Sauda Voice made such a challenge when she posted, "For the past several years, black women have comprised the largest number of new HIV-AIDS cases in America. *Didn't know?* I'm not surprised. Little to no attention has been paid to this growing epidemic by the mainstream media (MSM). Is it because the devastation is primarily affecting people of color? Perhaps, but one can only speculate at this point" (July 2, 2009, emphasis in original).

Brown Sista and The Sauda Voice, in the vein of the Combahee River Collective and other Black critical scholars, are challenging the use of the social construction of Black womanhood in the organization of society. By challenging the racialization of HIV/AIDS, they highlight the possible damage—from both hypervisibility and invisibility—that can result from these often employed constructions. It is posts such as these, the notes between the silences, that hint at Black feminist practice. However, the posts simultaneously ignore how gender influences Black women's vulnerability to the virus. Thus, Black women who are HIV positive and those with AIDS are simultaneously visible and not visible; they are there but not there. This is the process that renders them shadow bodies in politics.

With respect to HIV/AIDS and its relation to social class there are also limited, and often indirect, references appearing in Black women's talk. Throughout the 113 blog posts, there was one explicit reference to social class made by A Lady's Perspective. In this post, she states,

The HIV/AIDS epidemic in African American communities is a continuing public health crisis for the United States. At the end of 2006 there were an estimated 1.1 million people living with HIV infection, of which almost half (46 percent) were black/African American. While blacks represent approximately 12 percent of the U.S. population, they continue to account for a higher proportion of cases at all stages of HIV/AIDS—from infection with HIV to death with AIDS—compared with members of other races and ethnicities. The reasons are not directly related to race or ethnicity, but rather some of the barriers faced by many African Americans. These barriers can include poverty (being poor), and stigma (negative attitudes, beliefs, and actions directed at people living with HIV/AIDS or people who do things that might put them at risk for HIV). (A Lady's Perspective, February 7, 2010)

Ignoring the relationship between economic status and susceptibility to HIV/AIDS can limit our response to the spread of the virus. While it is important to recognize that the virus is not bounded by economic class, in our desire to be universal we must remain mindful that there is a relationship between the prevalence of HIV/AIDS and individuals of a lower economic bracket (see Plowden, Fletcher, & Miller, 2005). Additionally, we also have to recognize that an individual's economic resources influences how she can live with HIV and AIDS in terms of access to care for example (see Watkins-Hayes, 2008).

Black congresswomen very rarely explicitly integrated poverty and class in their talk—that is, specific use of the terms. Instead, access to health care appears to serve as the proxy to discuss issues of class and poverty and HIV/AIDS. Congresswoman Maxine Waters (Ryan White AIDS Care Act, 151 Cong. Rec. H21592, 2005) articulated one such frame when she stated "The Ryan White CARE Act is critical for minorities who often lack access to traditional health care and support services. About half of all Ryan White Care Act clients are black, and that proportion is much higher in some care settings" (p. H21592).

What was often missing from this frame is an explicit understanding and/or questioning of how the lack of access to care influences Black women's vulnerability to and experiences with HIV/AIDS. This silence I interpret as a manifestation of the *spiritual/supernatural strength* subscript ascribed to Black women's bodies. This script, which is part of the *Strong Black Woman* metascript, suggests that Black women somehow are able to cope regardless of the structural violence levied against them (see chapter 2). Thus, Black women who are affected by HIV/AIDS, because its understanding is coupled with a narrative of transcendence, cannot be talked about as they challenge the narrative of progress and respectability that is often relied upon by many in the Black community (Cohen, 1999; Hammonds, 1992).

Over the 10-year period covered in this study, there were three explicit references to economic class and its relationship to HIV/AIDS within the pages of *Essence* and *Ebony*. In the article on "An HIV cure?" (2001), it was asserted:

Community Outreach in the United States, HIV/AIDS treatment dollars are available, and most people who need care get it. But what of the groups that show increasing infection rates—namely women of color and young gay Black men? "Many factors have led to the upsurge, including poverty, drug abuse, lack of education and jobs," says Arboleda. Activists are lobbying to ensure that appropriate education and treatment reach people of color. (p. 80)

Another reference to class stated , "Along with ending the silence, experts say prevention efforts must address socioeconomic factors, such as poverty, that discourage Black women from getting diagnosed and seeking treatment. 'The epidemic disproportionately affects people who are poor,' says Dr. Gayle. 'They have poor access to information, poor access to health care and services'" (Starling, 2000, p. 136).

The above two quotations focused on issues of poverty. However, the third reference was different in comparison to the above two. The third referenced the intersection of class and HIV/AIDS by centering middle-class Black women. Accordingly, it stated:

Unfortunately, many Sisters make that same mistake, experts say. "Part of the problem reaching middle-class Black women who have achieved a certain level of success is that they think AIDS is for other women of color," says Dr. Cargill. "They think if he's a nice guy with a nice car and lives in a nice neighborhood, he couldn't possibly be infected with HIV. But HIV doesn't care if he has a Rolex watch or if he went to the premier college in the land. It's about risk behavior." (Starling, 2000, p. 136)

Given the minimum references to the relationship between class and the spread of HIV/AIDS, I assume that *Essence* and *Ebony* sought to show the universality of the spread of the disease regardless of economic class. The unwillingness to talk about the relationship between economic class and HIV/AIDS must be read in context of Black women's politics. Such politics often responds to the negative construction of Black womanhood and engages in actions to not perpetuate already-existing negative constructions. However, in failing to explore the relationship between HIV/AIDS and economic class, these women might not be taking advantage of the possibility of connecting HIV/AIDS to already-existing issues that tend to be mainstays on the Black political agenda—issues such as access to housing and education, for example. The failure to link AIDS to such issues is but another form of silence.

With regards to HIV/AIDS, researchers confirm a systematic relationship between HIV/AIDS incidence and prevalence to economic deprivation (Farmer, 2005; Fife & Mode, 1992a, 1992b; Parker, Easton, & Klein, 2000; Plowden, Fletcher, & Miller, 2005; Simon, Hu, Diaz, & Kerndt, 1995; Zierler et al., 2000). Poverty and its resulting manifestations such as unequal access to education, employment, and livable wages (due in part to segregation and access to jobs); limited access to health clinics; and heightened exposure to violence influences women's ability to make decisions over their lives and their abilities to negotiate power in their relationships at both micro and macro levels. At the micro level, Leone et al. (2005) show that HIV-positive Black women (in North Carolina) who were financially dependent on their partners tended to engage in risky sexual behavior because they were unable to negotiate condom use (in part). Consequently, the approach most often taken to address HIV/AIDS—prevention through behavioral modification and education—continues to be challenged. Failure to speak on Black women's economic situation might prove difficult in convincing some women to change their sexual behaviors. Poverty, at the macro level, also limits HIV-positive Black women's ability to negotiate their care. Simply put, income influences access to health care. In a 1998 study, Bozzette and colleagues stated that HIV-positive adults in the United States, relative to the general population, are one-fifth more likely to lack health insurance. Additionally, these individuals are three times as likely to be insured by Medicaid and nine times as likely to have Medicare coverage. Women, in comparison to men, are more likely to be covered by Medicaid—61 percent women, 39 percent men (Bozzette et al., 1998). A 2010 report indicates that "African-American women are less likely to receive health care. When they do get care, they are more likely to get it late" says a report on Minority Women's Health (Madlock Gatison, 2016, p. xvi). Financial barriers are one of the major factors that limit Black women's access to health care. Financial restrictions include, for example, health care costs for out-of-pocket expenses and medications. Some women are also often financially limited in their ability to afford transportation to seek care (National Alliance of State and Territorial AIDS Directors, 2008).

Black women's failure to systematically and critically engage the interrelatedness of class and HIV/AIDS is the result of the controlled morality talked about by scholars such as E. Frances White (1990). Given African Americans' commitment to "respectability politics (Higginbotham, 1993), there is an attempt to control the public presentation of Blackness in particular and Black womanhood specifically. Black womanhood in relation to class and its intersection with HIV/AIDS does not permit for the type of control necessitated by respectability politics. As I argue in the concluding chapter, to bring such women out of the shadows would suggest that Black womanhood is "flawed" and as such the Black community has failed. It has failed in the sense that the Black community has not lived up to its notions of strength and respectability—which is also connected with the *Ass* metascript.

The issue of sexual identity also represents another discreet silence in Black women's talk. Heterosexuality, although not prominently talked about, was privileged in the discourses. The discourses centered the spread of HIV/AIDS via heterosexual sex and the failure to use condoms. This can been seen when Representative Millender-McDonald (Women's Health Issues, 143 Cong. Rec. H1966, 1997) asserted "Among minority women, the most prevalent modes of contracting HIV are injecting drug use, 37 percent, and heterosexual contact, almost 38 percent. . . . In the inner-city community, there are often greater perceived notions that sex is not as good if a condom is used. Frequently women do not encourage their sexual partners to use condoms for fear of retribution?" (p. H1966). Congresswoman Clayton (HIV/AIDS, 147 Cong. Rec. H3839–40, 2001, p. H3839) also centered heterosexuality when she stated, "Rates of infection continue to grow among adolescents among women, with heterosexual contact as their primary mode of transmission."

Black lesbians were rendered completely invisible in the discourses of Black female congressional members. The HIV/AIDS and sexuality frames focused on the Black male homosexual. While not widely used (only one reference), there was a mention of the phenomenon related to "men on the down low": "There has been a lot of discussion about many facts and a lot of individuals and communities and a lot of individuals and communities really heap a lot of blame on men who are considered on the 'down low.' . . . Some people feel that the down low is contributing to these statistics. But the truth is, we just do not know" (Supporting Goals and Ideals of National Black HIV/AIDS Awareness Day, 151 Cong. Rec. H432, 2005). The dominant sexual identity frame tended to be employed in the "celebratory" frame discussed above. In this frame the work of gay organizations was highlighted and celebrated. However, there was very little discussion about either the needs of transgendered or lesbian individuals who are HIV positive or the extent and the impact of the disease among these populations. These women are in essence the shadow bodies of this discourse.

Sexual identity, unlike economic class, did receive a bit more attention by Black female bloggers. Bloggers tended to focus on the issue of men who have sex with men. To a lesser extent a few bloggers discussed the issue of prison sex and its implications once the men are released. More often than not, women were projected as the prey/victims of these men. Consider Brown Sista's post, which said:

Best-selling novelist Terri McMillan shares her emotionally-charged testimony on the controversial BET News documentary, 'The Down Low Exposed,' premiering March 28 at 10 p.m. ET/PT. "I think that what [BET is] doing should be applauded because I think more than anything there are women out there that are victims," the author of 'Waiting to Exhale' said during the one-hour news special—a probing look into the world of men with wives or girlfriends who also secretly engage in sex with other men. "I think we need to hold men accountable for their actions," McMillan added, in what she said is her final public interview on the subject. Last year, her marriage to Jonathan Plummer publicly unraveled with a nasty divorce as a result of his admission to a secret gay life. "I think that he should be charged with attempted murder for risking my life without my knowledge or consent," the chick-lit diva said in the documentary.

Helmed by Park Hill Entertainment President Shirley Neal, 'Exposed' examines this divisive subject from a variety of angles including prison sex and its impact on the spread of HIV/AIDS; the Black church; the impact of HIV and AIDS on women infected by men who hid their homosexuality; and the crucial importance of being tested for the disease. (March 27, 2006)

Such posts sought to expose the secrecy around men who have sex with men but who do not consider themselves gay. This type of talk, prevalent over the time period of this study, is reflected in Brown Sugar's 2009 post.

According to Brown Sugar (January 3, 2009), "Sex in prison is normative." She then goes on to talk about men on the "down low." On December 10, 2007, Brown Sugar explicitly links prison sex and the HIV/AIDS epidemic. As stated, "Many men contract HIV and other diseases in prison. And we know what those numbers are like for black males. They get out and voila we've got ourselves an epidemic."

In *Ebony* and *Essence* the framing of the intersection of sexuality and HIV/AIDS focused on how women contract the disease from homosexual or bisexual men. For instance, Foston (2002) said

Contributing to the alarming rate of infection are a variety of factors, including unprotected sex, sex with multiple partners, needle sharing among intravenous drug users, and the growing population of "down-low Brothers"—men who do not consider themselves gay or bisexual, but engage in sex with both men and women. The return of previously incarcerated men into our communities also affects the rate of infection among Black women. "We have a huge population of African-American males who go into prison HIV-negative and come out HIV-positive," says Thornton. "When these men get out, they come back to our daughters, our mothers and our sisters. They don't go back to men because they don't consider themselves gay." (p. 17)

Dr. Gwendolyn Goldsby Grant (2000, p. 66) in "Safe, Soulful Sex" asserted, "Statistics show that nationwide Black women have the highest rate of reported AIDS cases among any racial or gender group. And we're getting the virus largely from having unprotected sex with bisexual men and drug users." Beyond the so-called men on the down-low phenomenon and how women have sex with these men unknowingly, there was one story that explicitly discussed homosexuality, with a particular focus on lesbians.

Readers were informed, "Homophobia kills. It would be bad enough if it killed only lesbians and gay men. But the impact it has on the battle against AIDS in Black communities is devastating" (Wilson, 1998, p. 62). Wilson (1998) further writes,

> A contributing factor is the veil of secrecy and the disgrace surrounding homosexuality in the Black community. "If we really are going to be serious about helping to end HIV infections and building a proud and strong Black community, we are going to have to begin by making it clear that there can't be any space for discriminating against gays and lesbians," says A. Cornelius Baker, executive director of the Whitman-Walker Clinic, an influential non-profit lesbian and gay community health organization based in Washington, D.C. (p. 62)

Across the diverse platforms that I used to analyze talk on HIV/AIDS (and for that matter the other two public issues), this was the only instance that explicitly discussed protecting homosexual individuals (most of the talk focused on how to protect oneself from homosexuals—particularly men "on the down low").

Once again, Black lesbians and transgendered individuals are not included in the talk. There is a silence with regard to this population. In explaining the absence of women who have sex with women and self-identified lesbians, Goldstein (1997, p. 90) argues that it is "impossible to construct an HIV-infected person with a complex identity from within the confines of the CDC-regulated AIDS discourse." She further argues that, "Although the CDC surveillance definitions play a significant role in obscuring the rate or cause of HIV infection among women who have sex with women, the construction of risk categories, and hence, responsibility for lesbian invisibility in the AIDS epidemic, also lies with other sectors of the scientific community" (p. 91).

While she focuses on the scientific community, I would argue that "everyday" individuals and those in some relative position of power to frame discourses on HIV/AIDS also contribute to the invisibility of some who are affected and infected by the disease. I posit that such exclusion is a result of Black women's protectionist politics, which is an outgrowth of the scripts ascribed to Black women's bodies. Thus, Black lesbians, for example, are not seen as epitomizing the "good" elements of Black womanhood. Consequently, they are not included in the agenda—which is a manifestation of the *piece of ass* and the *ass question* subscripts discussed in chapter 2. While this protectionist approach (i.e., not displaying perceived "negative" images of Black women) can be read as liberatory, it can also be read as oppressive. A protectionist politics limits who we can advocate on behalf of and it fails to open spaces that can facilitate a more trans-formative and inclusive integration of intersectionality.

LIVING WITH AIDS: SUGGESTIONS ON HOW TO CONFRONT THE DISEASE

Two frames, couched under the umbrella of behavioral modification, dominated Black women's approaches to addressing HIV/AIDS. Black congresswomen, Black female bloggers, and *Essence* and *Ebony*, as a means of fighting the spread of HIV/AIDS, instructed their listeners and readers to know their status and that of their partners. Additionally, women were instructed to "take care" of themselves—either in terms of seeking medical attention when seeing their pri-mary care physicians or in terms of their intimate relationships. Another element of the behavioral modification approach involved the promotion of condom use and the call for women, in particular, to "wake up" and learn about the dangers of HIV and AIDS. This I refer to as the "education frame." Beyond the educa-tion frame, and among Black elected officials only, there were policy demands made for increased funding of the Ryan White Care Act. The policy demands also included specific requests for how such funding would benefit communities of color. While I highlight the use of these frames, it is not to suggest that they were frequently or abundantly employed in the talk on how to confront HIV/AIDS among Black women.

Particularly evident in Black women's talk was the marked absence or limited references to structural factors as contributing to the spread of HIV/AIDS—this shows the discreet silences deployed by the women. Below, I present the "Take care of yourself" frame followed by the "Education" frame. These frames suggest the types of political action engaged in and encouraged. They also speak to notions of citizenship, who is included and how and who is excluded, and the role of the state as it relates to HIV and AIDS.

Take Care of Yourself: Know His and Your Status

As part of the larger behavioral modification frame, Black women are instructed to "take responsibility for their bodies" (Hughes, 2004, p. 64). Such instruc-tion may be read as a response to the *piece of ass* subscript and the notion of the hypersexual/irresponsible Black sexual being. However, the framing of the policy responses, in the manner of take personal care, tends to ignore sexual power rela-tions within the Black community. Taking responsibility for their bodies involves Black women screening their "sexual partners carefully. If he doesn't want to be honest about his sexual history, then he should be history. And latex condoms are a must when you are sexually involved" ("HIV," 2004, p. 140). Readers were also cautioned about the factors they use to evaluate their sexual partners.

But it's not just the insidious nature of AIDS that gets us in trouble, observes Wyatt. Most of us simply use the wrong criteria to evaluate our partners. "Women are looking at jobs and clothes and appearance and what the person says and how much money he makes," she says. Those may be appropriate criteria for deciding whether to have dinner with someone, but they're hardly worth considering when it comes to deciding whether to have unprotected sex. Instead, says Wyatt, you should ask: *Is this person a player? Has he been in prison? Does he use drugs? Is he sleeping with more than one person? Does he have my well-being at heart?* And most important: *Has he been tested recently, and does he practice safe sex?* Keep in mind that one in 50 Black men is HIV-positive or has full-blown AIDS. "Once the virus becomes prevalent in a community, as it is in ours, your risk of bumping into it becomes much higher," says Helene Gayle, M.D., M.P.H., senior adviser for HIV/AIDS with the Bill & Melinda Gates Foundation in Seattle. As a result, she says, Black women need to evaluate their sexual partners much more carefully. (Amber, 2002, p. 118, emphasis in original)

While Amber discussed the prevalence of the virus, she fails to address the factors (beyond behaviors) that influence the spread of the disease among Black women. This approach to dealing with HIV/AIDS relies heavily on a language of self-help and individual behavior, a trend that runs throughout the suggestions on how to address HIV/AIDS. Ignored are those women who cannot readily protect themselves—the women who are not strong enough or who are treated as a *physical ass* or a *piece of ass*. These women become problematic because they challenge Black racial advancement in the sense that they do not fit the model of the "strong" Black woman. Also, they are damaged and consequently cannot be used in the racial uplift project, thus the silence.

Education Is Key: A Means of Protection

As suggested in the naming of this frame, its primary purpose is to provide general education to readers. Such information draws attention to how HIV is contracted and how it could be prevented. The education frame varied across the three areas of talk, but covered related topics. For example, there was the focus on how one can contract HIV and testing options. Below, I offer a few illustrative examples of the education frame.

This quote, taken from blogger Is it Just Me, highlights one aspect of the education frame which focused on protecting one self. Is it Just Me wrote:

My humble opinion says, why not fight the urge for sudden instant physical gratification and see if the person is really worth giving so much of yourself to? Trust and believe I know it's hard, but it's a far cry better than doing something of minimal value and not having anything of merit to show for it than waiting. It's sad that people are more willing to shed their clothes than to share their true selves . . . Blog fam, we're already a community broken and this behavior trend plays a key role in why. Yes, I realize other races probably have this issue to, but I'm speaking on *my* community. With the HIV rate skyrocketing, it's one more reason to slow your roll. (August 28, 2008)

This approach encourages women to look after their sexual health in general. A similar approach was taken in *Essence* and *Ebony* magazines, which often inform readers:

> But thanks to faster and more convenient methods of testing, you and your partner can now go to the doctor and get results in as little as 20 minutes. To get your partner on board, Know HIV/AIDS, a national campaign to raise awareness of the disease, suggests this: Tell your partner you want to talk about testing so that the two of you can be closer and worry less. Emphasize that sex will be less stressful once you both know your status. Then together go over the information below so that you know what your alternatives are. (Carter, 2004, p. 99)

The article then lists and discusses various types of testing options, such as rapid testing. As a final example of the education frame, I offer the following: "Dr. Yolanda H. Wimberly, assistant professor of clinical pediatrics for Grady Health Systems and Morehouse School of Medicine in Atlanta, says schools, churches and parents must assume a larger role in educating young people about AIDS and other sexually transmitted diseases like bacterial vaginosis, trichomonas, Chlamydia, herpes, syphilis and gonorrhea" (Bullock, 2003, p. 136).

Black Congresswomen, such as Johnson, often stated, "We must continue to educate/prevent and care for our members who have been affected by [this] atrocious epidemic and continue to fight against HIV/AIDS" (Supporting the Goals and Ideals of National Black HIV/AIDS Awareness Day, 2007, p. H1166). Representative Waters (HIV/AIDS, 152 Cong. Rec. H7504, p. H7504), in articulating the actions of the Congressional Black Caucus, asserted that the organization "has and continue to assume a leadership role in addressing the issue through AIDS education and other actions. We are increasing our efforts to insist on personal responsibility, mandatory testing, outreach and education, advocating for increased funding, more legislation." Representative Waters's approach is one of: educate, prevent, and increased access. Embedded in this frame (implicitly and explicitly) are notions of behavioral modification as a means of limiting the spread of the infection. It centers, minimally, on addressing structural issues that heighten Black women's susceptibility to HIV/AIDS. Furthermore, such a frame limits the role of government in addressing the spread of the virus to simply offering education, and does nothing to call on the government to pursue gender or race equity policies or other policies designed to challenge systemic inequality.

It should be of no surprise to learn that Black female bloggers, in general, tend to promote and encourage an individualistic response, one of personal responsibility, to HIV/AIDS. When HIV/AIDS is framed in a manner that does not recognize the intersection of HIV/AIDS and multiple systems of oppression, then it is more difficult to challenge these systems. The majority of the blog posts did not offer specific suggestions for addressing HIV/AIDS. This is a result of the "laundry list" approach where HIV/AIDS is referenced as another ailment, among several, that plagues the Black community. Or, it could be the result of the bloggers, in a rather neutral manner, simply citing the impact and extent of HIV/AIDS in the Black community. Whatever the rationale, bloggers tended to encourage support of various charities and for individuals to engage in sexually healthy practices as means for confronting HIV/AIDS.

Support for various charities and encouraging readers to purchase various products was a somewhat typical call to action. Readers were informed, by Ari (on Brown Sista's Blog):

> A couple days ago I decided to go to Dillard's and visit the Mac counter for new cosmetics I hadn't tried yet. During my visit I picked up an amazing lip gloss by Viva Glam called Tinted Lipglass. There are three distinctive shades to choose from depending on your personality and style. It's long-lasting effect will keep you wanting more. Despite its great color and shine, all proceeds of Viva Glam lipstick and lipglass is donated to M-A-C Aids Fund. This fund supports men, women, and children living with HIV and AIDS. This gloss is so rich and stunning you're bound to fall in love. (Brown Sista, August 12, 2009)

As suggested in this post, not only will you get a great lipstick, but also your purchase would be put to a greater good. I Like her Style also encouraged her readers to shop at the Body Shop in order to support various HIV/AIDS charities. She suggested to readers that they make such purchases their "good deed for the day and look great doing it!" (I Like her Style, September 25, 2006). This approach seems to fit the model of the woman as consumer and by extension consumerism as "activism." Consequently, other forms of activism and organizing remain invisible.

There was one blogger who went beyond the personal sexual healthy frame and consumer activism. In 2008, blogger A Lady's Perspective wrote:

> "Leadership-Stop AIDS. Keep the Promise" is this year's theme. People living with HIV and AIDS (PLHIV) and their supporters are the driving force in the fight against the disease. They have taken the lead in asking questions and getting global leaders and governments fully involved in the fight, but the struggle continues. Without PLHIV leadership, universal access to prevention, treatment

and care will remain a dream. To achieve the goal, everyone must do his/her part in the fight. Governments must get involved and keep the promises they made. Community leaders must encourage its members to take leadership roles in sharing information. Individuals must get tested, know their rights to prevention and treatment, and take action against stigma and discrimination, because HIV/AIDS does not discriminate.

She made a similar call to governments, community leaders, and individuals in 2009. Although this post does not explicitly address the intersection of HIV/AIDS and multiple systems of oppression, it does hint at recognizing that individual-level behavior alone cannot stop the spread of the disease.

The only post that suggests a Black feminist politics recognized the organization Women Alive. This post, contributed by Kim Anthony for Black Girls Give Back, stated:

> Another "story" that is close to Cookie Johnson's heart is the plight of the women served by the evening's beneficiaries, Women Alive. Created in 1990 by a group of women living with HIV/AIDS who recognized the need to provide a more specialized gender specific AIDS service organization for women, Women Alive reaches nearly 150 HIV+ clients and their families, and over 1,000 individuals through their outreach endeavors, out-patient clinics, health fairs, home visits, posters, brochures, and role model stories. (October 24, 2010)

In the words of Michele Berger (2004, p. 187) the policy suggestions offered by Black women fail to recognize "the multifaceted response to injustice that galvanize women" to act in response to HIV/AIDS and its relation to structural and systemic oppression. Not only do the policy suggestions fail in the manner suggested by Berger, but they also fail because they do not recognize the modalities of Black womanhood. The pervasive silence around structural violence and HIV/AIDS in Black women's talk leaves us to wonder who is this group muting and why? The "activism" around Black women and HIV/AIDS among Black congresswomen, Black female bloggers, and *Essence* and *Ebony* magazines erases the broader social structures that impact the lived realities of diverse Black women who are affected with HIV/AIDS. Such Black women seem to have no political efficacy. Their political efficacy is stymied; as there is a perception that such women cannot be "innocent" and used in the project of racial uplift—they are too closely aligned with the negative aspects of the *Ass* script and fail to satisfy the requirements necessitated by the *Strong Black Woman* script. Consequently, Black HIV-positive women cannot be used to organize activism and political change among Black women and the larger Black community.

CONCLUSION

As articulated by Berger (2004, p. 7), "the degree to which women have been affected by the disease is inseparable from the historical scars of inequality in American society." Black women are susceptible to HIV and later AIDS as a result of a number of factors including gender inequality, race/racism, age, poverty, marital status, geographic location, and work-related issues. Singularly and combined, these factors play a vital role in increasing women's vulnerability to the disease (see Albertyn, 2003; Quinn, 1993; Schiller and Lewellen 1994). Overwhelmingly, these women tend to be poor, solo-parents, and residents of urban communities (Connors, 1996; Schable, Chu, & Diaz, 1995).

However, in the face of the growing AIDS epidemic among African American women and the relationship between the virus and the legacy of inequality, they have been rendered both invisible and hypervisible. In discussing the invisibility and hypervisibility of African American women who are affected by and infected with HIV/AIDS, Evelynn Hammonds (1992) said

> African-American women with AIDS are constantly represented with respect to drug-use—either their own or their partners. They are largely poor or working-class. They are single mothers. Media portrayals of these people with AIDS allude to the specter of drug abuse and controlled sexuality coupled with welfare "dependency" and irresponsibility. Such allusions undermine any representations of African-American women with AIDS that would allow them to be embraced by the larger public. (p. 11)

The Black response to AIDS, because of its conscious or unconscious reliance on negative images of women and its inability to incorporate gender into its freedom struggle, has also contributed to the neglect of HIV-positive Black women (Cohen, 1999).

Part of being made invisible and at the same time hypervisible means that these women are often denied access to care and their plight does not make it to the public agenda. While it appears that they are being talked about, in essence they are not being talked about—thus rendering them shadow bodies in the framing of HIV and AIDS. Relying on a negative construction, which result from scripts ascribed to the Black feminine body, of Black womanhood, HIV-positive African American women are viewed as sexually and morally impure and as vectors in the spread of the disease. AIDS-related discourses, both inside and outside of the Black community, tend to construct these women in a rather negative light. Public health officials and government decision makers' response to AIDS and its relation to race, class, and gender is generally one of neglect. According to Rodriguez, there was a systematic failure to recognize the relationship between the disease and "poverty, economic hardship, or sexual oppression" (Rodriguez,

1997, p. 35). Additionally, the social construction of HIV/AIDS as resulting from deviant behavior and the fact that it appears to disproportionately affect marginalized members of society have resulted in a state of complacency in governments' response and general neglect.

In addition to the challenges of gender inequality in the Black community, neglect, and the avoidance of an AIDS discussion, according to Dalton (1989, p. 205), is "less a response to AIDS, the medical phenomenon, than a reaction to the myriad social issues that surround the disease and give it meaning. More fundamentally, it is the predictable outgrowth of the problematic, mutual fear and mutual disrespect, a sense of otherness and a pervasive neglect that rarely feels benign."

The discourse of HIV/AIDS captures much of what Frantz Fanon (1967) describes in *Black Skin, White Masks*. In this work, Fanon demonstrates the enormous power of the discursive and political effects of responses to the Black body. Running through much of the construction of HIV/AIDS discourse is the concern over the Black female body. The Black female body remains a site of contestation in our discussions of HIV/AIDS not only in Africa, but also in the United States. Patricia McFadden (2004, p. 23), in characterizing the body of research on HIV/AIDS and Africa, asserted "everyone is researching and analyzing the drama that is unfolding on the bodies and in the lives and deaths of Africans, but of special interest is the besieged body and life/death struggle of the black woman and the black girl." She captures the silences I discussed above and, while she speaks of the silence as it relates to Africa, I argue that the same can be said of U.S. discourses.

Cohen (1999) says that "A more accurate characterization of the political positioning of most black Americans is that of a qualified linked-fate, whereby not every black person in crisis is seen as equally essential to the survival of the community, as an equally representative proxy of our own individual interests" (p. xi). Hegemonic discourse, birthed from the scripts ascribed to Black women's bodies, results in Black women who are positive or who have AIDS as being disqualified for inclusion into the understanding of the survival of the larger Black community. They are not useful to sell commodities (the *physical ass*), they are not useful as sexual partners (*piece of ass*), and as such they are treated as the troubling *ass question*. The result is that there is a tendency to focus on individual-level sexual and cultural practices of Black women. Consequently, individuals constructed as outside of the "norm" find themselves the recipients of moralizing rhetoric and policies. Much of the response to HIV/AIDS has been heavily concentrated in normalizing sexuality, promoting heterosexual behavior, and changing women's behavior. Lane et al. (2004) challenge this conceptualization of HIV/AIDS and the resulting response. They suggest that the "individual-level risk factors" approach ignores structural violence and the resulting spread of HIV/AIDS among racially marginalized groups. Using this understanding of structural violence, researchers posit that to better understand and address the spread of HIV/AIDS among Black women, we should look at macrolevel risk factors that include: disproportionate incarceration rates of African American men, residential segregation, gang turf, constraints on access to sexually transmitted disease services, and commercial sales of douching products, among others.

While extant research highlights the relationship between structural violence and HIV/AIDS, the public discourse of Black congresswomen, *Essence* and *Ebony*, and Black female bloggers seem to ignore such understandings. To incorporate such an understanding into to their talk would require that these Black women challenge the "original" construction of HIV and AIDS. Additionally, they need to confront how the understanding of the Black female body is intimately used in the dominant narratives of HIV/AIDS—a narrative of deviance that predated the spread of HIV/AIDS. Beyond confronting such usage, Black women also need to investigate how their talk is influenced by the larger project of "respectability," which in part is a response to the scripts ascribed to Black women's body, the *Ass* and *Strong Black Woman* scripts. The devastating impact of HIV/AIDS provides us with a unique, albeit sad, opportunity to address the systems of oppression resulting from gender, race, and class relations and practices.

5 · KILLING ME SOFTLY

Narratives on Domestic Violence and Black Womanhood

As I revised this chapter, there were two very distributing cases of violence against women/domestic violence in the news. At the 2013 National Rifle Association (NRA) meeting, a life-sized ex-girlfriend mannequin was unveiled. "Alexa Zombie," the mannequin, is billed as "the ex" who bleeds heavily when shot. As this life-sized target mannequin is being marketed, 64-year-old Brenda Belle (of Barbados) died at the hands of her estranged husband. It is alleged that he repeatedly stabbed and mutilated Ms. Bell, after what now appears to be an earlier failed attempt. This type of cultural representation of violence and women's lived experiences with violence has sparked many in both the United States and Barbados to ask how do we prevent the actual physical violence of women and a culture that often celebrates such violence.

Indeed, both of these cases are sensational, and it is expected that they will garner such attention. They make visible, even if momentarily, what is often invisible. Although these cases bring attention to the issues of violence against women and domestic violence, much of the talk is framed in a rather monolithic manner—the category of woman is treated in an essentialist manner, and this has implications for how society responds. Domestic violence knows no boundaries—it touches individual lives regardless of the person's social location (Rennison & Welchens, 2000; Straus & Gelles, 1986). But as the statistics in the Introduction belie, black women are disproportionately affected.

Research on women of color, and in particular Black women's, experience with domestic violence suggests that it is not simply gender (especially gender inequality) that influences these women's experiences. Blackwomenshealth.com (n.d.), in discussing the relationship between structural violence and domestic violence, asserted:

Factors such as the breakdown of families, unemployment and underemployment, poor schools, inadequate vocational skills and training, bad housing, the influence and use of drugs, and the density of liquor stores in the inner city contribute to the problem of domestic violence. All of these ingredients may compound and coalesce into a strong undercurrent of frustration that can lead to domestic violence.

These data suggest that the intersection of race, class, and gender influence Black women's experiences with domestic violence. Yet, these women and this particular understanding of domestic violence are shrouded in silence, and as such they remain in the shadows both within and outside their communities.

Over the course of the book, I argue that the scripts ascribed to Black women's bodies provide the templates for Black women to define and understand domestic violence. The scripts and the resulting construction of domestic violence embody power structures within the Black women's community. This chapter begins to show how such power structures are represented in the talk and silence related to domestic violence and its intersection with Black womanhood to show how shadow bodies are produced. The primary purpose of this chapter is to:

- Understand and analyze the framing employed by Black congresswomen, Black female bloggers, and *Essence* and *Ebony* magazines. Specifically, I ask: How is intersectionality integrated into the domestic violence frames?
- Understand the policy suggestions made by Black women for addressing and responding to domestic violence. To this end, I interrogate the discourse by asking: How and if the talk is contextualized by Black women's social location and the relationship between racial loyalty and structural violence and domestic violence?

Asking these questions of the data revealed the following frames that were used by Black female congresswomen, *Essence* and *Ebony*, and Black female bloggers: (a) disaster/impact and (b) testimonial. When these women, and those speaking on behalf of women, spoke to how to address domestic violence, they tended to use the frames of: (a) learn to love yourself, (b) surviving, (c) government accountability, and (d) community call out. While there are nuances, as reflected in the subthemes of these general frames, they are indicative of the rhetorical devices used across the time span of the study, 1997–2007. These themes are not only repeating articulations across time and space, but are indicative of the larger question that guides the research—how do discursive practices, both speech and silences, support and maintain hegemonic understandings of Black womanhood, thereby rendering some Black women as shadow bodies? The frames show how the scripts ascribed to Black women's bodies (see Figure 3.1) shape Black women's talk on domestic violence.

These questions make it possible for me to identify and analyze which categories of difference are deployed in the talk and if there are discreet silences. Once I am able to determine how differences are employed, I am then able to interpret how Black women make sense of domestic violence and its intersection with Black womanhood. Focusing on which bodies are included and excluded in the talk, and on what types of actions are advocated for and what types of actions are excluded from the talk (that is, the discreet silences) I can then show how intragroup Black women's politics functions.

To aid this analysis, I first present a brief review of social science research that theorizes domestically abused Black women's experiences—I emphasize theoretical developments focused on structural inequities and violence, as this is where I tended to see the discreet silences. In the second section I offer an analysis of if and how Black women integrate the conceptual understanding of the relationship between structural inequalities and domestic abuse in suggestions on how to confront domestic violence. As discussed below, in the talk of Black congresswomen, Black female bloggers, and *Essence* and *Ebony*, there is silence in terms of: (a) the limited talk on domestic violence, (b) the universal frames used in the talk that treat all women as the same, and (c) the suggested actions that center personal growth and development as opposed to demanding a response on behalf of the government.

THEORIZING BLACK WOMEN'S EXPERIENCE WITH DOMESTIC VIOLENCE

Generally, literature highlights four dominant elements or structures to explain Black women's experiences with domestic violence. These four elements/structures are: notions of racial loyalty, housing segregation and its impact on the availability of resources, lack of culturally competent service providers, and gender entrapment. Similar to the HIV/AIDS and mental health literatures, within this growing body of research social structural elements (specifically structural violence) are used to help explain Black women's exposure to domestic violence, the impact of domestic violence on their lives and on the lives of their families, and their coping mechanisms, and to offer policy suggestions on how to address domestic violence within this community. Such an approach allows, by focusing on the intersection of race, class, and gender and domestic violence, for a more nuanced understanding of domestic violence.

In addition to gender, Kanuha (1994, 1996), Richie (2000), and West (1999) center other oppressive structures and resulting inequalities, such as racism, heterosexism, and classism in their analyses of domestic violence. This body of research challenges the often-universalistic understanding of not only expo-sure to violence, but also our theorizing and understanding of its impact. It is argued that "intersectionalities color the meaning and nature of domestic vio-lence, how it is experienced by self and responded to by others, how personal and social consequences are represented, and how and whether escape and safety can be obtained" (Bograd, 1999, p. 276). Using gender entrapment theory, Richie (1996) argues that the social construction of gender identity limits black women's options for responding to violence in their intimate relationships, thus forcing them to engage in illegal activities. Gender entrapment theory seeks to analyze and explain an invisible group of women (often labeled as criminals and not victims) by centering women's participation in illegal activity as a response to domestic violence, the ongoing threat of violence they experience in their intimate relationships, and state/institutional/cultural violence that they experi-ence (neglect and oppression of these women). According to this gender entrap-ment argument, institutional practices in combination with social relationships function in a manner that results in the regulation of individuals, according to gender (and I add race and class) norms and practices.

Ammons (1995, p. 5) suggests that abused women of color must also confront "the complex phenomenon of racism . . . which stems from the basic assumption that people of color are inherently more violent." Consequently, in addition to dealing with abuse, women of color must also deal with "an overwhelming sense of hopelessness and low self-esteem" (p. 5), resulting directly or indirectly from racism. West offers this insight on shame as a response to domestic violence. According to West (1999, p. 67), women of color who have suffered abuse tend to experience self-blame and shame "because shame has a psychic identity, it can readily merge with the social stigmas based on race and gender that are usually already at work on black women's psyches." Combined, the sense of hopelessness, low self-esteem, self-blame, and the structural constraints faced by these women tend to trap them in violent situations—where they are simultaneously victims of crime (particularly intimate partner violence) and perpetrators of crimes.

Racial loyalty, in addition to gender entrapment, is also used to explain Black women's experiences with domestic violence (Bent-Goodley, 2001; White, 1994). Black men, depicted in novels such as Ralph Ellison's (1952) *Invisible Man*, James Baldwin's (1968) *Tell Me How Long the Train's Been Gone*, and Rich-ard Wright's (1940) *Native Son* are sometimes portrayed as victims of a racial state, and it is suggested that they are emasculated as a result of the interaction of various racial structures. These men have become constructed as "endangered" (Alexander-Floyd, 2007; Wallace, 1990). According to Bent-Goodley (2004):

> Being acutely aware of police brutality and other forms of injustice, the woman forgoes her needs for fear of the criminal justice system. This increases her chances of physical injury and mental anguish. She is almost expected to sustain

the abuse to protect the family, maintain the relationship, and spare the larger community of embarrassment, all the while denying her mental health needs and physical safety. Maintaining racial loyalty can have devastating physical and mental health effects. (p. 309)

It is thus expected that men, at the intrafamily level, be protected via the actions of "their" women.

Racial loyalty is a defense mechanism that results in silencing about domestic abuse. It has been suggested that Black women might remain silent in response to abuse as a means of protecting Black men from a racist state response. This "loyalty trap" (Ammons, 1995) not only describes the tension confronted by abused Black women, but also helps us understand how they confront abuse. One, Black women remain silent about abuse because they do not want to be viewed as perpetuating negative stereotypes of Blacks, particularly Black men, that suggest they are violent. Second, Black women who recognize how their communities are simultaneously underserved by the police while being subjected to hyper-aggressive surveillance tend not to reach out and seek protection. Part of their decision is a result of a cost-benefit analysis that includes paying attention to the effects of reporting violence on the Black community in general and Black men specifically. Third, loyalty might prompt these women not to seek counseling. This is often related to the notion that one should not air the community's "dirty laundry." As such, their ability to heal and recover may be stymied.

Another variation of racial loyalty presents itself in Black women's internalization of the *Strong Black Woman* script. Potter (2006) shows how this script is harmful to abused Black women:

For many of the participants, assuming the role of the Strong Black Woman, as well as being perceived as a Strong Black Woman, had policy implications for battered women's shelter and counseling services. The women who capitalized on using shelters and therapy to assist them with terminating the abusive relationships were often singled out because of their distinguishing experiences with abuse and as Black women. When the participants' experiences with intimate partner abuse were pointed out by the other clients, it tended to be done for the purposes of placing battering and abuse in a hierarchical sequence and served as a perverse source of competition for the other battered women. When the participants were singled out by counselors, it was for the seemingly innocuous purposes of benefiting the battered Black women, to highlight how they are stronger than the other women (i.e., the White women) and strong enough to get out of the relationships. Even if these assertions by other battered women and service providers were true, they often served as a detriment to battered Black women's inclination to leave abusive relationships. Undervaluing battered Black women's violent encounters because they are not in abusive relationships as long as White women or because their injuries are not (or do not appear to be) as severe as other women's essentially justifies battering to a certain degree. Furthermore, it perpetuates battered Black women's impression that they do not need to seek alternative or supplemental assistance to their familial and personal resources. (Potter, 2006, p. 115)

Internalization of this script has led some Black women to reject some services in their attempts to respond to intimate partner violence. This script is used to convey the message that Black women, in comparison to other women, are resilient and strong and as such are not in need of care and sympathy.

Racialized stereotypes according to Gillum (2002) and West (1999) influence the nature and extent of services offered to abused Black women. As Kanuha (1994, p. 441) posits, the "limited options for battered women of color . . . is primarily related to the inaccessibility and racial insensitivity of existing social, psychological, and domestic violence services." Furthermore, racism affects "how African-American women receive treatment through domestic violence resources and how they perceive resources" (Martinson, 2001, p. 259). Race-gendered scripts and the resulting stereotypical images of Black womanhood—such as strong, aggressive, and resilient—impeded women's access to domestic violence services, in part, because these scripts and stereotypes prohibit them from being viewed as "victims" (see Ammons, 1995; Martinson, 2001).

Services are also often inaccessible to battered Black women as a result of poverty and their residence in highly segregated communities that offer very little services, such as legal services and domestic violence shelters (Brice-Baker, 1994). According to Taft, Bryant-Davis, Woodward, Tillman, and Torres (2009, p. 54) "African American victims of IPV [inter-partner violence] lacking financial resources may thus find themselves trapped in situations marked by a high likelihood of revictimization without access to the institutional and personal resources to which they would have access elsewhere." Service utilization is an issue for not only lower income Black women, but also their middle-class and upper-class sisters who face a number of constraints in terms of accessing services:

These women in particular may face intimidation and pressure from their partners and other individuals within the community to keep silent as to their abuse. Furthermore, community-level resources available to other victims, such as police protection and support from the church, may be unavailable to them, thereby hindering their ability to garner assistance and leaving them vulnerable to further violence. (Taft et al., 2009, p. 54)

Battered women face a systematic lack of accessible material and tangible resources, including, for example, safe housing, financial resources, emotional support, and employment (Gelles, 1979; Sullivan, Tan, Basta, Rumptz, & Davidson,

1992). What is explored below is if and how such understandings of domestic violence are integrated into the talk of Black women. I do not expect that Black women necessarily use the language used by academics, but that they integrate the understandings of the intersection of Black womanhood and domestic violence. Furthermore, I would expect that Black women would critically address the heterogeneity of Black women's experiences, as this would be a means of countering the process that results in shadow bodies.

"YOU GONNA STAND THERE AND WATCH ME BURN?"[1]: HOW BLACK WOMEN TALK ABOUT DOMESTIC VIOLENCE

Between the various groups of women and within their talk there were no dominantly used frames on domestic violence. Black congresswomen spoke of domestic violence 61 times (see Table A.1, Appendix), in *Essence* and *Ebony* magazines it was referenced 84 times, and Black female bloggers discussed the issue a total of 33 times. I offer below a few snapshots that provide brief insights into how Black women's subjectivity was discursively constructed in a manner to respond to the negative connotations associated with the *Ass* and *Strong Black Woman* scripts. The deployment of these scripts in reflected in the frames used by Black women. Black women's talk on domestic violence centered human disaster/prevalence of domestic violence or they focused on what I refer to as testimonials. Testimonials are stories of women who survived domestic violence. Minimally used by bloggers was the recognition frame, which focuses on the actions of celebrities and their related domestic violence causes. By bringing to the forefront the used frames, I am able to show the discreet silences on which these frames are dependent and how shadow bodies emerge as a result. Below are randomly selected representative quotes for each of the aforementioned frames.

Disaster/Impact Frame

There was silence on the extent of domestic violence in the Black community and how Black women are impacted by domestic violence. In the talk on the prevalence of domestic violence, Black women tended to treat gender in a general manner and relied on statistics to tell of the universal impact of domestic violence. Take for example Representative Christensen's (Motion to Instruct Conferees on H.R. 2215, 2002) claim, "Violence against women continues to remain a critical issue in our society that requires special attention. In the U.S., nearly 25% of women surveyed reported that they had been physically and/or sexually assaulted by a current or former intimate partner at some point in their lifetime" (p. H1996). In discussing the larger societal impact of domestic violence, elected officials also tend to utilize a more neutral approach. This can be seen in Congresswoman Millender-McDonald's (Drug-Free Workplace Act of 1998, 144 Cong. Rec. H4979–80, 1998) claim that domestic violence is harmful to society because of its effect on the workplace. Furthermore, Representative Watson (End Domestic Violence Week, 148 Cong. Rec. E299, 2002) told us of the indirect costs of domestic abuse and its wider societal impact when she argued that domestic violence "is more than a criminal offense, it is an attack on our families and our communities. . . . It is contributing to health care costs that are escalating, and it is tearing apart our communities." There is an attempt by Representative Watson and others to link domestic violence to larger issues that are not linked to race or class. While this approach might prove politically expedient, it fails to recognize how such violence is mapped onto some bodies as a result of their social location.

Representatives Christensen and Millender-McDonald did not explicitly mention Black women in their floor speeches. The result is that listeners are given permission to ignore the needs of abused Black women, who might experience domestic violence differently in comparison to their Asian American counterparts, for example, because they are simply not talked about, heard, or seen. The women are there but simultaneously not there—they are shadow bodies.

In the talk on Black women's experience with domestic violence there was no attempt to discuss the specific factors that increase Black women's exposure to domestic violence. *Essence* and *Ebony* also employed this type of neutral language, which fails to consider how factors such as gender entrapment or segregation contribute to Black women's exposure to violence. In the article "The Abuse Stops Here" (1999), it was asserted "Many Black women are in abusive relationships. . . . The rate of Black women murdered by a lover or spouse is three times what it is for White women." This frame, which relied on the use of statistics, represents the typical approach used to discuss the extent of domestic violence among Black women (again, it is worth mentioning that such a frame was not extensively utilized).

Blogger I'm Living Life Like It's Golden used a frame similar to that used by *Essence* and *Ebony*. She posted:

> According to the Institute on Domestic Violence in the African-American Community at the University of Minnesota, Black women reported more than 30% more cases of intimate partner violence than their White peers. In cases of domestic violence interventions are crucial, because Black Women are far more likely to be victims of homicides related to intimate partner violence. As a community, Black Americans account for 33% of such homicides with Black women specifically accounting for 22% of these cases (though they make up only 8% of the national population) and 42% percent of all female homicides related to domestic violence. (March 9, 2009)

Kanuha (1996) systematically critiques this approach of generalizing battered women's experiences. According to Kanuha, the notion that domestic violence affects "every person, across race, class, nationality, and religious lines" in an equal manner is "not only a token attempt at inclusion of diverse perspectives but also evidence of sloppy research and theory building" (p. 40). Although Kanuha critiques social science research, one could apply her critique to public talk on domestic violence. The generalization that suggests that domestic violence impacts all women equally is dangerous because it "trivializes both the dimensions that underlie the experiences of these particular abuse victims and more important, the ways we analyze the prevalence and impact of violence against them" (Kanuha, 1996, p. 41).

It is worth mentioning that there were two posts that actively engaged gender stereotyping and domestic violence. Both posts were in response to the Rihanna/Chris Brown domestic abuse case in 2009. Chris Brown pled guilty to assaulting Rihanna; however, in the court of public opinion there was much discussion about who was at fault. In response to this type of public talk, AfroBella's post questioned the use of gender-related stereotypes and assumptions in her analysis of the response to Rihanna and Chris Brown:

> Where do these kinds of twisted interpretations and stereotypes even begin? When did we get to this point, where we instantly blame the victim? It's like people don't know what to say about this sad situation, so they're just talking out of ignorance and stereotypes and assumptions. It seems people are saying anything to try to explain why R&B music's it couple wound up missing what should have been one of their most magical evenings together. . . . Second of all, domestic violence is never OK. It's never to be explained away, dismissed, or most shamefully of all, celebrated. No matter how much you may love someone's music or style or ability, to explain away Chris Brown's alleged crime by saying "she probably started it" or "I heard she gave him herpes," or whatever the excuse of the moment is, is woefully inappropriate and misguided. It reveals volumes about how women are valued in this society. . . . Domestic violence is a serious societal ill, and our collective attitude towards it should be examined and improved. (February 9, 2009)

This was one of two posts that explicitly mentioned gender and the socially constructed value of women's influence on the construction and treatment of women who have been battered. For the most part there was silence on the intersection of gender, race, class, and domestic violence. The *ass question* subscript helps in interpreting this discreet silence. This subscript speaks to notions of racial loyalty as discussed in academic literature. The *ass question* subscript suggests that there is no place for gender (and specifically gender inequality in the Black community) on the policy agenda. To insert such into the discourse would suggest a break in Black politics, as it would be perceived as substantiating the stereotype of the violent Black man. So like Mary (a character in *Invisible Man*, see chapter 2), no one seems to want to discuss the concerns of this group of women as it might reflect negatively on Black men (see Cole and Guy-Sheftall, 2003).

The universalizing of abuse along the identity marker of gender is also apparent along the spectrum of race and racism. Consider the publications that appeared in *Essence* and *Ebony* magazines. Across the various articles, there were little to no explicit references to race or racism and their relation to domestic violence. One explicit reference to race/racism states, "While many victims share painful similarities in the cycle of domestic abuse, African-American women in particular often face staggering cultural and racial odds, which may hamper their ability to seek professional help, according to experts" ("Ending and Surviving an Abusive Relationship," 2000, p. 48). There was one other explicit reference to racism—this shows the use of discreet silence among Black women.

In terms of race and its intersection with domestic violence, Black elected officials made two explicit references to race/racism. Within these two references, race was mentioned in a universal manner. For instance, we were told by Representative Watson, "Communities of color and Native American communities remain at higher risks of domestic violence. They also have fewer services than other communities to deal with the violence and negative economic consequences that frequently result" (Supporting the Goals and Ideals of Domestic Violence Awareness Month, 151 Cong. Rec. H8372, 2005). In their talk, Black women failed to connect the issue of domestic violence to the larger issue of racial justice and the limits of democracy to be inclusive of minoritized groups. This talk fails to recognize how domestic violence is a social practice that is maintained and perpetuated by multiple systems of oppression, one of which is racism.

Similarly to Richie (1996), I also argue that the construction of gender identity tends to circumscribe the options available to Black women to escape abusive relationships. To integrate the issue of race/racism in relation to domestic violence would challenge the notion of Black racial progress, vis-à-vis the *Strong Black Woman*. A failure of this woman to overcome difficulties and more importantly, the crack in the notion of the *Strong Black Woman* suggest that these women are not suited to participate in the racial uplift project required of Black women. The construction of the *Strong Black Woman* results in these types of discreet silences that in turn limit not only how Black women talk about the intersection of race, gender and domestic abuse but also how they suggest it should be confronted.

Class, as a system of oppression, and its intersection with domestic abuse was also absent in the talk on domestic violence. I read and reread the blog posts for any reference to the relationship between class, gender, race, and domestic violence. All of my reading yielded no examples of this relationship. Additionally, both publications also reflect this type of discreet silence as they typically stayed away from issues of class. *Ebony* magazine's "Ending and surviving an abusive relationship" (2000, p. 48) limited treatment of class took the following form: "There has been this perception that domestic abuse is a White woman's or a poor woman's issue. . . . But, it's every culture's issue. And in reality, it's the middle and upper-middle-class African-American women who aren't doing too well." One does not see another reference to class in the publication. In the transcripts analyzed for this study, I did not find any reference to class in the articles appearing in *Essence* magazine.

This silence on the intersection of class and domestic abuse was also evident among Black elected officials. There were only three explicit references to class made by Black congresswomen over the 10-year time period that was studied. Representative Clayton (National Domestic Violence Awareness Month, 143 Cong. Rec. H8447, 1997) said, "Poor women are still far more likely to be victims of domestic violence than other women, and domestic violence endures as the leading cause of injury to women." In keeping with this type of framing, Representative Majette (Speaking Out Against Administration's Record in Combating Violence Against Women, 150 Cong. Rec. H4746, 2004) posited, "the President has refused to include protections for battered women in the marriage proposal programs that are integral to his welfare proposal, despite the risk that poor women could be pressured to remain in abusive relationships." According to Representative Millender-McDonald,

> While domestic violence occurs in all income levels, low-income women are significantly more likely to experience violence than any other women . . . women who head poor families experience severe physical violence as adults at the hands of male partners. . . . The problem faced by low-income battered women can be particularly acute and complex. Often they are financially dependent on their batterer and require an immediate source of support and shelter in order to escape from a dangerous situation. In many communities, emergency shelters are simply not available; where they are, they are frequently forced to turn victims away due to overcrowding as too often battered women and their children are forced to return to the home that they share with the batterer because they have nowhere else to go. (Departments of Commerce, Justice and State, the Judiciary, and Related Agencies Appropriations Act, 146 Cong. Rec. H4977–78, 2000)

Richie (2000) speaks to how discreet silences results in another layer of violence that is enacted on the bodies of Black women. She challenges this notion of universal risk and the failure to pay attention to the relationship between domestic violence, class, and race. As she argues, poor women of color are "most likely to be in both dangerous intimate relationships and dangerous social positions" (Richie, 2000, p. 1136) Accordingly, the failure to pay attention to such a relationship, according to Richie, "seriously compromises the transgressive and transformative potential of the antiviolence movement's potential [to] radically critique various forms of social domination" (p. 1135). In order to be able to pay such attention to the needs of these women, they must be brought out of the shadows. But to do such would challenge the racialized-gender ideologies that inform Black women's politics.

Finally, the analysis of sexual identity and domestic violence shows that domestic violence is generally constructed as primarily a heterosexual matter. There is silence on the topic of Black lesbians and domestic violence. While heterosexuality was mentioned in the talk, in a very limited way, it was not employed in a transgressive and transformative manner. The heterosexual frame tended to be employed in discourses that centered the prevalence or impact of domestic violence—and even this was limited. Representative Carson was one of the few who explicitly framed domestic violence in a heterosexual manner (for the others it was more implied). In discussing the impact of domestic violence and lack of protection encountered by many women, Carson told this story, "We had a tragic situation where a young man went to court, was convicted of domestic violence, was allowed to leave the courtroom and go home and prepare himself for prison. Instead, he visited his wife's job and killed her and another day care provider."

She followed up by stating, "domestic violence is the leading cause of injury to women in this country, were they are more likely to be assaulted, injured, raped or killed by a male partner than by another type of assailant" (Domestic Violence, 148 Cong. Rec. H6921, 2002). Carson, like so many others, relies on the heteronormative construction of domestic violence. Meanwhile, she ignores other groups who are also abused.

In terms of heterosexual domestic abuse, no intragroup or intergroup comparisons were provided as a means of contextualizing the impact of domestic abuse within various groups. For example, there was no mention of how many Black women are abused by males in comparison to White women who are abused by males (this type of frame was employed in the HIV/AIDS talk). Additionally, there were no references to violence among same-sex couples. Finally, ignored in the talk were transgendered and intersexed survivors of domestic violence. These individuals were explicitly omitted from all discourses.

Among bloggers, one post discussed domestic violence among lesbian couples. The Sauda Voice (October 26, 2010) was the only blogger who dealt with the issue of domestic violence and sexuality:

Before I get into this story, I have to get something off my chest. In my opinion, had this been a former NBA player shot and killed by a girlfriend in a domestic dispute, this story would have been all over the major network and cable stations (and print media)—with heavy rotation—for days and likely weeks. But since the victim in this case had the "misfortune" of being a *woman* in a *lesbian* relationship, her tragic death received virtually no media attention whatsoever. Ridiculous! (emphasis in original)

The Sauda Voice calls attention to the social location of lesbians in society—their invisibility—when she compared and contrasted the status of the NBA and WNBA. Her critique brings center stage how and why Black lesbians face a double form of silence in our conversations of domestic violence.

Besides the silence that I describe above, lesbians' experience with domestic violence is just not talked about. Additionally, Black lesbians experience a type of self-imposed silence. While some lesbians may be open about their sexuality, they may remain silent about any abuse they experience in their intimate relationships (Butler, 1999; Ristock, 2002). Renzetti (1998) argues that while there exist similarities between heterosexual and lesbian battering—specifically, the exercise of power and control—they are indeed not the same. Homophobia and the threat of disclosure, or outing, are important factors of lesbian battering. Both homophobia and the threat of outing may prevent many lesbians from leaving abusive relationships. Lesbians might choose to remain in these relationships as a result of fear—particularly the fear of how they will be treated and responded to, not only by family, but also by societal institutions and processes. These women violate notions of good Black womanhood as some might perceive them as violating sexual norms, and as such they are not available to be the *sacrificial, Strong Black Woman* necessitated by the larger Black community. When we fail to talk about these women and the issues they confront, because of a perception that they deviate from the notion of good Black womanhood, we are in essence failing to offer a more democratic critique of society.

Testimonial/Recognition Frame

In addition to the human disaster frame, I also analyzed the testimonial/recognition frame to determine where silence was evident among the talk. This frame was used primarily by *Essence* and *Ebony* and by Black female bloggers. The testimonial frame is used to tell the story of abused women who have triumphed. Indeed, this testimonial frame, second only to the recognition frame, dominates much of the discourse on domestic violence.

One assumes, given the nature of the publications, that the women profiled in the stories—those who triumphed over domestic violence—were Black women. In "Her Toughest Case" (Harrison & Johnson, 1999), a type of testimonial frame, we come to know Scherryl Jefferson Harrison:

> I am the last person anyone would've thought of as a battered wife. I am a domestic-violence prosecutor who, after battling for my life the night before, would march into court and indict *other* women's abusers. To everyone around me, my life seemed picturesque: I had a beautiful house on nine acres of Alabama land, two well-mannered sons and a charming, handsome husband who seemed to adore me. But behind the pretty portrait, my life was spiraling into disaster. When I tell sisters that my husband beat me, they often ask, "Why did you stay?"

The simple answer is that I wanted my dream of a happy family to be real, and when I discovered it wasn't, I chose to overlook that reality. But the deeper reason has to do with who I was before meeting my husband: a 19-year-old girl who longed to be in love and to be loved. I subconsciously longed for someone, *anyone*, to fill a void in my heart. In 1965, the year I entered college, I gave my heart to the man I thought could do that. (p. 96, emphasis in original)

This domestically abused prosecutor, while advocating on behalf of abused women, had to keep her own abuse hidden. The article describes how and why Harrison rationalized her behavior, her attempts to leave, and how she was persuaded to return to the marriage (primarily for the sake of her children). By the end of the article Harrison instructs us that "Now I don't see myself as a victim but as a survivor. Instead of regretting that I chose to stay for so long, I use my pain to grow strong and to begin nurturing myself. And by openly telling my story to other women, I'm helping them see that they don't have to wait as long as I did to reclaim their lives" (Harrison & Johnson, 1999, p. 96). The testimonial frame is used to tell the story of women who not only survived domestic abuse, but also have thrived. They are used as a means of celebrating Black women in general and the *sacrificial/nurturing, Strong Black Woman* and the *spiritual/supernatural, Strong Black Woman* specifically.

This narrative of surviving and thriving is filled with the notion of the *Strong Black Woman*. While this can be uplifting for some, the use of this script can be crippling for others. Focusing on the surviving and thriving domestically abused woman ignores a substantial group of women. What about those women who might have escaped domestic violence but have not thrived in the way that *Essence* and *Ebony* advocate? What about those women who as a means of dealing with domestic abuse might have escaped the situation, but turn to drugs or sex (as was the case of the young woman my mother told me about) as a means of coping? Where are their stories? More importantly, we have to ask what work is being done when such stories do not appear in the pages of *Essence* and *Ebony*.

Similar to the testimonial frame is the recognition frame. "Whatever happened to the Black Miss America?" exemplifies one type of recognition frame. In this article, we are told that Marjorie Vincent, the 1991 Miss America, "used the spotlight as Miss America to spread her message about domestic violence" ("Whatever happened to the Black Miss America?," 2002, p. 108). Additionally, the recognition frame was also presented in this manner:

When it comes to pleasing the ladies, Spinderella—aka Deidre Roper—of Salt-N-Pepa fame has just the ticket. Her new She Things Salon and Day Spa, (718) 276–5212, in Queens, New York, is a soothing sanctuary where clients can get massages, facials and herbal wraps in addition to hair and nail services. There's even a psychologist on hand for when sisters need that extra support, as well as

information on women's issues like breast cancer, child care and domestic violence. To top it all off, a portion of the salon's monthly profits will be donated to
charity. How's that for keeping it real? ("Places to go," 1997, p. 17)

Beyond acknowledging the works of individuals, the publications also recognized the work of organizations such as the Learning Institute of Family Education, a Detroit company that offers workshops on how to deal with issues such
as domestic violence (Cash, 2000, p. 501). Another version showcased the work
of celebrities. It appears that the major goal of this form of the recognition frame
is to show the reader what celebrities, such as Sheryl Lee Ralph, among others
("Front Row," 2005, p. 18), are doing in the name of domestic violence. This construction of domestic violence relies heavily on a language of individual action
and not on language that encourages collective action around this issue. The
scripts ascribed to Black women's bodies influence our policy suggestions often
by taking some types of actions off of the agenda. In this case, because domestically abused Black women are perceived as failing to represent the prototypical
Black woman and her relationship to the narrative of Black progress, individual
approaches to combatting domestic abuse become the action that is sanctioned.

Black female bloggers' posts on domestic violence centered on recognition and
more specifically "celebrity watch," of which the Rihanna/Chris Brown posts fall
into. As an example of the "celebrity watch" frame I offer the following post:

Glenda Cook has fought against domestic violence for more than 13 years. As a
compassionate provider of guidance and support to victims, Cook works with
the city of Detroit to build greater awareness of domestic violence and the devastating impact it has on the community. She is a driving force in the recently
formed dating violence program, "Diamond in the Rough," and hopes to start a
nonprofit to assist the ever-growing group of youth unfairly exposed to domestic
violence. (Black Girls Give Back, December 14, 2010)

On October 5, 2009, Brown Sista posted,

October is Domestic Violence Awareness Month. According to statistics, every 15
seconds a woman is physically assaulted within her home. Remember that suffering is OPTIONAL! You have a voice. You have a choice. You don't have to suffer. If
you are a victim of domestic violence, please get help! The National Domestic Violence hotline is 1–800–799-SAFE (7233). Anonymous & Confidential Help 24/7.

More often than not the testimonial and recognition frames were employed
in a manner that discusses the universality of domestic violence. Embedded in this testimonial frame, which employs gender in a nontransformative way, is the script of strength. This notion of strength is used to suggest

that "good" members of the Black community reach back and pull others up. Women who are unable to "lift while climbing" are therefore not worth talking about because they represent a failure of the Black narrative of progress. Consequently, there is silence around abused Black women who are perceived as not being able to triumph after abuse. While highlighting the activities of celebrities and organizations can assist in consciousness raising, it is limited in the sense that it fails to move beyond the individual approach to addressing domestic violence. Additionally, this frame fails to engage a Black feminist analysis of violence, which would highlight the relationship between multiple oppressive structures and domestic abuse—this is but another form of discreet silence. Doing such could expand the proposals for addressing domestic violence in this community.

LEARN TO LOVE OURSELVES: PERSONAL RESPONSIBILITY AS A MEANS OF ADDRESSING DOMESTIC VIOLENCE

Below, I consider what methods and approaches (policy frames) are used to promote individual and collective action regarding domestic violence against women. It is by looking at the talk that the discreet silences are revealed. To facilitate this analysis, I consider how Black women's talk integrates the relationship between abuse and wider social behaviors and structures that I identified in the introduction as racial loyalty, segregation, lack of culturally competent service providers, and gender entrapment. The extent to which these social behaviors and structures are integrated into policy suggestions is a reflection of how the *Ass* and *Strong Black Woman* scripts influence the hierarchy of bodies in Black women's politics. Policy frames, following from the frames used to describe the issue of domestic violence, did not employ a particular intersectional approach. Additionally, the frames were markedly nontransformative in the sense that they avoided structural issues and violence. While I offer a series of quotes as examples of the types of approaches offered to address domestic violence within the Black community, I would be remiss if I did not state that these frames were minimally employed in the talk. Among Black elected officials, the dominant policy frames focalized government accountability—in terms of the protection of women from further harm; law and order—with calls to make the legal system more responsive to the needs of the women and their families; and requests for increased funding. Within the pages of *Essence* and *Ebony* and Black female bloggers, the following frames were used to suggest how to address domestic violence: survival skills and community call outs.

Learning How to Survive Domestic Abuse

The survival skills frame sought primarily to educate readers. This frame took various forms such as:

If you find yourself in the middle of a violent episode, stay alert. Think of yourself as a lion tamer. Don't get backed into a corner. Try to keep something between you and your abuser. Also, says Marjors, stay out of the most dangerous rooms, such as the bathroom and kitchen. They're filled with easy weapons and hard counters on which you might hit your head if you are knocked down. If you're going to run out of the house, have in mind a safe destination, like a convenience store, fire station or anyplace where there are other people. (J. A., 1997, p. 68)

Publications also proffered to readers a list of resources (usually national hotlines) that they could access for help to escape violent relationships. In "The Ebony Advisor" (2003, p. 25), a response to a letter written by a reader, it was proclaimed,

There are shelters for victims of domestic violence and their children in most cities. Check your local telephone book, directory assistance or police station. You should be given a number to call anonymously, interviewed on the phone and, once you agree not to disclose the location to ANYONE, directed to a nearby shelter. Once you and your children are physically safe, you must take steps toward emotional safety. Establish a relationship with a mental health professional in your community. This can provide you and your children with much needed support and you with additional insight into your comfort in the role as caretaker.

Additionally, articles provide numbers and lists of places to call to seek help. This format, in *Essence* for instance, tended to dominate and often held titles such as: "The Abuse Stops Here" or "Taking Action Against Abuse." Readers of *Essence* are duly informed that

If a person you know is the victim of domestic violence, encourage her to turn to these organizations for help: National Domestic Violence Hotline (800) 799-SAFE (7233) (800) 787-3224 (TDD), National Resource Center on Domestic Violence (800) 537-2238, Resource Center on Domestic Violence, Child Protection and Custody (800) 527-3223, Battered Women's Justice Project (800) 903-0111. ("The abuse stops here," 1999, p. 96)

I recognize the importance of providing women such information. However, this approach, of providing a list of numbers, assumes that once women leave, the abuse ceases. The silence in this frame is that it does not address the challenges and angst some women might face in terms of being able to "pick up the phone." In a sense this proposal is a rather simplistic approach to ending abuse. Knowingly or unknowingly, this recommendation relies on the script of the *Strong Black Woman* as it assumes that women have the strength to pick up the phone and leave.

Black female bloggers used a similar format in their posts. "Learn to love ourselves" dominated bloggers' suggestions on how to confront and deal with domestic violence among Black women. In line with this approach, readers were provided with a list of resources/places that they could access for assistance. "There are some tremendous domestic violence resources online," AfroBella tells her readers. She then informs them, "If you've been a victim, or know someone who has, I encourage you to visit the Safe Space Foundation, the National Domestic Violence Hotline (call 1–800–799-SAFE), Women Called Moses, and the YWCA, or the Family Violence Prevention Fund at endabuse.org" (Feb. 9, 2009). Similar to the approach taken regarding HIV/AIDS, this approach also supports and privileges an individual-level intervention. There are multiple silences embedded in this frame. For one, this tactic addresses domestic violence after women have been harmed. Second, one is left to wonder, what about offering proposals designed to prevent domestic violence? Finally, such a frame fails to address batterers, also making them invisible in our conversations on domestic abuse. The *Ass* and *Strong Black Woman* scripts buttress these discreet silences as they demark the boundaries of the community and consequently whose cause can be championed and how it should be advanced (see Bent-Goodley, 2004; Potter, 2006).

Another manifestation of the survival skills frame sought to encourage women to seek spiritual help as a means of overcoming abuse. Starling (1998, p. 92) states, "[T. D.] Jakes says the search for meaning that has led people back to the altar is the same quest that created an audience ripe for authors to heal them with their words. People seek hope as they confront the weighty problems of AIDS, domestic violence, drugs, child abuse and everyday disappointments that come with living and loving." Gordy (2006) recounted Yvette Cade's[2] experience with domestic violence and her miraculous survival in the piece "A Survivor's Tale." Gordy quotes Cade who said, "I get by through prayer and knowing that God can heal me" (p. 220). This survival skills frame centers the individual in the fight against domestic violence and often suggests that it was their religious faith that led them to a place of healing. This approach is frequently employed in the storytelling of domestic abuse and Black womanhood in both *Essence* and *Ebony* magazines. *Strong Black Women* rely on faith to transcend oppression—regardless of what they encounter—the use of this script suggests that they can survive. Although this is a dominant narrative of Black progress, often playing a key role in Black protectionist politics, it can result in some women being excluded from the Black community as they are perceived as failing to embody strength.

A Call for Government Accountability

Beyond personal transcendence and the individual approach to fighting against domestic violence, Black congresswomen approached domestic violence by calling attention to the actions of government. The government accountability frame appeared in a number of different forms, but generally it called attention to the need to protect the women from further abuse by the "system." For example, Representative Moore (Announcing Introduction of the Shield Act, 151 Cong. Rec. H4194, 2005) said,

> I know of the victims that have finally built up the courage to leave their abusive relationships and have nowhere to go but to a homeless shelter. I know of the women who every day are scared for their lives because their abusers are trying to track them down. I know of the victims who are so scared that they can be tracked down by their predators, and they probably would not seek housing assistance if they knew that HUD required them to disclose their personal information, their Social Security numbers, birth date and location into the homeless management information system database. . . . I ask my colleagues to please support H.R. 2695, the SHIELD Act, to exclude personally identifying information. Reaching out for assistance is a really big step for these victims. Let us not put them in grave danger.

Some of the women, such as Representative Moore, stood in support of the Shield Act (H. R. 2695), which would allow for the exclusion of the victim's personal information from public record as a means of protection.

Representative Majette (Speaking Out Against Administration's Record in Combating Violence Against Women, 150 Cong. Rec. H4746, 2004) also pleaded for the protection of the women from further abuse, resulting from government policies, when she asserted:

> It would shock the conscience of this Nation to know that this administration has placed individuals hostile to women's interests on expert advisory committees, including those responsible for providing advice on domestic violence and reproductive health. It simply reveals a disregard for the National Advisory Committee on Violence Against Women to appoint members to this body who represent organizations that have outspokenly criticized the Violence Against Women Act. Yet that is exactly what this administration has done.

Beyond this, there were challenges made to the Unborn Victims of Violence Act of 2003, by Representative Jones:

> A pregnant woman is one of the most vulnerable members of our society . . . H.R. 1997 does nothing to protect pregnant women from violence; rather, it creates a new cause of action on behalf of the unborn. The result would be a step backward for victims of domestic violence by once again diverting attention of the legal system away from efforts to punish violence against women. Recognizing the fetus as an entity with legal rights independent of the pregnant woman would create future

fetal rights that could only be used against a pregnant woman. (Opposition to H.R. 1997, the Unborn Victims of Violence Act of 2003, 150 Cong. Rec. H658, 2004)

While this government responsibility approach is universal in nature, I see such calls as positive in offering a more comprehensive approach to addressing do- mestic abuse. Frames such as this begin to move us away from the individual- level response and provide an opening for incorporating structural violence in our understanding of and response to domestic violence. Furthermore, they move us beyond the script of the *Strong Black Woman*, thereby allowing for the possibility of a different framing and policy suggestions that are outside the boundaries of the individual level approach.

A second policy frame focuses on legal responses and services offered to vic- tims of domestic violence. For instance, Representative Carson asserted:

> However many politicians, intentionally or unintentionally, have not dealt with this serious and destructive epidemic. In my district alone, judicial levels have been totally insensitive to the plight of victims of domestic violence to the extent of sending perpetrators home on home monitors, with ankle bracelets; and they eventually go out and kill the victim without being noticed by the system until it is way too late. (Violence Against Women, 147 Cong. Rec. H1065, 2001)

Furthering the call for legal sensitivity, Representative Watson (2002, p. E299) suggested that law enforcement be made "sensitive to the cultural, social, eco- nomic and personal issues that complicate domestic violence cases." This was not a common call issued by Black female elected officials. She does what so many others do not do in their talk on domestic violence: speak to structural violence and neglect.

Funding requests also dominated the policy proposals offered by the vari- ous Black congresswomen. Representative Watson (2002, p. E299) asked for additional funds to ensure that "law enforcement has the monetary resources to tackle" domestic violence. Additionally, it was argued by Representative Norton:

> They need residential shelters, shelters for their children, but we are able to han- dle only 1 of 5 women who needs somebody to take them in from an abusive part- ner. With just $6 billion or 15 percent of the tax cut, we would have had shelter and transitional services for these women and their children. I do not know how Members can continue to talk about women and children and then wipe away all of the funds that they need to do what it is that we are talking about. (History of Women's Rights, 149 Cong. Rec. H5462, 2003)

These quotations from the various Black congresswomen indicate the majority of the policy proposals offered to address domestic violence were presented in a neutral manner. They failed to systematically address issues of class and even racial inequalities and their relationship to domestic violence and as such cannot be considered as transformative. However, there are the silences around the notes that show a possibility for how the talk can be expanded. Although limited, there were instances where the talk did not rely on the script of the *Strong Black Woman* and instead focused on structural and policy issues. The key is to center such frames in our talk on domestic violence to encourage a more transformative approach.

Essence magazine minimally encouraged its readers to contact their congressperson as a means of advocating on behalf of abused women. For instance, in 2000, Yolanda Gault Caviness informed readers that "The National Violence Against Women Act is up for reauthorization. Passed as part of the Crime Act of 1994, it provides government money for domestic-violence safety-and-awareness programs. Lobby your congressperson to make sure funding keeps flowing to help support battered women and their children" (2000, p. 30). These limited attempts at looking beyond the individual do little to reconfigure "neoliberal" state practices that result in further residential segregation and economic inequality—factors that contribute to domestic violence. In addition, this frame does not challenge a patriarchal state that often renders Black women simultaneously visible (think of the welfare reform of the 1990s) and invisible (also think of the treatment of Black women's access to health care).

Community Call Out

Beyond this, there were a few calls made to the community to actively challenge domestic violence. Specifically *Essence* pleaded for the (Black) church to become more involved in the fight against domestic violence. This plea took the following format:

> The Black church has a tremendous role to play in ending the silence around domestic violence and breaking through the mythology that allows too many of us to think that beating women is acceptable. By working through church and community groups to identify the warning signs for domestic violence, we may be able to help prevent it. In cases where violence already exists, our churches must become sanctuaries, providing shelter, counseling and referrals. We must also reach out to abusers *and* their children, teaching them more peaceful ways to resolve conflict. We must all finally act as rivers flowing into a single ocean where all of us are respected. (Williams, 2002, p. 252)

This community call out frame is a plea for help. *Essence* and *Ebony* magazines petition their readers to demand help from various organizations and/or institutions. Again, this proposal hints at intersectionality; additionally, it provides an opening to expand our talk as it moves us beyond the realm of the personal response that result from the *Ass* and *Strong Black Woman* scripts. However, because of its focus on the recognition of domestic violence victims' need for help, the proposal tends not to demand systematic changes that center gender inequality, poverty, and sexuality, for example, as contributing factors that fuel and promote domestic violence. Thus, still evident is how the *ass question* sub-script continues to shape Black women's responses to domestic violence.

Gina the Blogmother encouraged readers to move beyond the "survival skills" approach by asking where are Black institutions in the response to domestic abuse. She posted,

> Today is October 1st, a National Day of Unity as part of National Domestic Violence Awareness Month. If you are an African American woman, you should be AWARE of the fact that Black women are three times as likely to be the victim of domestic violence than our non-Black counterparts. But don't hold your breath waiting for our leading social or civic organizations to hold vigils, public forums, or community outreach events. (October 1, 2007)

She challenges the institutional silence surrounding domestic violence. While Gina the Blogmother does not delve into explaining the existence of such silence, one can speculate, based on the literature on domestic violence and the Black community, that the silence may result from a sense of racial loyalty and the functioning of patriarchy.

CONCLUSION

Indeed, most of the talk on domestic abuse centered the individual and individual "self-help." Running throughout this frame is the script of the *Strong Black Woman*. The danger of relying on this script is that it focuses on individual healing/self-love (calling Black women to be individually strong) with no focus on the context—the structural violence—that Black women confront. Silenced in the talk among Black women are state institutional processes and practices, ideological power, and how they contribute to the abuse faced by Black women.

Talking about domestic violence is painful. The mere utterance can be traumatic. For those who have been abused, such talk can result in feelings of shame, fear, or even ambivalence. For those who talk about domestic violence, such talk can also result in similar feelings. Among Black women feelings of shame and fear can result from a sense of racial loyalty; consequently there is no place on the agenda for Black women. As such, women can remain quiet for fear of perpetuating racial stereotypes such as the violent Black man and for suggesting that Black women are not strong—this is how discreet silences are manifest. Regardless of the source of the silence, such silence results in a general failure to address the cumulative trauma experienced by domestically abused women. If we are to engage in a progressive, transformative and a more democratic politics around Black women and domestic violence, we must systematically challenge and change social beliefs, attitudes, and behaviors that perpetuate all forms of violence against women. Domestic violence, as argued by Bograd (1999, p. 276) is not a monolithic phenomenon and as such, "intersectionalities color the meaning and nature of domestic violence, how it is experienced by self and responded to by others, how personal and social consequences are represented, and how and whether escape and safety can be obtained."

Failure to consider how multiple oppressive structures influence and affect Black women's experiences with domestic violence results in a passive, yet active, neglect of domestically abused Black women—this is how they are "made" into shadow images in the larger Black freedom struggle. Internal and external oppressive structures have often resulted in a silencing about domestic violence. This silence is both perpetuated by and fuels the neglect that these women encounter. Silence is the result of a rather complicated process that involves the larger society's views of Black women, the Black community's response, and how Black women internalize all of the race-gender expectations they experience on a daily basis. This might be the case, as noted by Briggs and Davis (1994), because the African American community does not view domestic violence as an issue of concern. Domestic violence seldom appears on the political agenda, and the affected women are seldom viewed as victims in need of protection. Such limits are an outgrowth of the failure of talk to challenge normative aspects of social control that are deeply entrenched in our social relations and our political practices and processes. This, I argue, is in part the result of the scripts ascribed to Black women's bodies and the manner in which these scripts are read by those in power (this is discussed in more detail in chapter 7).

6 · "WHY SO MANY SISTERS ARE MAD AND SAD"[1]

Talking about Black Women with Mental Illnesses

In 2010, Surgeon General Dr. Regina Benjamin, in conjunction with the Substance Abuse and Mental Health Services Administration (SAMHSA), the Ad Council, and the Stay Strong Foundation, launched a mental health campaign aimed at bringing attention to mental health in the Black community. This mental health campaign involves a series of public service announcements (PSAs) geared towards encouraging young individuals to discuss the various challenges of mental illness and mental health that they face on an everyday basis. The campaign was launched at Howard University and coincided with the first Historically Black Colleges and Universities (HBCU) National Mental Health Awareness Day. The launch of this campaign embodies the issue of mental illness in the Black community. First, it speaks to the growing need to address the issue of mental health—a call to bring it to light. Second, the launch of the campaign shows how the media, mainstream and nonmainstream, tend to address the issue of mental health in the Black community. There was very little coverage of this campaign. The campaign is a battle to make visible what has too often been kept invisible in the Black community—mental illness. It is an attempt to challenge that silence that cloaks mental illness.

The taboo subject of mental illness is "slowly" being brought into the public sphere. First-person narratives and autobiographies (see Danquah, 1998; S. L. Taylor, 1995; Williams, 2008), clinical, and other academic treatments (Beauboeuf-Lafontant, 2009; Brown & Keith, 2003a; Cannon, Higginbotham, & Guy, 1989; Tomes, Brown, Semenya, & Simpson, 1990) have done much to address the issue of the intersection of race, class, gender, and mental illness.

Various organizations such as the Stay Strong Foundation and the California Black Women's Health Project, among others, have also engaged in action to publically address mental illness among African Americans. However, "African American women [are] virtually nonexistent because gender differences in mental disorders in the African American population [are] rarely the focus of analysis" (Brown & Keith, 2003b, p. 25). Consequently, the extent of the impact of mental illness among Black women is not a settled issue. Nevertheless, from these diverse literatures, a portrait of mental illness and Black womanhood is emerging, and that portrait is one of Black women being disproportionately affected by depression (Department of Commerce & Office of Management and Budget, 2011) and experience it more acutely in comparison to other racialized women (National Alliance on Mental Illness, 2009). Data also suggest that Blacks' socioeconomic status, among other factors, also increases their vulnerability to mental illness (Keith, 2003). The emerging portrait (although limited) tells us that Black women are hurting and that societal silence around mental illness must be broken in an attempt to care for these women.

Below, I analyze Black women's talk to determine how they give voice to Black women, from different social locations, who suffer a mental illness. The following are the central concerns of this chapter:

- Analyzing and understanding how Black congresswomen, Black female bloggers, and *Essence* and *Ebony* magazines frame the issue of mental illness. Specifically, I ask: How is intersectionality integrated into the mental illness frames?
- Understanding the suggestions made by these women for addressing and responding to mental illness. Thus, I interrogate the discourse by asking: How and if the talk is contextualized by Black women's social location?

These questions make it possible for me to identify and analyze which categories of difference are deployed in the talk and if there are discreet silences. They produced the following frames used across the platforms of talk: (a) education and (b) stargazing. Additionally, the talk showed that the frames (a) treatment availability and (b) love your body/love yourself dominated the talk on how to address mental illness. The titling of these frames captures not just the general nature of talk, but also the subthemes that might be evident in the talk. In developing these themes, I centered the voices of those talking on mental illness and my sense making of the talk in a manner that was reflective of the central purpose of the research—to uncover discreet silences that result from the scripting of the Black female body (see Figure 3.1).

By determining how differences are deployed across the various platforms of talk, I can then interpret how Black women make sense of Black womanhood and its intersection with mental illness. By focusing on which bodies are included and excluded in the talk—that is, become shadow bodies—and on what types of actions are advocated for and what types of actions are excluded from the talk, I am able to demonstrate how intragroup Black women's politics functions. Over the time period 1997–2007, Black female elected officials discussed the issue of mental health/illness a total of 71 times (see Table A.1, Appendix). The search for stories on mental illness/health in *Essence* (a total of 60 stories) and *Ebony* (42 total stories) yielded 102 stories. The issue of mental health/illness accounted for 30 blog posts. I start the analysis with a brief overview of the factors, at both the system and individual levels, that affect Black women's experiences with mental illness. The next section addresses Black women's talk on mental illness. The analysis shows that Black women framed mental illness using what I refer to as (a) star gazing—which focused on the actions of celebrities and other public figures and (b) education—that is, learning to identify mental illness. In terms of recommendations for addressing mental illness, Black women, across the various spaces of talk, spoke to the availability of services and the commitment to loving your body and yourself. In general, the talk centered individual-level behaviors and often remained silent with respect to some Black women, such as Black lesbians, and to challenge the systemic factors that influence Black women's vulnerability to mental illness.

MENTAL ILLNESS: THEORIES ON INDIVIDUAL- AND SYSTEM-LEVEL CHALLENGES

In my assessment of mental illness, I focus not only on the psychological aspects, but also on the social and political aspects. Mental illness, as defined by the National Alliance on Mental Illness (n.d.), and as used in this study, is understood as "Medical conditions that disrupt a person's thinking, feeling, mood, ability to relate to others and daily functioning. Just as diabetes is a disorder of the pancreas, mental illnesses are medical conditions that often result in a diminished capacity for coping with the ordinary demands of life." I recognize that mental health is influenced by a number of factors both biological and socio-structural. In this brief overview, as this is an analysis of power, I focus more on the socio-structural factors.

Various researchers point to structural violence as a means of explaining Black women's experience with mental illness. According to D. R. Brown (2003, p. 1), "Although medical science endeavors to identify biological and genetic bases for mental health and mental illness, we contend that societal factors are the most salient influences on the mental well-being of African American women." Racism, cultural alienation, violence (sexual and physical), poverty, housing segregation, and in general what we consider structural violence contribute to Black women's experiences with mental illnesses. Housing segregation and its limits on available resources, as asserted by D. R. Brown (2003), influence mental well-being. Poverty also influences well-being, according to the White House report *Women in America* (Department of Commerce & Office of Management and Budget, 2011), "Poverty level also has an impact on the mental health status of all Americans. In 2006, adults living below the poverty level were four times more likely to have serious psychological distress as compared to adults over twice the poverty level" (n. p.). This suggests that there is a relationship between poverty and mental illness. However, like HIV/AIDS and domestic violence, mental illness knows no class boundaries. Thus, middle-class and upper-class Black women are indeed not immune from the various stressors that can challenge their mental well-being (see Chisholm, 1996).

Black women with a mental illness who are seeking help encounter a number of challenges and barriers at both the (a) system level—those that are created by systems designed to provide mental health service, and (b) individual level—how individuals view and experience their encounters with the system (interpersonal and intrapersonal) (Cristancho, Garces, Peters, & Mueller, 2008). It is suggested that stigma influences both the system- and individual-level barriers faced by these women. Stigma is often cited as one of the major challenges in confronting mental illness. "Women's internalization of stigma related to mental illness can also have grave social consequences. Expectations of rejection can lead to reduced confidence, impaired social interactions, constricted social networks, low self-esteem, depressive symptoms, unemployment and income loss" (P. Y. Collins, von Unger, & Arbrister, 2008, p. 390). It has been shown that African Americans tend to hold particularly negative views of the mentally ill (see Diala et al., 2000; Silva de Crane & Spielberger, 1981). This cycle, resulting from stigma, is made that much more difficult to break because of the silence that cloaks the issue. Instead of publically addressing mental illness, Black women at times try to personally and individually address their illness. Overeating is one such means used by Black women to cope with their mental illness (see T. M. Williams, 2008). Additionally, some women who experience mental illness women engage in high-risk sexual behavior as a coping mechanism (see Randolph et al., 2007). Stigma results in silence, which can cause further harm to these women. T. M. Williams (2008, p. 1), in discussing this silence, writes, "The folks who wrote to me were scared—some of them terrified—to breathe a word to anyone; they were paralyzed by the fear that no one would understand or accept them." Williams (2008, p. 22) asserts that silence has become a "cultural habit." The outcome of this cultural habit is that Black women remain untreated and unheard.

Beyond stigma and the resulting silence, other system-level barriers include access to care (which could result from limited to no transportation, lack of or inadequate medical insurance, and no child care, for example), the availability of services, and poor quality of care (limited access to culturally competent clinicians and case management) (Cristancho, Garces, Peters, & Mueller, 2008; Miranda et al., 2003; Tidwell, 2004).

"Although there has been increased interest in understanding barriers to the use of mental health services among minority populations, specific studies on Black women are few and often limited in scope" (Caldwell 2003, p. 258). The literature consistently informs us that Black women face a number of barriers that limit their access to treatment. In discussing what women of color face in seeking psychiatric treatment, Olmedo and Parron (1981, p. 108) state, the "typical structural situation not only reflects the biases inherent in our society but also increases the likelihood that these biases will become an integral aspect of the therapeutic process." For example, Black women are expected to conform to "traditional" gender (sex roles and performance of these roles) and race norms (notion of the *Strong Black Woman*). These norms can at times become incorporated into how these women are diagnosed and ultimately treated. Consequently, the biases Black women face in their everyday lives are also apparent within the psychology profession. These women become shadow images both within and outside of the mental health profession.

Black women who experience mental illness are also made shadow images as a result of how we understand mental illness and their lack of trust in the medical profession as a whole. Olmedo and Parron (1981) argue that while there exists a wide range of projective and objective instruments for clinical and personality assessment, and that although test results have become an integral part of diagnosis, their applicability for Black women remain limited and suspect because these measures were typically developed within rather narrow cultural, racial, and ethnic perspectives. Beyond being excluded from the general understanding of mental illness, which can influence how they are treated, Black women must also confront their fear of the medical profession. Rusert (2009) and Whaley (2001), among others, hypothesize that the African American fear of the medical system can be explained, in part, by the legacy of their experience with the Tuskegee Experiments.[2] This legacy has fostered mistrust between African Americans and the medical profession in general.

Combined, these system-level and individual-level barriers that result from the intersectionality of oppressive structures produce a shadow of Black women who experience mental illness and often construct them as unavailable to the community—in terms of racial uplift—as they fail to embody the notion of the *Strong Black Woman*. "Today, most of us are not in jeopardy of disappearing from the record books of our cities and states. But we are dying, and we are at risk of being emotionally and spiritually unavailable to ourselves as well as absent in meaningful ways from the lives of our families and communities" (Williams, 2008, p. 247). The California Black Women's Health Project (2003) reports that 60 percent of African American women experience symptoms of depression. However, in comparison to White women and African American men, African American women's use of outpatient mental health services is considerably lower (Breslau, Kendler, Su, Gaxiola-Aguilar, & Kessler, 2005; Mays, Caldwell,

& Jackson, 1996; U.S. Department of Health and Human Services, 2001). Black women's existence is challenged as a result of undiagnosed and untreated mental illnesses. While Black women affected by mental illness are dying, being misdiagnosed, and being mistreated, and even incarcerated, there is very little outcry from the mainstream Black community.

"YOU CRY OUT AND NO ONE CAN HEAR IT"[3]: MENTAL ILLNESS, SILENCE, AND REPRESENTATION

In the words of the singer Phyllis Hyman,[4] Black women with mental illnesses are crying out, but "no one can hear." Black congresswomen spoke little on the intersection of mental health, race/racism, class, sexuality, and gender. Mental health, when discussed, was generally done in a manner that did not link mental illness to structural violence and inequalities. Black women in essence failed to incorporate an intersectional approach in the framing of mental illness and Black womanhood, thereby failing to open up the discourse for inclusion of diverse Black women. The data on mental health among Black elected female officials were so scant that I ran the search multiple times to ensure that I had not missed a speech. Multiple search terms, including *depression, suicide,* and *stress,* were used in hope that more data could be generated. Black female bloggers have a tendency to treat mental health via reflections on celebrities' accounts/actions (star gazing frame); comments on what some refer to as a "blah" day and how to get through it; and the recognition of campaigns to raise awareness of mental health. Both *Essence* and *Ebony* magazines used the following types of frames in their construction of mental illness: education, which encompasses how to find help and identify mental illness, and star gazing, which centers celebrating the works of individuals and/or organizations. In general, the frames used by Black women were not particularly progressive and transformative. This I argue is a result of the discreet silences, resulting from the *Ass* script—particularly the *ass question* subscript and the *Strong Black Woman* metascript, used to frame the intersection of mental illness and Black womanhood.

Star Gazing

A dominantly employed frame by the women centered on the recognition of the acts of individuals, celebrities, and/or organizations. For example, Representative Gwen Moore (In Tribute to the Legal Aid Society of Milwaukee, 152 Cong. Rec. E2240, 2006) in paying tribute to the Legal Aid Society of Milwaukee asserted, "Since 1916, this non-profit organization in my district has provided invaluable legal services to low-income people and other vulnerable members of society. . . . the Legal Aid Society specializes in advocating for children, people living with HIV/AIDS, the elderly, immigrants, those with mental illness, prisoners, and victims of domestic abuse." This stargazing frame does a few things.

For one, it recognizes actions—often in a superficial manner. Second, it tends to treat mental illness as part of a list of "ailments" and/or issues. As I discuss below, this limits the framing of the claims for addressing mental illness among Black women.

As part of the star gazing frame used to discuss mental illness by bloggers, Brown Sista (July 5, 2010) wrote of Mary J. Blige's "hardships . . . faced, from clinical depression" and how she expressed herself in her music. According to Brown Sista, Blige, in response to the question on how she expressed her battles with depression in her music, said, "The 'My Life' album was when I started to cry out for help. I was confused and on the verge of suicide and being abused in relationships that I had drawn to myself that were negative. I began to speak on that album publicly; it was a cry for help. And so many women spoke back to me." Beyond the stargazing frame, there was what I refer to as the public service announcement frame. This frame focused on discussing various campaigns designed to raise awareness of mental health within the Black community. Blogger Black Girls Give Back (February 24, 2010) wrote on the "PSAs debut at Howard University and Black Colleges and Universities Nationwide as part of the First Annual HBCU National Mental Health Awareness Day." This post discussed the extent of mental health in the United States and among African Americans 18 to 25 more specifically. While she discusses that "only 44.8 percent" of African Americans receive mental health services, Black Girls Give Back does not discuss why this might be the case. Additionally, Black Girls Give Back does little to address the impact of mental illness from a gendered perspective (this is discussed below in more detail).

While the star gazing frame is useful for at least starting a conversation on mental illness, overall it fails to tackle the issue in a critical manner by removing a cross-cutting understanding of the illness and its intersection with Black womanhood off the agenda (see Cohen, 1999; Schattschneider, [1960], 1975; Strolovitch, 2007). This becomes even more apparent when I sought to analyze whether Black women's talk integrated structural inequalities—race, gender, class, and sexuality—that constrain the lives of Black women with experiences of mental illnesses. I do not address sexuality because of the silence on this system and its interaction with mental illness in the lives of Black women. Across the spaces of talk, there was only one mention of the intersection of sexuality and mental health/illness. Gender leads the discussion, as this was the one axis of domination where there was a plurality of use in Black women's discourses on mental illness.

Education: Arm Yourself with Information to Fight Mental Illness

Often present in the Black woman's talk on mental health were attempts to encourage individuals to get educated and to seek help in order to recognize and treat mental illness. The minimum treatment of gender within this frame tends to portray women in a monolithic manner. Holloway's (2005) piece, which is part of the larger education frame, states, "You are not alone, especially if you are an African-American woman. Clinical depression is a serious medical illness that has a 15 percent chance of affecting a person during his or her lifetime. That figure is perhaps as high as 25 percent for women, according to the *Diagnostic Statistical Manual of Mental Disorders*, the reference guide for mental health professionals" (p. 154). She offers no reference to the extent of mental illness among Black women. However, the article concludes with "a brief description of some common forms of mental ailments that often affect Black women." Included in the list are: bipolar disorder or manic-depressive illness, postpartum depression, and panic disorder.

There were two articles that explicitly dealt with the issue of postpartum depression (a mental illness that is unique to women) that appear designed to educate women about the mental health challenges they might encounter during and after pregnancy. Representative of the framing is "Baby Blues" (Tharps & Cresto, 2004, p. 254). In this article women are instructed that "it is normal to have some anxious feelings" relating to impending motherhood. As such, pregnant/parenting women were instructed what to do before and after the birth of the baby. The article concludes by informing women what to do "when the blues won't go away." Specifically, this section discussed the stigma associated with mental illness and the general reluctance, among African Americans, to seek psychological help. Provided in one article is information for recognizing the various manifestations of "three separate postpartum mood changes that can occur after a woman gives birth" (Hughes, 2001, p. 72).

Beyond this, within the limited amount of talk that addressed gender and mental health, there was a tendency to focus on why Black women do not seek psychological help. Washington (2000, p. 61) informs us, "On the other hand Black women weren't thought to suffer from common mental-health issues. We were portrayed as matriarchal and castrating—and too strong to succumb to depression and suicide." Brenda Wade (1999), in "Rx for the Blues" states, "Unlike Ava, many African-American women who need professional help to cope with emotional difficulties—low self-esteem, divorce, addictive illness, relationship problems—fail to pursue it. One reason is the stigma of therapy and the belief that Black women should be able to handle whatever comes our way" (p. 53). Both Washington and Wade's framings indicate a challenge to the symbolic construction of Black women and can be read as being aligned with Black feminist thought. The framing of gender and mental health challenges the *Strong Black Woman* script and the stigma associated with mental illness. However, there is a failure to challenge macrostructural functioning of this script. Instead the focus is on the individual level, which encourages women to seek psychological help. Evident here is the functioning of protectionist politics designed to present a particular image of Black womanhood—an image of strength, coping, and survival. This is a trend that I also see among Black congresswomen and Black female bloggers. By no means am I suggesting that encouraging women to seek help should not be centered in our responses to mental illness. However, given the multiple factors believed to contribute to mental illness, the individual well-being approach should not be the only strategy.

The lack of integration of structural factors into the mental illness talk is also reflected in how issues of race and racism were integrated by the women in their talk. Black congresswomen, *Essence* and *Ebony*, and Black female bloggers' talk was generally deracialized. If we take the mentioning of the racial category of African American/Black as an attempt to confront race or to indicate the relationship between race and mental illness, then the silence is astounding. African Americans, over the course of 10 years, were explicitly mentioned three times by Representatives Jackson-Lee (America's Law Enforcement and Mental Health Project, 146 Cong. Rec. H10639 and H24029, 2000), Watson (2003), and McKinney (The Voice of Georgia's Fourth Congressional District is Back, 151 Cong. Rec. H3243–46, 2005). Representative McKinney (2005) discussed the relationship between race and mental illness when she claimed:

> In the United Kingdom, it is interesting to note that a psychiatrist was able to publish in the "British Medical Journal" that racism is harmful to one's health, is harmful to one's mental health . . . the result of a mere 1 percent increase in racial disrespect translates to an increase in 350 deaths per 100,000 African Americans. So not only is racism harmful to one's mental health; it is harmful to the fabric of our country. It is harmful to the very lives of the people who are impacted by it. (p. H2345)

Unlike the HIV/AIDS discourses or even domestic violence discourses, there was very little use of the term *minority* in the talk of Black congresswomen. In hopes that I could find a more comprehensive and fuller view of how race was deployed, I analyzed any talk on race in general and mental illness. Unfortunately, this did not result in an increased data set for Black congresswomen—this is another example of discreet silence. Representative Jackson-Lee's 2000 (America's Law Enforcement and Mental Health Project, 146 Cong. Rec. H10639) floor speech is one of the rare instances in which the term *minority* was included in the framing of mental health. According to Jackson-Lee, "in many minority communities there is a sense that to admit mental illness is to acknowledge a spiritual flaw or character deficit." There were limited references to other racial groups such as Asian Americans and Latinas. References to other racial groups (which occurred twice) took the following form: "Asian Community Mental Health Services (ACMHS) was founded in 1974 with the objective of providing community based mental health series to the East Bay's Asian Pacific Islander Community (Honoring Asian Community Mental Health Services, 150 Cong. Rec. E1602, 2004). Or, it took this form: "Hispanic adolescents are more likely to exhibit non-lethal suicide behavior. A 1999 report found that a shocking 1 in 3 Latina adolescents seriously considered suicide. Fifteen percent of Hispanic high school-age females actually attempt suicide each year" (Watson, 2003, p. H3853). Silenced in the talk was racial hierarchy. More often than not race was not gendered in the discourses. This pattern of race-neutrality in relation to gender and mental illness permeated the rather scant discussions of mental health among all of the women.

Essence and *Ebony* magazines also minimally addressed the intersection of race/racism and mental illness. Whitaker, who wrote one of the few articles addressing the intersection of race/racism and mental illness, states:

> But several barriers stand in the way of efforts to address Black America's mental health needs. First, there is the general suspicion that Black Americans have for the field of psychiatry. It is a suspicion rooted in the "legacy of racism" in the field of medicine in general and in psychiatry in particular, says Dr. Carl Bell, president and CEO of the Community Mental Health Council in Chicago, and a clinical professor of psychiatry at the University of Illinois School of Medicine.
>
> That racism has taken the form of research projects—most infamously the Tuskegee syphilis study—in which African-Americans were unwitting and unwilling subjects of medical experiments. Compound those incidents with the racist utterings and writings of many of psychiatry's towering figures, including Carl Jung, and you have, Bell says, a sense of distrust that you can't chalk up to mere paranoia. (Whitaker, 2000, p. 74)

Derrick (1997, p. 37) offers this analysis: "When African-Americans encounter discrimination, like the former Texaco employees, we have more at stake than our careers. Racism can also endanger our physical and emotional health." These two quotations represent the typical, but very limited, treatment of the intersection of mental illness and race/racism within the pages of *Essence* and *Ebony*. They speak to race/racism in a monolithic manner with very little attention paid to the differences resulting from the categories of sex and class, for example. However, both writers acknowledge racism as a structure that limits Blacks' use of medical care and how it impacts Blacks psychologically.

The framing of mental illness and class was done either in relation to homelessness or access to mental health care among Black congresswomen. Homelessness and access to mental health care, resulting primarily from a lack of insurance or availability of services, are taken to represent proxies of class. Take, for example, Representative Kilpatrick's (1998, p. H7612) claim that "we have not solved the problem of those persons who have mental illness and wander our nation's streets." Representatives Jackson-Lee and Waters also discussed the connection between mental illness and homelessness. Beyond this, access to health care was also used to discuss the intersection of class and mental health/illness. Claims such as "minorities are less likely to access mental health care, due to lack of insurance and other financial barriers and cultural stigma. For instance, only one third of African-Americans in need of mental health services actually receive them" (Watson, 2003, p. H3854) were often not deployed. A few women did speak of health disparities of which mental health is one.

Kelly Starling (1999, p. 140 emphasis added), in explaining why so many "sisters are mad and sad" asserts, "For some Sisters, the blues are caused by biological and genetic factors. But for an increasing number of Black women, depression is triggered by life's traumas. *Poverty*, dysfunctional relationships, loss of a loved one and job-related blues are a few of the top causes mental health professionals name." Beyond this, *Essence* and *Ebony* were silent on the issue of the relationship between class and mental health. Generally, the issue of class and access to mental health care tends to be deracialized and degendered. More often than not, Black women remained silent with regards to how structural factors, such as poverty, influence these health disparities.

Concerning the intersection of sexuality and mental illness, my analysis shows that this is the area where discreet silences were particularly prevalent. There was one reference to lesbianism in an article by Washington. Washington (2000, p. 61) discussed how lesbianism was considered a disease in psychiatrists' manuals. Beyond this and similarly to domestic violence, Black lesbian, transgendered, and bisexual women are not mentioned in the framing of mental illness.

The above framing of mental illness shows how African American women, like African Americans in general, have been socialized to engage in silence in relation to mental illness as a means of appearing strong and competent in relation to their peers (Joe, 2006). For many African American women, the script of the *Strong Black Woman* is internalized, consequently, "in the tradition of mammy, she acknowledges no personal pain, can bear all burdens, and will take care of everyone" (Greene, 1992, p. 152). Framing that integrates intersectionality fractures the public identity of Black womanhood as to do such might suggest that Black women are flawed and as such appear to support negative stereotypes of Black womanhood. This form of socialization also promotes an individual-level response to mental illness.

"ON THE ROAD TO HEALING": RECOMMENDATIONS FOR ADDRESSING MENTAL ILLNESS

It should be of no surprise that the policy suggestions, stemming from the frames discussed above, were relatively silent in terms of presenting a transformative approach to addressing the multiple factors influencing Black women's experiences with mental illness and were also relatively silent in terms of directly addressing the needs of Black women. The diversity of Black women's experiences with mental illness was not included in the frames of these women. The *Strong Black Woman* and the Black woman affected by mental illness represent two conflicting identities. Black womanhood tends to be marginalized and stigmatized; consequently, adopting an additional stigmatized identity such as mental illness proves to be particularly challenging for this community. This conflict is reflected in both the framing of mental illness and Black womanhood and policy proposals for addressing this issue.

The policy proposals articulated by Black women called for a different approach to treating those affected by mental illness (often in a degendered and deracialized manner); mental health parity, or addressing the lack of mental health services in underserved communities; and for mental health service providers to be culturally competent. It is worth noting that each of these policy suggestions was generally referenced once or at most twice by Black congresswomen. On the pages of *Essence* and *Ebony*, proposals focused on individual self-help—the love your body/love yourself frame. When Black female bloggers discuss approaches to dealing with mental health among Black women, they are also apt to privilege the self-help frame—which could include the call for a religious/spiritual intervention. Again, the policy proposals reflect how Black women are responding to the *Ass* and *Strong Black Woman* scripts. The approach minimizes presenting Black women in a manner that might suggest that they are "flawed" or "broken."

Treatment: Availability and Access

Delegate Norton asked for the mentally ill to be treated in a less "restrictive," community-based setting. She also advocated for recognizing the rights of these individuals (District of Columbia Mental Health Civil Commitment Modernization Act of 2004, 150 Cong. Rec. H8258, 2004). In discussing posttraumatic stress associated with victims of Hurricane Katrina, Representative Lee demanded that mental health professionals "be sensitive to . . . the diversity of the affected populations and understand the cultural background of those who have been traumatized" (Hurricane Katrina Disaster, 151 Cong. Rec. H7718, 2005). This policy suggestion is related to Watson's (Mental Health Caucus, 149 Cong. Rec. H3853–54, 2003) assertion that "there is a serious lack of mental healthcare providers, and an even greater lack of minority providers, who are more likely to practice in communities with high minority populations." As a means of addressing this shortage, Representative Kilpatrick (Introducing the Health Care Access Improvement Act, 143 Cong. Rec. E2182, 1997) introduced "the Health Care Access Improvement Act," which was designed to "provide a

$1,000 per month tax credit over 5 years for primary health care providers who are located or will establish practices in health professional shortage areas." She identified mental health as one of the underserved areas. Additionally, there were a few calls made to increase funding for the provision of mental health services. Consider the plea made by Representative Jackson-Lee (America's Law Enforcement and Mental Health Project, 146 Cong. Rec. H24029, 2000): "I believe mental health is an issue that people do not speak about. They are our neighbors. We need more funding."

The pages of *Essence* and *Ebony* were relatively silent concerning suggestions on how to confront mental illness among Black women. Whitaker (2000) wrote one article on this issue. It stated,

> Improving the access to mental health professionals and facilities will help. With too few psychiatrists and psychologists serving Black communities, delivering treatment, even to those who want it, is difficult. "We have to close a fairly significant gap between the institutions and leadership in mental health and the underserved communities that need those services," says Dr. Bell, who is serving on a task force established by the surgeon general that will issue a report this summer on the mental health needs of minority communities. "It's a matter of connecting the dots between these entities and creating an infrastructure to support them. When we do that, we will have better mental health treatment for Black America." (p. 74)

Given the dearth of stories on mental illness in both *Essence* and *Ebony*, it should not be particularly surprising that there was minimum discussion of Black women's access to mental health treatment.

Black women were efficient in linking mental illness to the larger issue of health access. Such talk, calling for filling the gaps in service provision, fits with the larger narrative of health access—a mainstay in the Black freedom struggle. Doing such provides them with access to the policy agenda without having to create a "new" language. While this is an efficient approach, it too can prove limiting. Such a method assumes a type of universality among the mentally ill. It does not allow us to see how Black women might experience mental health differently from Black men and therefore might require a different set of services. Furthermore, the frame does not explicitly address how poverty, for example, contributes to stressors that can perpetuate and/or worsen mental illness. This approach, like the approach to domestic violence, seeks to address mental illness after the fact while paying minimum attention to how to minimize socio-structural stressors that can exacerbate mental illness. It is possible that this response reflects Black women's mistrust of the medical profession. In fact, I will argue that is indeed a contributing factor as to why Black women do not engage socio-structural factors. However we also have to consider how socio-cultural factors, such as the scripts ascribed to the Black woman's body, contribute to this response. While many consider how stigma influences Black women's response to mental illness at an individual level (see Beauboeuf-Lafontant, 2009), what I reveal below is that stigma also influences the response at a macro level.

Love Your Body/Love Yourself

Beyond challenging Black women's access to mental health treatment, Black women also advocated that Black women learn to love themselves as a means of dealing with mental illness. One article suggested focusing on one's spiritual life as a means of addressing mental health. Accordingly, it was asserted, "That emotional and mental longevity, according to wellness experts, is directly impacted by your spiritual foundation. 'People who don't have a spiritual life or a spiritual practice actually suffer in their own mental health as opposed to people who have cultivated a spiritual practice and have a healthy and enriched spiritual life,' says Thompkins" (Foston, 2005, p. 138). Although not as prevalent, as was the case with domestic abuse, there were suggestions/resources offered on where to find help (N. I., 2001, p. 147). Additionally, women were instructed to seek professional help to determine if they were indeed suffering from mental illness. Consider the following as an example of such a frame: "Asking for help can be difficult for accomplished sisters. We often feel that reaching out is a sign of weakness. On the contrary, it is a sign of self-love. Good for you for seeking support. A mental-health professional can help determine whether your tense moments are actually panic attacks, for which there are effective treatments including medication" (Vanzant, 2004, p. 108).

Bloggers also assumed a similar approach as that used in *Essence* and *Ebony* magazines. For example, Is it Just Me posted, "Over the years, I've come to realize and recognize that suicide in any form is *not* an option. We all find ways to 'kill' ourselves and it must stop. We must find ways to reduce and eliminate pain in our lives. We must find a spiritual place to release ourselves and find the strength to go on and endure" (June 3, 2009). On June 28, 2007, she posted the following, "For everything I've been through in life good or bad, I've always been grateful to my heavenly father for His divine presense [*sic*] in my life. Even when I wanted to call it quits and say the hell with it all, I never let my faith falter and I held on regardless. *My Hope Is Built* is one of my favorite hymns and trust me when I say, it's literally saved me and others from being hurt." These two posts by blogger Is It Just Me embody much of how we are told to confront depression. It should be confronted on a personal level and primarily through faith. I could not possibly stretch my interpretation of how this general approach of "self-love" works to erase the broader social structures and processes that impact the lives of diverse Black women who are confronting mental illness.

As hooks (2003) argues, the script of the *Strong Black Woman* suggest that Black women have "built-in capacities to deal with all manner of hardship without breaking down, physically or mentally" (p. 70). In their policy suggestions we see Black women simultaneously trying to protect women from the stigma of mental illness and its intersection with Black womanhood (also a stigmatized identity) while perpetuating hooks's understanding of the *Strong Black Woman* script by promoting an individual response to addressing mental illness. In essence, while trying to prevent harm this group is perpetuating harm, as they are not offering a comprehensive approach to mental illness that would challenge many of the socioeconomic factors that can worsen Black women's experiences with mental illness because of their concern with cultural factors.

CONCLUSION

Representative Julia Carson (Medicare Prescription Drug Plan, 146 Cong. Rec. H6577–79, 2000) argued, "Mental health is an issue that has historically been kept quiet. It was sort of like a quiet storm within various households across this country and across this world. People were not inclined to talk about mental illness." For Black women who suffer from mental illness, the quietness remains. Indeed, the silence is deafening. What we see in the discourses on mental health and its intersectionality with Black womanhood is simply silence. As such, Black women who suffer from mental illness are omitted from our political deliberations—they are kept in the shadows.

The limited data left me with the question: How do I analyze what does not appear to exist? How do I speak of the silence around mental illness and intersectionality when overwhelmingly the talk fails to explicitly address this issue? My understanding of mental illness and its intersection with race, gender, and class focuses on the few notes (that is, the explicit references) and the silences that exist within the talk, unlike the prior discussed analyses of HIV/AIDS and domestic abuse.

This approach of challenging existing structures as a means of addressing the mental health concerns of African American women was indeed sparse. More typical were "policy" suggestions that focused on "self-help," a rather individual-level approach. Such an approach fails to be inclusive of a wide spectrum of Black women as it is constrained by the type of framing discussed above. The question that remains is, why? Why is it that *Essence* and *Ebony* could not move beyond the more individual and behavioral modification approach used to frame domestic violence, mental health, and HIV/AIDS? Why is it that there was more attention paid to recognizing the works of celebrities and minimum attention paid to the relation of systems of oppression to mental health? As I explore in more detail in the concluding chapter, it is the scripts ascribed to Black women's bodies that restrict how we can talk about Black women and these various illnesses and public issues. The *Ass* and *Strong Black Woman* scripts demarcate the boundaries of "good society." Those bodies that do not fit the prototypical woman that make up the "good society" are apt to be left in the shadows, where this is an appearance that they are on the agenda, but a closer look shows that some women are indeed missing in the discourse.

7 · SISTER SPEAK

Using Intersectionality in Our Political and Policy Strategizing

Nina Simone (1966) poignantly and hauntingly sings of the lives of four Black women in her song "Four Women." Combined, the bodies of these women personify the *Ass* script and *Strong Black Woman* script that I discuss throughout this book. In four stanzas Simone tells the story of: Aunt Sarah, Saffronia, Sweet Thing, and Peaches. Aunt Sara's back is strong, Saffronia is the product of rape and as such embodies the *Ass* script (Black women as a *piece of ass*), Sweet Thing belongs to anyone "who has money to buy" (also a part of the larger *Ass* metanarrative that commodifies Black women), and Peaches embodies strength (the *Strong Black Woman* but also thought of as the "angry" Black woman).

In telling of the lives of these four women, Simone not only speaks to the scripts ascribed to Black women's bodies, but she also tells of a number of issues that ail these women. These women have been abused, physically and emotionally; their needs have been neglected; they carry emotional scars that manifest in mental illnesses, among other manifestations (Peaches tells the story of her rough life and the resulting anger she feels); and they are susceptible to sexually transmitted diseases (as they are available for sexual pleasure). The script ascribed to these women's bodies, the *Ass* and *Strong Black Woman*, influences how they are seen and responded to by the larger community. Additionally, Nina Simone sings hauntingly of the silence that results from the process of muting that takes place within the Black community and among Black women more specifically. It is this song, in part, that led me to analyze HIV/AIDS, domestic violence, and mental illness and how Black women talk about these issues. Like Nina Simone, I wanted to bring to the forefront some of the issues that plague Black women and often render them as shadows to the women's movement, the Black freedom struggle, and even in the Black woman's freedom struggle.

By singing of the realities of these four women, Simone peals back the intricate web of race and gender relations and their operation both within and outside of the Black community. "Four Women" foregrounds both interracial and intraracial race, class, gender, and sexuality hierarchies. Simone exposes the ways race and gender work in relation to each other to subjugate and marginalize diverse Black women. She sings of the plurality of Black womanhood. Nina Simone sings of things often left unspoken, such as skin color and hair texture, sexuality, trauma, and diversity and sameness of oppression. Unmasked in this song is the trope of the universality of Blackness and Black woman-ness. She also sings about liberation. I see this song as liberatory in the sense that it gives voice to women who are often forced to be mute, invisible, or constructed as shadows to others. In essence, Simone offers a radical Black feminist intervention.

Black women have used protest literature, songs, and poems to reimagine a different construction of Black womanhood. Such works have questioned patriarchy, racism, sexism, and classism and their influence on the lives of Black women. While I recognize the depth and variety of said works, I use the work of Nina Simone, particularly the song "Four Women," as a starting point to reimagine an intersectional political and policy strategy that would allow us to confront the use of the *Ass* and *Strong Black Woman* scripts that are ascribed to Black women's bodies. Such an approach would allow us to question and challenge how scripts work as mechanisms for influencing Black women's subjectivity and representation. I bring into play Simone's song because it has a type of personal resonance with me. I am particularly fond of her delivery of the song, but more importantly, I appreciate the intervention she made on behalf of Black women. Thus, for me "Four Women" is a critical intervention for challenging what I found when I originally started this work some years ago—that we, Black women, continue to remain silent around some issues. We engage in a muting process that renders some bodies shadows, at best, in our talk.

In the first three chapters of the book I offer the theoretical foundation of the book. These chapters are designed to show the relationship between scripts and representation. I argue that scripts are the mechanisms that determine the positionality of Black women vis-à-vis Black women (see Figure 3.1). They reveal moments of fracture and of solidarity within Black women's politics. Consequently, scripts allow for an understanding of how "discreet silences" produce shadow bodies, thus showing the link between silence and power. In chapters 4–6 I present the analysis of Black women's talk and silences. The central purpose of these chapters is to identify and analyze which categories of differences are employed in the talk. In these chapters I reveal how identity intersects with representation to generate possibilities for social transformation in Black women's responses to HIV/AIDS, domestic violence, and mental illness.

In this concluding chapter, I demonstrate how the discreet silences manifest from the scripts ascribed to Black women's bodies. I first show how and why the

Ass and *Strong Black Woman* scripts influence Black women's framing of HIV/AIDS, domestic violence, and mental illness. From there, I demonstrate how the *Ass* and *Strong Black Woman* scripts produce shadow bodies by showing how they function (a) within groups of Black women, (b) between groups of Blacks in the larger Black community, and (c) in our practices and institutions, thereby limiting opportunities for a more democratic and inclusive Black women's politics. Focusing on how the scripts ascribed to Black women's bodies function at these various levels opens up and furthers our discussions of the intragroup performance of intersectionality. Finally, I craft an approach, grounded in intersectionality, for challenging the muting and silencing among and between Black women. This allows for the movement of Black women's bodies out of the shadows, thereby allowing them to be seen and valued for who and what they are (Berger & Guidroz, 2009; Carey, 2014; Crenshaw, 1989; Hancock, 2007; Wanzo, 2009). By doing such Black women are able to craft a more inclusive and democratic politics.

I analyze Black women's talk from various platforms on the effect of HIV/AIDS, domestic violence, and mental health on diverse Black women, and how multiple systems of oppression influence Black women's susceptibility and experiences with these public issues. Regardless of the platform that Black women are speaking from (or to Black women), magazines (*Essence* and *Ebony*), blogs, or on the floor of Congress, there is a type of silence around these issues. Indeed some Black women, such as Black lesbians, are completely ignored in the talk. More specifically, the talk does not employ an intersectional framework and neither is it transformative—these are also forms of discreet silences. Using Black feminist theory, muted group theory, and body studies, I argue that this silence is the result, in part, of the scripts ascribed to Black women's bodies.

These metascripts, the *Ass* and *Strong Black Woman*, provide the background information used to frame the issues of HIV/AIDS, domestic violence, and mental illness in such a manner that results in silencing. Scripts, borrowing from Goffman (1974, p. 210), serve as primary frameworks in the sense that they "appear to have no apparent articulated shape" but provide "a lore of understanding, an approach, a perspective." There is often a silence around the permanence of these scripts in understanding how we as Black women organize our politics. We talk about the damage that results from these scripts; however, we do not necessarily talk about how they are used to define our understanding of community, who we let in, and who we leave out. While not originally intended, my analysis has become one of understanding and unmasking this process and the resulting silence and the shadowing of Black female bodies. As such, I conclude this analysis with an attempt to "read" the silences as opposed to the words used to talk about and to Black women. It is through an analysis of these silences that we can add to our current approaches designed to confront these issues. Like

Nina Simone, I am disrupting the narrative of silence. Nina Simone recognized these silences and the ultimate (non)representation of the four women she sang about. She recognized how muted group theory worked to silence us and limit our ability and/or willingness to talk about and represent diverse bodies—in essence, she foreshadows Crenshaw's (1991) understanding of political intersectionality (see chapter 1). Furthermore, Simone understood how these bodies "disrupted" the dominant narratives, relating to Black gender politics and Black feminist sensibilities, of the 1960s.

"Four Women" addresses the notion of belonging and asks, who speaks for these women and to whom? This is indeed a song about community. To some extent, Black women remain silent and end up engaging in self-muting because we have yet to figure out and resolve what our community ought to look like. This is part of a long-standing dilemma faced by Black women, because we recognize that we operate from a point of intersectionality. However, we operate (for multiple reasons) from a notion of a universal experience that penalizes those of us who fail to conform—this can be thought of as a form of hegemonic Black womanhood. Our discursive practices support and maintain this hegemonic Black womanhood while simultaneously privileging other intergroup oppression (see Berlant, 1995; Durham, 2012; Wanzo, 2009). One example of how this behavior manifests itself can be seen in the recent work of Melissa Harris-Perry (2011). In this work Harris-Perry argues that misrecognition, stereotypes, and shame work to circumscribe African American women's lives and also influence their political decision making. She deploys the metaphor of Black women standing in a "crooked room" to explain how "distorted images and painful stereotypes about Black women . . . influence black women as political actors" (Harris-Perry, 2011, p. 32). This is indeed a substantive methodological intervention for understanding Black women's politics. However, there is a silence evident in the analysis. Harris-Perry, like the women I study, engages in a protectionist logic and therefore ends up reinscribing a particular understanding of what the Black (woman) community should look like. In the concluding chapter, she discusses Michele Obama and situates her as embodying "the most visible contemporary example of an African American woman working to stand straight in a crooked room "(Harris-Perry, 2011, p. 271). The use of First Lady Michele Obama as an example leaves little room for transformative politics— this is a form of silence. As visible as Michele Obama is, Harris-Perry does not show how her presence has fostered a fundamental paradigm shift that would be inclusive of diverse Black women. The analysis suggest that Black women's challenge of stereotypes occurs at an individual level and offers little room for those who are not as privileged relative to Michele Obama—in terms of class, sexual normativity, and education—to be able to engage in actions to stand in the crooked room. What is also silent is this analysis is how Michel Obama constructed and even reconstructed her image to be able to stand in the crooked room. So while Obama stands, the room remains crooked. Black feminists, as articulated in the Combahee River Collective and even in Nina Simone's song, have systematically challenged the crooked room by confronting and offering alternatives to the structures that make the room crooked. Furthermore, they have systematically worked to move our understanding of Black womanhood beyond the stories of women such as Michele Obama, to be more inclusive of the plurality of Black womanhood.

When faced with a plurality of Black womanhood, which can manifest in the form of cross-cutting issues, Black women (based on the talk analyzed in this book) fail to engage an intersectional approach in their strategizing around these issues. An intersectional political and policy strategy, one that would simultaneously challenge multiple systems of oppression, would require that we critically analyze our understanding of community. Toni Cade Bambara (1970, p. 7) said, "The first job is to find out what liberation for ourselves means, what work it entails, what benefits it will yield." Part of the process of defining what liberation would look like requires a critical analysis of our understanding of community. This process partially involves judiciously assessing how we use and respond to the scripts ascribed to Black women's bodies and how these scripts influence our intragroup subjectivity. Such a process can hopefully serve as a germinal introduction into a more pluralistic representation of Black women. Before discussing how we might construct a more pluralistic political and policy approach, I first want to address how the scripts ascribed to the Black female body influence the silences around HIV/AIDS, domestic violence, and mental illness.

"WE MIGHT PRAY ABOUT IT": READING SILENCES

While living in Maryland, I conducted research on domestic violence in Prince George's County. I searched the Internet for the county-level legislature—using the Legislative Information System—on domestic violence (during the period 2006–2008). I found nothing. Based on my assumption that I was conducting the search incorrectly, I called the Clerk of the Council to seek some assistance. She told me, "Dear, this is not discussed in the legislature. We might pray about it when someone gets hurt. That's about it" (personal conversation, August 15, 2007). At that time, I did not know that this was also a dominant approach advocated by so many others. Prayer seems to be the "policy" approach most strongly advocated—thus the title of this section, "We might pray about it." My aim in this section is to discuss the silences regarding HIV/AIDS, domestic violence, and mental illness. I start by addressing what is talked about in hopes that it will help us understand the silences and how the *Ass* and *Strong Black Woman* scripts influence these discreet silences.

Among the bloggers, Black female elected officials, and in *Essence* and *Ebony*, there is a tendency to use a narrative of race/racism to frame the discourses. Although the narrative of race/racism is heavily relied upon, for the most part there is no reference to how race, gender, and class work together to influence Black women's susceptibility and experiences with HIV/AIDS, domestic violence, and mental illness—this is the discreet silence that I explain below.

Singularity, where either race or gender was employed as opposed to a multiple system of oppression that show how these systems are interrelated, does not allow us to fully confront and address structural violence. The silence around intersectionality can worsen Black women's experiences with these social problems as it prevents us from engaging in a holistic approach—one that would simultaneously challenge multiple systems of oppression and individual well-being. Furthermore, the deployment of one axis of oppression allows for the perpetuation of privilege within our community, thereby limiting our chances of equality and justice for all. Below I address one source of these silences—the Black female body.

For some cultural theorists the body is thought of as key to understanding the deployment of the network of power structures (Morgan, 1997; Roberts, 1997; Wallace-Sanders, 2002b; Wanzo, 2009). Political power is embodied in our bodies via the ascribed scripts. Our strategizing—political and policy— embodies the *Ass* and *Strong Black Woman* scripts. From these scripts we are told that Black women's bodies are there to serve/please others. Their bodies are to be used for racial uplift and advancement. Black women's bodies are to be sacrificed if it means that others will advance to the "promised land." Thus, any body that fails to embody this performance of the Black female body is excluded from the community.

The silences that permeate the discourses on HIV/AIDS, domestic violence, and mental illness are the result of the perceived failure of the infected and affected women's bodies. These women fail to embody the central characteristics of the *Ass* and *Strong Black Woman* scripts. Their bodies are perceived as "diseased"; thus, they can be monitored, policed, controlled, and muted. As a result they become shadow bodies in the larger Black struggle for equality and justice.[1]

LINKING SCRIPTS, DISCOURSES, AND COMMUNITY

As stated at the start of this work, to address this silence we must recognize and confront the relationship between the scripts ascribed to Black women's bodies, the group muting process, and our strategizing. These scripts, the *Ass* and *Strong Black Woman*, function at multiple levels. The scripts (known and unknown) become part of our discursive practices that influence our politics (a) within groups of Black women; (b) between groups of Blacks in the larger Black community; and (c) our practices and institutions.

Scripts, Discursive Practices, and Within-Group Behavior

Black women, particularly those with some within-group power, determine who is more worthy of a circling of the wagons. This process can result in the perception that some Black women are nonprototypical members of the community of Black women. As Wanzo (2009) states, "African American women have struggled to gain political currency against narratives that often exclude them from stories about proper victims, and when they are visible, it is often because they powerfully illustrate one or more of the conventions in sentimental political storytelling" (p. 3). There is a type of code, scripted on the Black woman's body, used to determine who the prototypical Black woman is and subsequently, whose cause to take up. Consequently, some voices become more privileged relative to others and some voices are rendered mute. Narratives of sameness and universalism, usually couched in race and/or the racial family discourses, unfortunately hide this process.

Black women engage in policing and muting processes of other Black women in response to White middle-class patriarchal ideals (see Gaines, 1997; White, 2001; Wolcott, 2001). This is often thought of as the politics of respectability. During the Progressive Era, the project of racial uplift centered Black female deference, which promoted and encouraged "bourgeois values of thrift, sexual restraint, cleanliness and hard work" (Wolcott, 2001, p. 38). I add to this list not just sexual restraint, but also the privileging of heterosexuality. The manifestation of such deference was seen in the establishment of schools such as the National Training School that offered Black women courses on domestic service, cleanliness, and speech (Higginbotham, 1993; Wolcott, 2001), and citizenship schools that taught Blacks how to be "good" Black citizens (Hohle, 2009). Additionally, this approach was adopted in magazines targeting the Black community where proper dress, cleanliness, etc., were emphasized (Rooks, 2004).

Conflict is embedded in the politics of respectability. It is at once a form of resistance while simultaneously being a form of oppression. McKittrick (2000, p. 224) articulated this when she stated, "Black women produce diverse narratives that both reinscribe and debunk the racial tropes that emit from their bodies." The politics of respectability was intended to counter White's negative perceptions and portrayals of African Americans and it is predicated on the "aggressive shielding of the body; concealing sexuality; and foregrounding morality, intelligence, and civility as a way to counter negative stereotypes" (Thompson, 2009, p. 2). However, this approach also reified such negative understandings as it reflected an internalization of this construction of Black folk. Evelyn Brooks Higginbotham argued that the politics of respectability "equated non-conformity with the cause of racial inequality and injustice. The conservative and moralistic dimension tended to privatize racial discrimination thus rendering it outside the authority of government regulation" (1993, p. 203). Consequently, racial reform and uplift became a private, individual effort. The politics of respectability bred a certain understanding of community that was not inclusive of all Black women. It also explains the suggested approaches to confront HIV/AIDS, domestic violence, and mental illness—these approaches are grounded in personal and individual uplift. The individual approach apparent in the Black women's talk fails to bring to the forefront the functioning of the institutionalization of patriarchy and to encourage Black "women to organize politically to change society in conjunction with our efforts to transform our selves" (hooks, 1993b, p. 44).

Hegemonic Black womanhood results in the construction of Black womanhood that privileges middle-class, formally educated, heterosexual Black women in the understanding of the community of Black women. Wolcott (2001, p. 36) said that these women serve as the "guardians of bourgeois respectability." To this I add that their guardianship is predicated on the scripts ascribed to Black women's bodies. These scripts provide the framework used to demark the boundaries of the "good" Black woman. Nonprototypical Black women are treated to reform efforts as opposed to challenges to the systems that might foster certain types of behaviors among these women.

Scripts, Black Womanhood, and the Black Community

Scripts influence discursive practices where some members of the Black community and their voices are privileged. The status of some Black folk is ranked higher than the status of others (Alexander-Floyd, 2007; Hammonds, 1992; Higginbotham 1993; Isoke 2013). Status might be determined along multiple and intersecting axes such as class, sexuality, religious practices/affiliations, occupation, and gender, among others. In her discussion of this ranking process as it relates to gender, Cathy Cohen (1999) wrote

> In actuality, both inside and outside of black communities, certain segments of the population are privileged with regard to the definition of political agendas. For example, issues affecting men are often presented as representative of the condition of an entire community and thus worthy of a group response. Recently in black communities the troubling and desperate condition of young black men, who in increasing numbers face homicide, incarceration, and constant unemployment as their only "life" options, has been represented as a marker by which we can evaluate the condition of the whole group. The similarly disturbing and life-threatening condition of young black women, who confront teenage pregnancy, state backlash, and (increasingly) incarceration, however, is not portrayed as an equally effective and encompassing symbol of the circumstances of black communities. (p. 11)

Who speaks for Black women? Why is it that the challenges they face are not viewed as encompassing symbols of the challenges faced by the larger Black community? As I have argued thus far, the scripts ascribed to Black women's bodies, because they serve as a mechanism for demarking the boundaries of society, are useful for answering these questions.

In the dating/domestic abuse case involving pop icons Rihanna and Chris Brown, polling data reflected the outcomes of this discursive practice of privileging one group (primarily Black males) over another group (specifically Black females). A survey of 200 Boston youths, ages 12 to 19, on youths and dating violence, reported:

> 46% said Rihanna was responsible for the incident. 52% said both individuals were to blame for the incident, despite knowing at the time that Rihanna had been beaten badly enough to require hospital treatment. 35% said the media were treating Rihanna unfairly. 52% said the media were treating Chris Brown unfairly. In addition, a significant number of males and females in the survey said Rihanna was destroying Chris Brown's career, and females were no less likely than males to come to Rihanna's defense. (Boston Public Health Commission, 2009)

The results of the survey show the continuation of this ideology of Black male privileging. What is also reflected, implicitly, is the functioning of the *Ass* and *Strong Black Woman* metascripts that are ascribed to Black women's bodies. Consider that many of these young individuals believed that Rihanna was destroying Brown's career. Implicit in this argument is the notion that strong Black women protect their men primarily because they are able to transcend all forms of punishment/abuse. Like the character Lilith (in James's *The Book of Night Women*), Rihanna is expected to endure the beating, pick herself up, and carry on (see chapter 2). Similar to Mary and the other unnamed women of Ellison's novel, *Invisible Man*, Rihanna is expected to be a *piece of ass*, not just sexually but in terms of protecting the Black community. Rihanna's behavior is perceived as incongruous. A good Black girl would not involve the police—she would be silent. For some, Rihanna and not Chris Brown became the problem that needed to be solved.

Through the scripts ascribed to Black women's bodies, Black patriarchy flourishes and seems (at times) resistant to challenges. While there is some talk about patriarchy in the Black community, there is simultaneously a silence. Such silence

> demands collaboration and the tacit communal understandings that such collaboration presupposes. Although it is contractual in nature, a critical feature of this type of silence is that it is both a consequence and an index of an unequal distribution of power, if not of actual knowledge. Through it, various forms of power may be partly, although often incompletely, concealed, denied, or naturalized.

Although the type of silence I refer to may be a more or less stable and widely shared cultural convention, it is constituted through, and circumscribed by, the political interests of dominant groups. (Sheriff, 2000, p. 114)

The *Ass* and *Strong Black Woman* metascripts foster and encourage the type of silence discussed by Sheriff. Such silence hides within-group power structures, as it tends to normalize Black women's behavior, so that in the end neither men nor women know what ails her.

Practices, Structures, Institutions, and Discourse

Mills (1959) argued that individual-level problems arise in the context of broader social problems. Our macrolevel politics and policies, which are designed to organize the Black racial family, have implications for what happens at the level of the microfamily. The politics of representation, at both the macro and micro levels, is indeed a contested terrain that is influenced by social memory and notions of what the good community ought to look like and be comprised of. Sheriff (2000, p. 117) posited, "the production of social memory is anything but a neutral process; it can involve variously, struggles over what is considered socially or politically memorable, contested constructions and interpretations of history, and battles over the politics of representation." Our collective memory, which is socially constructed, teaches us how to recognize, classify, and categorize bodies. The process of reading the text inscribed on our bodies informs our institutional practices and procedures in a way that is simultaneously fluid and responsive but static in nature in terms of how we construct and use social memory. Our reading of the body influences our educational, religious, cultural, and political structures and discourses. It is our reading of the body that informs our understandings of the body politic, thereby linking our individual problems to our larger societal practices, processes, and institutions across time and space.

Our cultural schemas and narrative tropes of Black womanhood and Blackness serve as interpretive tools that allow us to make sense of our individual selves and our collective selves. They allow us to understand and interpret human behavior. Discourse and silence is but two ways that we use to make sense of our racialized, gendered, classed, and sexual behaviors. As I discuss in chapter 2, the *Ass* and *Strong Black Woman* scripts are used in determining good behavior at both the microlevel and the macrolevel of the collective Black "family." I expand upon this a bit more here.

There is a network of power structures that influence our discursive and ultimately our democratic praxes. Nikol Alexander-Floyd (2007) explicates how the discourse of Black cultural pathology and particularly the discourse of Black male endangerment fracture Black politics. As a result of these narratives Alexander-Floyd (2007) asserts, "Black politics is marked by an ongoing refusal of Black feminist politics, that is, a failure to recognize the mutually constitutive nature of identity and neglect of the need to have politics broadly defined to deal with this reality, both in practice and the study of Black politics" (p. 149). This network of power structures that include discursive practices such as "Black male endangerment" are designed to manage the public Black identity politically, culturally, and religiously.

While designed to manage the Black public image, some members who might enact their identities differently and who might engage in a different form of self-representation can be politically and culturally neglected and silenced. There is, at times, the illusion of inclusivity (consider the media kits of *Essence* and *Ebony* magazines; see chapter 3); however, careful analysis of discourse can reveal that some group members are advantaged in terms of the distribution of resources and the privileging of particular frames used to discuss the Black community.

> Indeed, the largest contradiction of black life, the elephant in the room that so many have tacitly agreed to ignore, is that for all the adoration, black women are under tight control, trapped in a cultural lockdown that offers few choices. There are requirements to being a Strong Black Woman [or adhering to the *Ass* metanarrative] that nobody says but everybody knows. They are allowed to be strong, but only for the good of others. (Parks, 2010, p. xvii)

The *Ass* and *Strong Black Woman* scripts play a similar role as the endangered Black man narrative discussed by Alexander-Floyd. These scripts, individually and combined, construct binaries of public/private behaviors. They are used to determine whose interests are presented in the public sphere. Accordingly, the *Ass* and *Strong Black Woman* scripts decide who gets sung about, how they are sung about, and the roles they are expected to play in society. They explain why some women "just don't stand a chance."

MOVING BEYOND THE SILENCES: A SONG FOR BLACK FEMALE SHADOW BODIES

Mary Husbands[2] is my name
My husband received a blood transfusion
And I got HIV
Who will want me; I am the "dirty one"?
So I live my life in the shadows of biological and societal illness.

Banita Jacks is my name
Demons, they were all possessed by demons
Four girls, ages 5 to 17 had to be changed for the demons to leave
They arrested me in January 2008 and told me that I killed my girls

But I tell them it was the demons
I lived with their decayed bodies for about six months
But the demons were gone.
So I live my life in the shadows of a prison cell for the next 120 years.

Yvette Cade is my name
I asked the judge to extend my protective order
He told me "Uh, this case is dismissed."
I felt the flames on my body
I saw my flesh on the ground
My ex-husband was sentenced to life in prison for attempting to burn me alive
Now I live my life a shadow of what I use to be.

The stories of these very real women not only speak to the challenges they face in their daily lives, but also they speak to how we as a society respond to these women. Mary, Banita, and Yvette, while much more than this, represent neglect. These might seem like extreme cases, but one has to wonder how many other stories are captured in their stories. When will these women get their songs? When will they no longer be shadow bodies in our cultural and political marketplaces?

Consider the story of Mary, whose husband contracted HIV/AIDS before society knew much about HIV/AIDS. After an accident, he received a blood transfusion. She lost her husband and later her son to HIV/AIDS-related complications. However, she received little to minimum assistance in dealing with her status. Community members also shunned her. Her neighbor, Alice, told me of a recent experience concerning Mary. Alice often gave Mary a ride since she did not have her own means of transport. One day she was approached by another neighbor who asked, "Do you know who you are putting in your car?" Alice asked, "What do you mean?" She was then told, "I wouldn't put her in my car. You know she has AIDS" (personal communication, June 15, 2009). This speaks to Mary's feeling of being "cast off" from society. She is scorned and often shunned although our medical understandings of HIV/AIDS have advanced and we now know more about how HIV is transmitted.

Beyond some members of the community shunning her, some in the medical profession have also mistreated Mary. Allegedly her husband's medical records are missing and are believed to have been destroyed. As such, there is no opportunity to determine if there was negligence on the part of the medical staff. Some medical personnel dismiss Mary while using her case as part of their public lectures. Her HIV-positive status has both public and private consequences. Mary's body is neglected. As a result of this, both her personal and public life has been limited. She is seen, but not really seen—she becomes a shadow image.

HIV-positive individuals are not included in the Black community, via our talk. This is a result of the perception that their bodies are diseased—literally and figuratively. The narratives used to discuss HIV/AIDS employ the scripts of "disease," "dysfunctionality," and "deviance." It is one of deviance: sexuality, drug use, and even poverty (often as a result of individual level behaviors). Combined, this suggests that these bodies are not useful for the project of racial uplift. In terms of the *Ass* script, these bodies are not useful for selling commodities and cannot be commodified as a signal of the vibrant and healthy Black woman. Additionally, an HIV-positive woman violates the *piece of ass* subscript because she is a danger to all those who seek her out sexually and to any offspring that may result from this union. Given our talk on HIV/AIDS, one that does not consistently challenge gender practices within the Black community, this woman is also rendered a shadow body in terms of the *ass question* subscript. To raise the issue of gender inequality and its relation to the spread of HIV/AIDS among Black women is to raise the *ass question*, which has proven troubling to the larger Black freedom movement.

Regarding the *Strong Black Woman* script, HIV-positive women and those living with AIDS also violate the characteristics of the script. Our HIV/AIDS talk does not permit us to see these women in this light of "strength." Affected women also violate the norms of the *sacrificial/nurturing, Strong Black Woman* script, as they are not perceived as "good" mothers. These women violate the notions of motherhood—biological and communal—as they have failed to use their bodies to protect the "offspring" from harm, specifically the physical dangers associated with HIV/AIDS and their inability to refract the negative stereotypes commonly associated with HIV/AIDS, gender, sexuality, and race. This is not a result of the individual women, but more a result of how we have framed HIV/AIDS in general and the long-standing stereotypes of Black women (particularly that they are sexually promiscuous). Thus, this suggests that these bodies are also perceived as violating the norms of the *spiritual/supernatural, Strong Black Woman* script. While there are a few stories of how HIV-positive women transcend via religion, this is generally not the case. I suspect that their stories will not be used in our collective stories of Black resistance, such as the case of Nanny in Jamaica or even First Lady Michelle Obama, because these women are perceived as not having made a racial sacrifice. These women will not become part of our collective memory.

Ava, the protagonist in Pearl Cleage's (1997) *What Looks Like Crazy on an Ordinary Day*, captures much of the lived realities of many Black women living with HIV/AIDS:

> I'm not buying into that shit. I don't think anything I did was bad enough for me to earn this as the paycheck, but it gets rough out here sometimes. If you're not a little kid, or a heterosexual movie star's doomed but devoted wife, or a hemophiliac who got it from a tainted transfusion, or a straight white woman who can prove she's a virgin with a dirty dentist, you're not eligible for any no-strings sympathy. (p. 4)

Mary, like the fictional character Ava, is not eligible for "no-strings sympathy." She is politically, socially, and culturally left on her own.

Jacks's story is also one of neglect. In a report issued after the discovery of the girls' bodies, it was reported that

> The family was supposed to receive monthly visits based on its housing place-ment; it never did. The school system didn't follow through when the girls dropped out of school. Police didn't fully investigate when they were called to the house. And health-care providers did not follow up on things that should have been red flags. . . . But when Jacks sought help with her mental health from a worker at D.C. Chartered Health Plan, a community health center serving Med-icaid patients, the worker never followed up to make sure that she got an appoint-ment and that her daughters were safe. (Dvorak, 2009)

Then D.C. mayor, Adrian Fenty, fired six social workers in the immediate days following the discovery of the bodies. What stood out to me during the mayor's press conference was his consistent claim that the system had failed the girls. Yes, there were systematic bureaucratic failures concerning the children that were murdered. However, no one seemed to ask the question (at least publi-cally), how did the system fail Banita Jacks? Where was her body (in its totality) in the discourses following the discovery of her murdered children? The story of Banita Jacks, as told by family and friends, was one that suggested a notice-able change in her behavior. From various accounts of stories retold on major news broadcasts and in newspapers, this was a woman who dutifully cared for her children. Then there was the death of her boyfriend and a resulting notice-able change in her mental state. Yet she remained unnoticed and did not receive adequate care. The legal system found her guilty; however, I find myself left with a series of questions—questions on her mental state. How do we as a society see women such as Jacks? Like Invisible Man wondered about Mary, I am left to wonder: What are Jacks's (and similar women's) concerns?

The bodies of those suffering a mental illness are troubling, as they do not necessarily fit into the narratives resulting from the *Ass* and *Strong Black Woman* scripts. "In black life, women are the fierce girlies, mamas, and grandmamas who hold together black families and neighborhoods through sheer determination" (Parks, 2010, p. xiv). Black women experiencing mental illness are not "fierce girlies"; they are not strong enough to hold together their communities. These women are perceived as either not being available or capable of doing the emo-tional work necessary for the progression of the Black community. Neither are they useful in the narratives resulting from the *Ass* scripts—in terms of availabil-ity to assuage the pain of the Black man as a *piece of ass*. They are not useful as commodities as they are not seen as "whole." In terms of the *ass question*, Black women, regardless of their mental health status, are often made invisible because of the patriarchal nature of representation. Black women experiencing mental ill-ness are further marginalized because of their status; consequently, they are not useful because they "fit" too closely with European notions of Black instability.

Yvette's story is also one of neglect. In the immediate period after the hor-rific burning of Yvette Cade, many focused on the Judge Palumbo's prior actions. *Washington Post* reporter R. Castaneda (2005) stated, "On Sept. 19, three weeks before Yvette Cade, 31, was doused with gasoline and set on fire, Palumbo dismissed a protective order she had obtained against her estranged husband, Roger B. Hargrave, 33. According to a recording of the hearing, Cade told Palumbo she was afraid of Hargrave, but the judge cut her off and, at the request of Hargrave, dismissed the protective order." The neglect of Yvette Cade extends beyond the actions of Judge Palumbo; the county government and their response to domestic violence also resulted in her being neglected. According to Mark L. (2007), "In 2001, Prince George's county accounted for more than 20 percent of deaths caused by domestic violence in the state. Since 2001, 48 people have died from domestic abuse in the county. Only Baltimore County has had more." The county government prayed about domestic violence while doing nothing to legislatively protect these women.

The bodies of abused Black women are also problematic for the racial uplift project because they show the fallibility of the claim of the *Strong Black Woman*. Additionally, this body is a visual reminder of the aggression script ascribed to the Black man's body (see Jackson, 2006). These bodies visibly, figuratively, and literally represent a break in the carefully crafted construction of Black society. Abused Black women also violate the norms of the *Ass* script. These bodies, similar to those affected with HIV/AIDS and those that are affected by men-tal illness, challenge and disrupt the constructed notion of good Black society. They are sometimes seen as supporting the stereotypes of Black aggression and anger. Furthermore, these bodies bring to the forefront Black patriarchy in a way that does not reconcile with notions of Black progress and an inclusive narra-tive (in the sense that the Black freedom struggle is inclusive of all regardless of gender)—the *ass question* subscript.

These three women, Mary, Banita, and Yvette, all operate from a point of intersectionality: class, race, sexuality, and gender. Yet they are consistently neglected. As I argue throughout this book, they are neglected because of the scripts ascribed to their bodies. Their bodies singularly and collectively "violate" the norms of Black life. The challenge that we all face is how to "rescue" these bodies from the shadows. How do we engage in a politics that allows us to value these bodies? For one, we must address why is it that we strive to construct our communities in the manner that we do. This requires that we look at both inter-group and intragroup factors to determine how we respond.

As I show in chapters 4–6, there is a failure among Black women to employ an intersectional framing in their talk on HIV/AIDS, domestic violence, and mental illness. This is the result of what the bodies that embody these "illnesses" represent to the community. We see that race dominated much of the framing of these issues across the posts of bloggers, the stories in *Essence* and *Ebony* magazines, and the floor speeches of elected Black congresswomen. Race allows for a continuation of a narrative that suggests cohesiveness around the Black body. It allows for the masking of differences, thereby allowing us to keep some bodies in the shadows. These bodies are kept in the shadows so that we can selectively use them as needed. This is not to suggest that individuals are sinister.

Dara Strolovitch (2006) shows that "In spite of sincere desires to represent disadvantaged members, organizations downplay the impact of such issues and frame them as narrow and particularistic in their effect, while framing issues affecting advantaged subgroups as if they affect a majority of their members and have a broad and generalized impact" (p. 894). There is a strategizing about the use of Black women's bodies, as reflected in the framing of HIV/AIDS, domestic violence, and mental illness, that is reflective of Strolovitch's conceptualization. I recognize that such universal framing might be appealing as part of the larger narrative of a Black equality movement that seeks to deflect the negative images and stereotypes imposed on Black men and women. However, there is a danger in deploying the language of universality in the quest for equality. It leaves some bodies out of the discourse.

Gender is often employed as a singular factor in the framing of HIV/AIDS, domestic violence, and mental illness. It is somewhat expected that gender would be used given that I am discussing the talk of Black women. However, there is a danger in how gender is used to craft the frames. It is deployed in a "universal" manner where differences between Black women, in terms of class and sexuality, are ignored.

Failure to talk about class in the framing of these issues is also a reflection of how the Black body politics is constructed. Poverty, and particularly class stratification, is a strain against racial progress. It is a challenge to the rhetoric of equality/progress, the abilities of the Black body to confront, exist, and master a capitalist system. It shows a tension within the Black community in the use of the legacy of slavery to construct their identity while being unable to confront poverty at the same time.

Sexuality is also problematic for the larger Black politic. Anyone who does not subscribe to heterosexuality is often viewed as violating the norms of Blackness (Shaw & McDaniel, 2007). Beyond the issue of homosexuality, sexuality and the stereotype of promiscuity among African Americans also limits the Black collective from addressing some issues. This stereotype renders us silent in terms of speaking about HIV/AIDS, for example, for fear that we might perpetuate the myth of the sexually loose Black woman and man. Ava (from Cleage's *What Looks Like Crazy on an Ordinary Day*) contests this inability to discuss sexual behavior when she declares "The audience was eating it up, but it got on my last nerve. The thing is, half these bitches are lying. More than half. They get diagnosed and all of a sudden they're Mother Theresa. I can't be positive? It's impossible! I'm practically a virgin! Bullshit. They got it just like I got it: fucking men" (Cleage, 1997, p. 3). By centering Ava's sexual agency, Cleage seems to be talking back to the dominant construction of HIV/AIDS and Black womanhood that tends to focus men on the down low, intravenous drug use, or some other notion of "innocence."

Finally, there needs to be a space where we can break these silences. Yes, "some of us are brave"; however, who are we brave for and under what contexts? We can no longer simply challenge external factors such as race/racism while ignoring internal pressures such as our inability to address sexuality and class differences in an open manner. While we often celebrate the work of individuals such as Audre Lorde, and while Black female elected officials tend to celebrate Black gay pride, we consistently do not do the work advocated by these individuals.

In the foreword to Bennett and Dickerson's anthology, *Recovering the Black Female Body*, Carla Peterson (2001) asks the following question:

> What can we say then about the representation of the Black female body as we begin the twenty-first century? Perhaps simply that history repeats itself given that this body remains a highly contested site of meaning both within and without the Black community and that African-American women still struggle with its representation, vacillating between the poles of sentimental normalization and the flaunting of eccentricity. (p. xv)

To address these tensions mentioned by Peterson, we should (re)examine the meaning of "community" and how our construction of such influences group rights that are shaped by the intersections of race, class, gender, and sexuality. Additionally, we have to systematically and honestly look at how the Black female body determines how we deal with these tensions and binaries that result in our silences. We have to ask ourselves, how does our act of silencing "non-prototypical" Black women allow for the perpetuation of their marginalization by us and by other groups? Then we can do the work of bringing these women, who are HIV-positive, who have AIDS, who are abused, and who are affected by mental illness, out of the shadows.

APPENDIX

TABLE A.1. Congressional Black women and the count of their speeches

Representative	Party/ State	Dates of Service	HIV/AIDS	Domestic Abuse	Mental Illness
Eleanor Holmes Norton	D-DC	1991–present	47	9	3
Maxine Waters	D-CA	1991–present	46	4	5
Carol Mosely Braun	D-IL	1993–1999	3	1	0
Corrine Brown	D-FL	1993–present	10	0	1
Eva Clayton	D-NC	1993–2003	20	1	3
Eddie Bernice Johnson	D-TX	1993–present	15	1	11
Cynthia McKinney	D-GA	1991–2003; 2005–2007	1	0	2
Carrie Meek	D-FL	1993–2003	15	0	2
Sheila Jackson Lee	D-TX	1995–present	8	2	4
Juanita Millender-McDonald	D-CA	1995–2007	35	15	4
Julia Carson	D-IN	1997–2007	8	5	4
Carolyn Cheeks Kilpatrick	D-MI	1997–2011	33	1	2
Donna Christensen	D-VI	1997–present	64	5	10
Barbara Lee	D-CA	1997–present	30	2	11
Stephanie Tubbs Jones	D-OH	1999–2008	26	6	6
Diane Watson	D-CA	2001–2011	26	5	1
Denise Majette	D-GA	2003–2005	2	1	0
Gwendolynne Moore	D-WI	2005–present	7	3	2

While the use of blogs in research has many positive aspects, their use is not without challenges. The primary challenge centers on how to ethically use the posts in research. The question that I had to first address is whether the posts are public or private. The answer to this question is important in determining whether informed consent is required. Kraut and colleagues (2004) assert that research, using blogs for example, is exempt from federal regulations protecting human subjects if "research involves the collection or study of existing data, documents, records. If these sources are publicly available or if the information is recorded by the investigator so that subjects cannot be identified." My test to determine if a blog was private or public relied on whether I had to subscribe or complete some form of registration before I could access the blog. Any blog that required such would then be excluded from the analysis.

Additionally, I confronted the issue as to whether the authors of the blog posts should be recognized or be treated anonymously. In its ethical guidelines, the Association of Internet Researchers (AoIR) suggested that the context of the computer-mediated communication be considered. They suggested that individuals participating in intimate chatrooms should be considered as human subjects. Alternatively, those who write publically, such as bloggers, should more than likely be considered as authors and as such recognized for their work (Ess, 2002, p. 7). Beyond this, in my reporting of the data, I strive at all times not to cause any harm to the bloggers.

For blogs to be included in the analysis, they had to meet the following criteria:

- Authorship: blogs were authored by Black women. In the event that the blog was written by a team of writers, then women had to represent the majority of writers.
- Geographic location: All blogs were based in the United States.
- Language: Posts had to be written in English.
- Accessibility: Keyword searches for archival materials had to be available.

TABLE A.2.   Black female bloggers

Title of Blog/Name of Blogger	About
Brown Sista / N/A	A word for my sistas; health & beauty; relationships; news; gossip
Share My World / Ms. Tee	Hi, I'm Ms. Tee. I am a 32 year old mother of two wonderful sons and I live in Miami, Florida. I am an inspirational journalist on a quest for my divine destiny. I am also studying to become a Relationship Therapist. My desire is to inspire you to live, love and dream fearlessly.
Afro Bella / Patrica Elizabeth Grell Yursik	*Afrobella.com* was created in August 2006 to fill a void that existed in print and in the blogosphere—a continual celebration of natural hair and women all shades of beautiful. If you love the skin that you're in and the beautiful natural texture of your hair, if you enjoy learning about different cultures and listening to eclectic music, if you have an obsession with makeup and fashion and all things fabulous—then this is the blog for you
Is It Just Me? / Blu Jewel	I'm filled with thoughts and often wonder, "is it really just me?"
Brown Girl Gumbo / N/A	N/A
I Like Her Style! / Sylvia	I have an incurable love of fashion. This is my medication. Enjoy!

TABLE A.2. Black female bloggers *(continued)*

Title of Blog/Name of Blogger	About
Young, Black, and Fabulous / Natasha E	It's the perfect mix of gossip, entertainment, and swagger. The focus is fashion, fabulousness, gossip, and foolywang. And if gossip were fashion, THE YBF would be couture.
Confessions of an Everyday Woman / Ms. Confessions	Hi, I am Ms. Confessions and I am the writer for this fabulous blog Confessions of An Everyday Woman. While there is no primary purpose other than to "air my personal dirty laundry," opinions and thoughts; I do hope that after reading my blog it's understood that you are never alone in any given situation.
I'm living my life like it's golden / Black Doll	Living this life has taught me wisdom is priceless and common sense is not all that common. In the end you can bend your actions to conform to your principles or you can bend your principles to conform to your actions. This is a choice we all must make. It is important to choose the path of integrity because all other roads ultimately lead to ruin.
Buzzology Surveys / N/A	Visit our blog daily to find the latest headlines about marketing efforts geared towards our community, view commercials, promos and other ad campaigns, read interviews with decision makers, and continue to stay informed!
Light-skinned-ed Girl / N/A	a mixed chick's mixed thoughts on a mixed-up world
Beautiful, Also, Are The Souls of My Black Sisters / N/A	A blogsite for the praising of all things beautiful and sublime in honor of all Black women. A blogsite to speak the truth of Black women's history and accomplishments in America.
The Adventures of an Urban Socialite / N/A	At UrbanSocialite.com we believe in great fashion, emerging design, and passionate artists. UrbanSocialite's approach to advertising is simple . . . we write about what we like . . . we promote brands, artists, musicians and products that we love.
A Lady's Perspective / N/A	N/A
Style Chile / Naki	Lawyer from NYC/Philadelphia
Two Jet Set Divas . . . and a Map / N/A	Hip. Chic. Funky. Urban. Cool. Life-expanding . . . Forward-thinking. . . . Jet-setting. This blog was created with these Divas in mind. Women who are ready to take on the globe, one trip at a time. Count on us to bring a fun and fresh twist on international travel commentary and information. We're Two JetSet Divas who are ready to explore the world, and we invite you to come along for the ride . . . we've got the map.

TABLE A.2. Black female bloggers (*continued*)

Title of Blog/Name of Blogger	About
Quarterlife Mocha Girl / Southern Lady	I'm a Southern girl living her life like it's golden. Well . . . most of the time anytime. Email me with any questions or concerns about my funny and downright weird journey at lishasu888@yahoo.com. Trust me, everything documented on this blog is REAL!
Black Gives Back / Tracey	BlackGivesBack features social entrepreneurs and everyday heroes, celebrity philanthropy, news of interest to the black community, coverage of charity and community events, and more. Although African Americans are viewed as passive recipients in philanthropy, my blog proves that we are active givers and major philanthropists, donating millions of dollars to issues impacting our community.
New Black Woman / The New Black Woman	A twenty-something professional black woman who is fed up with the portrayal, exclusion and degradation of black women. It's time for a revolution.
The Black Socialite / N/A	I'm a Super Socialite insider who enjoys having fun and making the world a better place! I live a fabulous life and encourage others to do the same. This blog will also include some of my junkets and musings about Black Socialite life. If you are a member of the tribe or aspire to become one, this rich dishy recipe should delight, entertain, and educate you!
apartment tbd, etc / kay	A 20something who's too complex to be summarized in a couple of short lines but ♥'s interior design, travel, history, a good book, pop culture and beautiful fabulous things. Working her way up the PR ladder in the entertainment industry but may say "f#@% it all" and take the path less traveled. Whatever that is. FINALLY decorating her first apartment & turning it into a chic abode on a budget. Sound like a diva?
The Sauda Voice / Stephanie M. Watts	The Sauda Voice represents a place where (1) the beauty, diversity and intellect of dark skinned people, especially black women, is always acknowledged and embraced, and (2) the issues important to them are given a voice and a platform by which to use it. The Sauda Voice is also a place where people of color are not constantly assaulted by information and opinion filtered through a lens of ignorance, bias, stereotypes, and at times, racism.

TABLE A.2.   Black female bloggers (*continued*)

Title of Blog/Name of Blogger	About
Beauty in Baltimore / BeautyinBaltimore	A very cute black chic who loves everything about fashion and beauty. I'm struggling through the ups and downs of being in my twenties. I am a recent graduate so I am doing everything on a really tight budget. That means no more Gucci or Louie Vuitton bags for now. I'll take a cat anyday over a dog. Travelling is my greatest love. I frequently discuss sex and how much I love a man with a average sized one. Mainly, this blog serves as a tool for me to get some things off my chest.
Brown Sugar / N/A	N/A
Young, Political & Fabulous / Lindsay Ross	Lindsay Ross I am a twenty-something political aficionada posing as a policy grad student and former Hill staffer in recovery. POLIFAB (pä-lē-fab) adj: A sublime quality that encompasses being political and civically-minded in nature and exuding poise, confidence and fabulousity.
What Tami Said / Tami	I am a writer, black woman, bibliophile, music lover, nappy head, geek, eccentric, Midwesterner, wife, stepmother, sister, aunt and daughter. I am a liberal progressive. I believe in equality . . . of gender . . . of race . . . of sexuality . . . and I believe in working PROACTIVELY toward same. I am anti-oppression. I believe in justice for ALL. (Knowing that, you may label me as you wish.) I am a genealogist and I believe there is strength and knowledge to be found in the lives of our ancestors. Good living, good food, good music, good books, good people and good conversation turn me on. In this space, I celebrate and discuss all that I am and all that I love.
Angelia's. . . . Ramblings. . . . / Angelia Vernon Menchan	I am a woman who has spent her life consumed by Love for the written word. My goal is to reach as many as I can through the written word and do what God has asked of me: Mentor by Writing.

ACKNOWLEDGMENTS

Needless to say, I did not write this book on my own. There are so many individuals who supported me along the way, some of whom are named below. To the anonymous reviewers, who took the time to offer amazing suggestions, thank you. My sincere gratitude to Kathleen Guidroz: you are an outstanding and dedicated editor. The cover art is the design of the talented photographer Carlens Therry Michel and the beautiful model Resana Rejeen Malone—thank you both for translating my vision of a Black woman's gaze. Thanks to Camille Wilson, Teri Fair Platt, Sekile Nzinga-Johnson, Ruth Nicole Brown, and Keesha Middlemass—always remember the peacock and never forget that we are Nupe Women Warriors. Monica Simal and Tuba Argatan supported me by sustaining me in what has been a rather oppressive institution. I thank you both. I am grateful for having Viviane Saleh-Hanna who carried me and offered me her undying support. I will always be grateful to my grandmother Kathleen Griffith and my mother Monica Jordan for the stories they gave me along the way. I write because they speak. And finally, I have to thank my daughter who often kept me grounded and challenged me to think critically about what it means to be a Black woman in the age of social media and the Obama administration. My dear Makeen because you often (re)affirmed me and kept me grounded as I fed off your commitment to racial justice and freedom, my sincere gratitude.

NOTES

INTRODUCTION

1. The analysis of blogs does not conform to this time period as I was cognizant of the emergence of blogs as part of larger evolving computer-mediated communication technologies.

2. I identified the 27 blogs from a list of blogs provided by a Mahogany Butterfly Network site titled "BlogsbyBlackWomen" (http://www.mahoganybutterfly.com/bloggers.aspx). This site, at the time of the data collection process, offered 80 blogs written by Black women. It represented one place for locating a variety of blogs of this nature. However, some of the blogs were not included in this study because they were no longer available or could not be searched. Given the fluid nature of blogs, I make no claim that this is the most comprehensive or exhaustive list of blogs hosted by Black women. However, I do believe that the listed blogs are representative of the varied nature of Blogs by these women—and I wanted, relatively speaking, a list of blogs encompassing a range of types of blogs.

3. McCall's focus is on research categories, particularly on which categories inform and are selected for analysis and how said categories are employed. To this end, she distinguishes between anti-, intra-, and intercategorical approaches. According to McCall, anticategorical approaches reject the idea of identity categories and instead focus on homogenizing and essentializing differences. Intracategorical approaches critically evaluate common categories in order to focus on complexities *within* given social groups to understand their marginalization. Intercategorical approaches, her chosen approach, assess the complexity of relations among multiple social groups. Accordingly, these approaches empirically study "whether meaningful inequalities among groups even exist in the first place" as opposed to presupposing the nature of such relations. (McCall, 2005, p. 1785).

CHAPTER 2

1. It should be noted that while I treat these as individual subscripts of the much larger *Ass* and *Strong Black Woman* metanarrative scripts, there is an interrelationship between the subscripts.

CHAPTER 3

1. I do not include *Jet Magazine* in this analysis as it is published weekly. The goal was to analyze comparable publications with similar publication histories—which also explains why other magazines, such as *Today's Black Woman,* are not included in the study.

2. The Jena 6 case began in August 2006 when a Black male student sat under a tree known to be spot where Euro-American students gathered. In response, White students hung three nooses in the tree. Previously existing racial tensions escalated in the months following the display of the nooses. There were a number of confrontations between Black and White students. Additionally there was a fire that destroyed the central wing of the Jena High School. Six Black males, in response to a statement one of them overheard that involved a White student bragging about a racial assault, responded by assaulting Barker (a White male student). Barker sustained minor injuries. The six Black students were arrested and initially charged as adults with felony offenses, including attempted murder and aggravated assault. The White students' punishment involved limited school suspensions. Civil rights advocates protested the charges levied against the Black male students. Eventually the charges were reduced to battery for all but one the offenders. This case raised the issue of the continuing functioning of race in the U.S. justice system.

3. At a celebration for Senator Strom Thurmond (a known segregationist), Senator Trent Lott made a comment in support of racial segregation. Senator Lott, at that time, was thought to be the most powerful Republican. He was eventually forced to resign.

4. Given the standards of both qualitative research and IPA, I do not rely on techniques such as intercoder reliability, which suggest that there can exist an accurate/true analysis of the data that can be captured through coding or thematic analysis. Instead, I utilize Guba and Lincoln (1981) criteria for designing qualitative research, which relies on credibility, fittingness, auditability, and confirmability to ensure the "trustworthiness" of the analysis.

CHAPTER 4

1. Title taken from article in *Essence* Magazine (Grant, 2000, p. 66).

CHAPTER 5

1. The title was taken from the song "Love the Way You Lie," which was recorded by rap artist Eminem (Winters, Mathers, Grant, & Haferman, 2010) featuring Rihanna. Interestingly, Rihanna sang the hook to this song which included the line "you gonna stand there and watch me burn. . . . I love the way you lie," in spite of her experience with domestic violence.

2. In 2005, Cade's ex-husband, Roger B. Hargrave, doused her with gasoline and lit her on fire at her place of work in Upper Marlboro, Maryland.

CHAPTER 6

1. Title taken from Starling's (1999, p. 140) *Ebony* article "Black Women and the Blues: Why So Many Sisters Are Mad and Sad."

2. The "Tuskegee Study of Untreated Syphilis in the Negro Male" began in 1932 with the goal of recording the natural history of syphilis. The experiment was conducted on approximately 600 Black men, some with syphilis and others who were free of the disease. The study was conducted without the benefit of patients' informed consent. And in fact patients were misguided and mistreated as they were told that they were being treated for "bad blood" and were denied medications to treat syphilis. The original study was slated for a six-month period. In actuality, it lasted for 40 years.

3. From the CD, *I Refuse to Be Lonely* (Friedman, Hyman, Rich & Martinelli, 1995) performed by Phyllis Hyman. Philadelphia: Volcano Records.

4. On June 30, 1995, Hyman, at the age of 45, committed suicide.

CHAPTER 7

1. I am not suggesting that all individual bodies are treated in this manner. I do believe that it is possible for some individuals to be treated in a different manner, where their stories are selected to show how indeed they embody either the *Ass* and/or *Strong Black Woman* scripts.

This is what I discuss in chapter 2 as the possibility for these scripts to be used for either a positive or a negative frame. However, when I consider the various discourses in totality, it was indeed more common to see more, often implicit, frames suggesting how these women violated the norms of the scripts.

2. This is a pseudonym used to protect the identity of this woman.

REFERENCES

5 questions for: Dr. Lorraine Cole, president and chief executive, Black Women's Health Imperative. (2005, October). *Ebony*, 26.

The abuse stops here. (1999, August). *Essence*, 96.

Adimora, A. A., & Schoenbach, V. J. (2002). Contextual factors and the Black-White disparity in heterosexual HIV transmission. *Epidemiology, 13*(6), 707–712.

Adimora, A. A., & Schoenbach, V. J. (2005). Social context, sexual networks, and racial disparities in rates of sexually transmitted infections. *Journal of Infectious Diseases, 191*(Supplement 1), S115–S122.

AfroBella. (2009). As an "Island Woman . . ." [Web log post]. Retrieved from http://www.afrobella.com

Afrobella. (2010, March 10). Are you rocking red pumps today [Web log post]? Retrieved from http://www.afrobella.com/2010/03/10/are-you-rocking-red-pumps-today/

AIDS Epidemic, 147 Cong. Rec. E1035 (daily ed. June 6, 2001) (statement of Rep. Meek). Retrieved from http://thomas.loc.gov

Albertyn, C. (2003). Contesting democracy: HIV/AIDS and the achievement of gender equality in South Africa. *Feminist Studies, 29*(3), 595–615.

Alexander-Floyd, N. (2007). *Gender, race and nationalism in contemporary Black politics.* Basingstoke, UK: Palgrave Macmillan.

Alexander-Floyd, N. (2010). Critical race Black feminism: A "jurisprudence of resistance" and the transformation of the academy. *Signs: Journal of Women in Culture and Society, 35*(4), 810–820.

Alexander-Floyd, N. (2012). Disappearing acts: Reclaiming intersectionality in the social sciences in a post-Black feminist era. *Feminist Formations, 24*(1), 1–25.

Alexander-Floyd, N., & Jordan-Zachery, J. (special eds.). 2014. Black women in politics: Identity, power, and justice in the new millennium [special issue]. *National Political Science Review, 16.* New Brunswick, NJ: Transaction.

Amber, J. (2002, August). Why don't you use a condom? *Essence*, 118.

America's Law Enforcement and Mental Health Project, 146 Cong. Rec. H10639 (daily ed. October 24, 2000) (statement of Rep. Jackson-Lee). Retrieved from http://thomas.loc.gov

America's Law Enforcement and Mental Health Project, 146 Cong. Rec. H24029 (daily ed. October 24, 2000) (statement of Rep. Jackson-Lee). Retrieved from http://thomas.loc.gov

Ammons, L. (1995). Babies, bath water, racial imagery and stereotypes: The African-American woman and the battered woman syndrome. *Wisconsin Law Review, 5*, 1003–1080.

Announcing Introduction of the Shield Act, 151 Cong. Rec. H4194 (daily ed. June 8, 2005) (statement of Rep. Moore). Retrieved from http://thomas.loc.gov

Anthony, K. (2010, October 4). CJ by Cookie Johnson: A champagne celebration with a cause [Web log post]. Retrieved from http://www.blackgivesback.com/2010/10/cj-by-cookie-johnson-champagne.html

Ardener, E. (1975). Belief and the problem of women. In S. Ardener (Ed.), *Perceiving women* (pp. 1–17). London: Malaby Press.

Ardener, E. (1978). Some outstanding problems in the analysis of events. In G. Schwinner (Ed.), *The yearbook of symbolic anthropology* (pp. 103–121). London: Hurst.

Armstrong, E. (2001). Gangsta misogyny: A content analysis of the portrayals of violence against women in rap music, 1987–1993. *Journal of Criminal Justice and Popular Culture*, 8(2), 96–126.

Atwater, D. F. (2009). African American women's rhetoric: The search for dignity, personhood, and honor. New York: Lexington Books.

Auerbach, C. F., & Silverstein, L. B. (2003). *Qualitative data: An introduction to coding and analysis*. New York: New York University Press.

Augello Cook, A., Perry, L., & Mostyn, S. (2007). Superwoman [Recorded by A. Keys]. On *As I Am* [CD]. New York: Sony BMG.

Avery, B. (1990). Breathing life into ourselves: The evolution of the National Black Women's Project. In E. C. White (Ed.), *The Black women's health book* (pp. 4–10). Seattle: Seal Press.

Bachrach, P., & Baratz, M. (1963). Decision and non-decisions: An analytic framework. *American Political Science Review*, 57, 632–642.

Baird, K. L. (2010). Agenda setting, social construction of populations and problems, and marginalized groups. Paper presented a the Annual Meeting of the American Political Science Association meeting, Washington, D.C.

Baker, C. N. (2005). Images of women's sexuality in advertisements: A content analysis of Black- and White-oriented women's and men's magazines. *Sex Roles*, 52(1–2), 13–27.

Baldwin, J. (1968). Tell me how long the train's been gone. New York: Dell.

Bambara, T. C. (1970). *The Black woman: An anthology*. New York: Washington Square Press.

Banks-Wallace, J., & Parks, L. (2004). It's all sacred: African American women's perspectives on spirituality. *Issues in Mental Health Nursing*, 25, 25–45.

Bardhan, N. (2001). Transnational AIDS/HIV news narrative: A critical exploration of overarching frames. *Mass Communication & Society*, 4, 283–310.

Barrett, E. J. (1995). The policy priorities of African American women in state legislatures. *Legislative Studies Quarterly*, 20(2), 223–247.

Barthes, R. (1972). *Mythologies*. (A. Lavers, Trans.) New York: Hill and Wang.

Baumgartner, F. R. & Jones, B. D. (2002). *Policy dynamics*. Chicago, IL: University of Chicago Press.

Beauboeuf-Lafontant, T. (2009). Behind the mask of the strong Black woman: Voice and the embodiment of a costly performance. Philadelphia, PA: Temple University Press.

Beck, S. A. (1991). Rethinking municipal governance: Gender distinctions on local councils. In D. L. Dodson (Ed.), *Gender and policymaking: Studies of women in office* (pp. 103–114). New Brunswick, NJ: Center for the American Woman and Politics.

Becker, A. (1995). *Beyond translation*. Ann Arbor, MI: University of Michigan Press

Belkhir, J. A. & Barnett, B. M. (2001). Race, gender and class intersectionality. *Race, Gender and Class*, 8(3), 157–74.

Bennett, V & Dickerson, V. D. (2001). Recovering the Black female body: Self representation by African American women. New Jersey: Rutgers University Press.

Bent-Goodley, T. B. (2001). Eradicating domestic violence in the African American community: A literature review and action agenda. *Trauma, Violence, & Abuse*, 2(4), 316–330.

Bent-Goodley, T. B. (2004). Perceptions of domestic violence: A dialogue with African American women. *Health and Social Work*, 29(4), 307–316.

Berger, M. T (2004). Workable sisterhood: The political journey of stigmatized women with HIV/AIDS. New Jersey: Princeton University Press.

Berger, M. T. & Guidroz, K. (2009). *The intersectional approach: Transforming the academy through race, class and gender*. Chapel Hill: The University of North Carolina Press.

Berlant, L. (1997). The queen of America goes to Washington City: Essays on sex and citizenship. Durham, NC: Duke University Press,

Bilby, K., & Steady, F. C. (1981). Black women and survival: A maroon case. In F. C. Steady (Ed.), *The Black woman cross-culturally* (pp. 458–460). Cambridge, MA: Schenkman.

Black college queens 2003. (2003, April). *Ebony*, 138.

Black Diamond. (2006–2007, December–January). *Complex*, 90–95.

Black Girls Give Back. (2010, December 14). Allstate honors 2011 Give Back Day heroes [Web log post]. Retrieved from http://www.blackgivesback.com/2010/12/allstate-honors-2011-give-back-day.html

Black Girls Give Back. (2010, February 24). Mental health campaign launches targeting African American community [Web log post]. Retrieved from http://www.blackgivesback.com/2010/02/mental-health-campaign-launches.html

Blackwomenshealth.com. (n.d.). *Domestic violence: When love becomes hurtful!* Retrieved from http://www.blackwomenshealth.com/2006/articles.php?id=35

Black, R. W. (2006). Language, culture and identity in online fanfiction. *E-Learning, 3*(2), 170–184.

Blood, R. (2000). *Weblogs: A history and perspective.* Retrieved from Rebecca's Pocket: http://www.rebeccablood.net/essays/weblog_history.html

Blood, R. (2002). Weblogs: A history and perspective. In R. Blood (Ed.), *We've got blog: How weblogs are changing our culture* (pp. 7–16). Cambridge, MA: Perseus.

Bobo, J. (1995). *Black women as cultural readers.* New York: Columbia University Press.

Bogle, D. (2001). Prime time blues: African Americans on network television. New York: Farrar, Strauss and Giroux.

Bograd, M. (1999). Strengthening domestic violence theories: Intersections of race, class, sexual orientation, and gender. *Journal of Marital and Family Therapy, 25,* 275–289.

Bositis, D. (2001). *Black elected officials: A statistical summary 2000.* Retrieved from www.jointcenter.org

Boston Public Health Commission. (2009, March 12). *Public Health Commission surveys youths on dating violence.* Retrieved from http://www.bphc.org/Newsroom/Pages/TopStoriesView.aspx?ID=60

Bowleg, Lisa. (2008). When Black+lesbian+woman ≠ Black lesbian woman: The methodological challenges of qualitative and quantitative intersectionality research. *Sex Roles 59*(3): 312–25.

Bowleg, L., Lucas, K. J., & Tschann, J. M. (2004). "The ball was always in his court": An exploratory analysis of relationship scripts, sexual scripts, and condom use among African American women. *Psychology of Women Quarterly, 28,* 70–82.

Boyd, E. B. (2011, January 31). *How social media accelerated the uprising in Egypt.* Retrieved from http://www.fastcompany.com/1722492/how-social-media-accelerated-the-uprising-in-egypt

Boylorn, R. M. (2013). Blackgirl Blogs, Auto/ethnography, and Crunk Feminism. *Liminalities: A Journal of Performance Studies. 9*(2), 73–82

Bozzette, S. A., Berry, S. H., Duan, N., Frankel. M. R., Leibowitz, A. A., Lefkowitz, D., . . . Richman, D. (1998). The care of HIV-infected adults in the United States. HIV Cost and Services Utilization Study Consortium. *New England Journal of Medicine, 339,* 1897–1904.

Bratton, K. A. (2005). Critical Mass Theory revisited: The behavior and success of token women in state legislatures. *Politics and Gender, 1*(1), 97–125.

Bratton, K. A., & Haynie, K. L. (1999). Agenda-setting and legislative success in state legislatures: The effects of gender and race. *Journal of Politics, 61*(3), 658–679.

Breslau, J., Kendler, K. S., Su, M., Gaxiola-Aguilar, S., & Kessler, R. (2005). Lifetime risk and persistence of psychiatric disorders across ethnic groups in the United States. *Psychological Medicine, 35,* 317–327.

Brice-Baker, J. R. (1994). Domestic violence in African-American and African-Caribbean families. *Journal of Social Distress and the Homeless, 3*, 23–38.

Briggs, J., & Davis, M. D. (1994). The brutal truth: Putting domestic violence on the Black agenda. *Emerge, 57*, 5–50.

Brock, A. (2007). Race, the internet, and the hurricane: A critical discourse analysis of black identity online during the aftermath of Hurricane Katrina. (Unpublished doctoral dissertation). University of Illinois at Urbana-Champaign.

Brocki, J., & Wearden, A. (2006). A critical evaluation of the use of interpretive phenomenological analysis (IPA) in health psychology. *Psychology and health, 21*(1), 87–108.

Brooks, D. E., & Hébert, L. P. (2004). *Lessons learned or bamboozled? Gender in a Spike Lee film.* Unpublished manuscript.

Brooks, D. E, & Hébert, L. P. (2006). Gender, race and media representation. In B. Dow & J. T. Wood (Eds), *Gender and communication in mediated texts* (pp. 297–317). Thousand Oaks, CA: Sage.

Broussard, J. (2004). Giving a voice to the voiceless: Four pioneering Black women journalists, Studies in African American history and culture. New York: Routledge.

Brown, D. R. (2003). A conceptual model of mental well-being for African American women. In D. R. Brown & V. M. Keith (Eds.), *In and out of our right minds: The mental health of African American women* (pp. 1–22). New York: Columbia University Press.

Brown, D. R., & Keith, V. M. (Eds.). (2003a). *In and out of our right minds: The mental health of African American women.* New York: Columbia University Press.

Brown, D. R., & Keith, V. M. (2003b). The epidemiology of mental disorders and mental health among African American women. In D. R. Brown & V. M. Keith (Eds.), *In and out of our right minds: The mental health of African American women* (pp. 23–58). New York: Columbia University Press.

Brown Girl Gumbo. (n.d.). World AIDS Day [Web log post]. Retrieved from http?/browngirldgumbo.blogspot.com

Brown, N. E. (2010). *The intersection of race and gender on representation: Black women legislators' impact on legislation* (Unpublished doctoral dissertation). Rutgers, The State University of New Jersey, New Brunswick.

Brown, N. E. (2014a). Black women's pathways to the state house: The impact of race/gender identities. *National Political Science Review, 16*, 81–96.

Brown, N. E. (2014b). Sisters in the statehouse: Black women and legislative decision-making. New York: Oxford University Press.

Brown, R. N. (2008). Black girlhood celebraton: A hip-hop feminist pedagogy. New York Peter Lang.

Brown, R. N. (2013). *Hear our truths: The creative potential of Black girlhood.* Urbana: University of Illionois Press.

Brown Sista. (2006). Terry McMillan still upset with gay ex husband! [Web log post]. Retrieved from http://brownsista.com

Brown Sista. (2008, August 13). Commentary: Stop saying I'm diseased [Web log post]. Retrieved from http://brownsista.com/commentary-stop-saying-im-diseased/

Brown Sista. (2009, October 5). How come you hit on me? [Web log post]. Retrieved from http://brownsista.com/?s=October+is+domestic+violence+awareness

Brown Sista (2010, July 5). Mary J. Blige debuts new fragrance [Web log post]. Retrieved from http://brownsista.com/mary-j-blige-debuts-new-fragrance/

Bruneau, T. J. (1973). Communicative silences: Forms and functions. *Journal of Communication, 23*(1), 17–46.

Bullock, L. (2003, December). The explosive health crisis that no one talks about. *Ebony*, 136.

Butler, J. (1990). Gender trouble: Feminism and the subversion of identity. London: Routledge.

Butler, J. (1993). Bodies that matter: On the discursive limits of 'sex.' London: Routledge.

Butler, L. (1999). African American lesbian women experiencing partner abuse. In J. McClennan & J. Gunther (Eds.), A professional guide to understanding gay and lesbian domestic violence (pp. 181–205). Pittsburgh, PA: Edwin Mellen.

Caldwell, C. H. (2003). Patterns of mental health services utilization among Black women. In D. R. Brown & V. M. Keith (Eds.), In and out of our right minds: The mental health of African American women (pp. 258–276). New York: Columbia University Press.

California Black Women's Health Project. (2003). Healing for the mind, body & soul. News notes. Retrieved from http://oldsite.cabwhp.org/pdf/oct2003.pdf

Campbell, D., Sharps, P. W., Gary, F., Campbell, J. C., & Lopez, L. M. (2002, January 31). Intimate partner violence in African American women. Online Journal of Issues in Nursing. Retrieved from http://www.nursingworld.org/ojin/topic17/tpc17_4.htm

Cannon, L. W., Higginbotham, E., & Guy, R. F. (1989). Depression among women: Exploring the effects of race, class, and gender. Tennessee: Center for Research on Women, Memphis State University.

Canon, D. (1999). Race, redistricting and representation. Chicago: University of Chicago Press.

Cappella, J. N., & Jamieson, K. H. (1997). Spiral of cynicism. The press and the public good. New York: Oxford University Press.

Carabine, J. (1998). New horizons? New insights? Postmodernising social policy and the case of sexuality. In J. Carter (Ed.), Postmodernity and the fragmentation of welfare (pp. 121–135). London: Routledge.

Carastathis, A. (2008). The invisibility of privilege: A critique of intersectionality models of identity. Les Ateliers de l'Éthique, 3(2), 23–38.

Carby, H. (1987). Reconstructing womanhood: The emergence of the Afro-American woman novelist. New York: Oxford University Press.

Carey, T. L. (2014). Take your place: Rhetorical healing and Black womanhood in Tyler Perry's films. Signs, 39(4), 999–1021.

Carey, T. L. (2016). Rhetorical healing: The reeducation of contemporary Black womanhood. Albany: State University of New York Press.

Carroll, S. J. (1994). The politics of difference: Women public officials as agents of change. Stanford Law and Policy Review, 5, 11–20.

Carroll, S. J. (2002). Representing women: Congresswomen's perceptions of their representational roles. Retrieved from http://www.capwip.org/readingroom/congroles.pdf

Carter, S. R. (1991). Hansberry's drama: Commitment amid complexity. Urbana and Chicago: University of Illinois Press.

Carter, Z. M. (2004, December). Know your status. Essence, 99.

Cash, R. (2000, February). Good works: Building strong foundations. Essence, 50.

Castaneda, R. (2005, October 14). After burning of woman, judge's cases are limited. Washington Post. Retrieved from http://www.washingtonpost.com/wp-dyn/content/article/2005/10/13/AR2005101301940.html

Caviness, Y. G. (2000, October). Act now: Keep sisters safe. Essence, 30.

Centers for Disease Control and Prevention. (1997). Ten leading causes of death, 1994. Atlanta: National Center for Injury Prevention and Control.

Centers for Disease Control and Prevention. (2010, March 7). National Women & Girls HIV/AIDS Awareness Day. Retrieved from http://www.cdc.gov/Features/WomenGirls HIVAIDS/

Champions for a cause. (2003, October). Ebony, 92.

Chattopadhyay, R., & Duflo, E. (2004). Women as policy makers: Evidence from a randomized policy experiment in India. *Econometrica, 72*(5), 1409–1443.

Chen, G. M. 2013. Don't call me that: a techno-feminist critique of the term *mommy blogger. Mass Communication and Society, 16*(4): 510–532.

Chisholm, J. F. (1996). Mental health issues in African-American women. *Annals of the New York Academy of Sciences, 789*, 161–179.

Cho, S., Crenshaw, K, & McCall, L. (2013). Toward a field of intersectionality studies: Theory, application, and praxis. *Signs, 38*(4), 785–810.

Chomsky, N. (1987). *The Chomsky reader.* New York: Pantheon.

Christian, B. (1985). Black feminist criticism: Perspectives on Black women writers. New York: Pergamon.

Christian, B. (1988). The race for theory. *Feminist Studies, 14*(1), 67–79.

Chun, J. J., Lipsitz, G., & Shin, Y. (2013). Intersectionality as a social movement strategy: Asian immigrant women advocates. *Signs, 38*(4): 917–940.

Clark, M. D. 2014. *To tweet our own cause: A mixed-methods study of the online phenomenon "Black Twitter"* (Unpublished doctoral dissertation). University of North Carolina, Chapel Hill.

Clarke, J. N. (2010). The portrayal of depression in the three most popular English-language Black-American magazines in the USA: *Ebony, Essence,* and *Jet. Ethnicity and Health, 15*(5), 459–473.

Cleage, P. (1997). *What looks like crazy on an ordinary day.* New York: Avon Books.

Cohen, C. (1993). *Power, resistance, and the construction of crisis: Marginalized communities respond to AIDS* (Unpublished doctoral dissertation). University of Michigan, Ann Arbor.

Cohen, C. (1999). The boundaries of blackness: AIDS and the breakdown of black politics. Chicago: University of Chicago Press.

Cole, H. (2007, November). Alicia bares her soul. *Ebony,* 68.

Cole, J. B., & Guy-Sheftall, B. (2003). *Gender talk: The struggle for women's equality in African American communities.* New York: One World, Ballantine Books.

Collins, P. H. (1986). Learning from the outsider within: The sociological significance of Black feminist thought. *Social Problems, 31,* S14–S32.

Collins, P. H. (1991). Black feminist thought: Knowledge, consciousness, and the politics of empowerment. New York: Routledge.

Collins, P. H. (1998). It's all in the family: Intersections of gender, race, and nation. *Hypatia, 13*(3), 62–82.

Collins, P. H. (2004). Black sexual politics: African Americans, gender, and the new racism. New York & London: Routledge.

Collins, P. Y., von Unger, H., & Arbrister, A. (2008). Church ladies, good girls, and locas: Stigma and the intersection of gender, ethnicity, mental illness and sexuality in relation to HIV risk. *Social Science and Medicine, 67,* 389–397.

Combahee River Collective. (1977). *The Combahee River Collective statement.* Retrieved from http://circuitous.org/scraps/combahee.html

Combating HIV/AIDS in the Black Community, 145 Cong. Rec. H9180 (daily ed. September 30, 1999) (statement of Rep. Waters). Retrieved from http://thomas.loc.gov

Connors, M. (1996). Sex, drugs and structural violence: Unraveling the epidemic among poor women of color in the United States. In P. Farmer, M. Connors, & J. Simmons (Eds.), *Women, poverty, and AIDS: Sex, drugs, and structural violence* (pp. 91–123). Monroe, MD: Common Courage Press.

Cooper, A. J. (1995). The status of woman in America. In B. Guy-Sheftall (ed.), *Words of fire: An anthology of African-American feminist thought* (pp. 44–49). New York: New Press.

Cottle, S. (2000). *Ethnic minorities in the media.* Philadelphia: Open University Press.

Couch, G. (2010, May 24). Venus baring all in race to be number 1. Retrieved from http://www.tennisforum.com/12-general-messages/409831-venus-baring-all-race-number-1-article.html

Crenshaw, K. (1989). Demarginalizing the intersection of race and sex: A Black feminist critique of antidiscrimination doctrine, feminist theory and antiracist politics. *University of Chicago Legal Forum, 139–167.*

Crenshaw, K. (1991). Mapping the margins: Intersectionality, identity politics, and violence against women of color. *Stanford Law Review, 43*(6), 1241–1299.

Crenson, M. (1971). The un-politics of air pollution: A study of non-decision making in the cities. Baltimore, MD: Johns Hopkins University Press.

Creswell, J. W., & Plano Clark, V. L. (2007). *Designing and conducting mixed methods research.* Thousand Oaks, CA: Sage.

Cristancho, S., Garces, D. M., Peters, K. E., & Mueller, B. (2008). Listening to rural Hispanic immigrants in the Midwest: A community-based participatory assessment of major barriers to health care access and use. *Qualitative Health Research, 18,* 633–646.

Crovitz, L. G. (2011). Egypt's revolution by social media: Facebook and Twitter let the people keep ahead of the regime. *Wall Street Journal.* Retrieved from http://online.wsj.com/article/SB10001424052748703786804576137980252177072.html

Dahmoon, R. K. (2008). Considerations on mainstreaming intersectionality. *Political Research Quarterly, 64*(1), 230–243.

Dalton, H. L. (1989). AIDS in blackface. *Daedalus. 118,* 205–227.

Danquah, M. N. (1998). Willow weep for me: A Black woman's journey through depression. New York: One World.

Dates, J., & Barlow, W. (1990). *Split image: African Americans in the mass media.* Washington, DC: Howard University Press.

Dauenhauer, B. P. (1980). *Silence: The phenomenon and its ontological significance.* Bloomington: Indiana University Press.

Dawson, M. C. (1994). *Behind the mule: Race and class in African-American politics.* Princeton, NJ: Princeton University Press.

DeLoach, A. D. (2007). *Breaking boundaries: Black magazines reconstructing Black female identity* (Master's thesis). Retrieved from http://u2.gmu.edu:8080/bitstream/1920/5609/1/DeLoach_Anita.pdf

Departments of Commerce, Justice and State, the Judiciary, and Related Agencies Appropriations Act, 146 Cong. Rec. H4977–78 (daily ed. June 22, 2000) (statement of Rep. Millender-McDonald). Retrieved from http://thomas.loc.gov

Derrick, R. C. (1997, March). Healing the wounds of racism. *Essence, 37.*

Diala, C., Muntaner, C., Walrath, C., Nickerson, K. J., La Veist, T. A., & Leaf, P. J. (2000). Racial differences in attitudes toward professional mental health care and in the use of services. *American Journal of Orthopsychiatry, 70,* 455–463.

Diamond, I. (1977). *Sex roles in the state house.* New Haven, CT: Yale University Press.

Digby-Junger, R. (2005). Ebony. In T. Pendergast & S. Pendergast (Eds.), *St. James Encyclopedia of Popular Culture.* Farmington Hills, MI: Gale, Cengage.

Dill, B. T. (1983). Race, class, and gender: Prospects for an all-inclusive sisterhood. *Feminist Studies, 9*(1), 131–150.

Dill, B. T., & Zambrana, R. E. (2009). Critical thinking about inequality: An emerging lens. In B. T. Dill & R. E. Zambrana (Eds.), *Emerging intersections: Race, class, and gender in theory, policy and practice* (pp. 1–21). New Brunswick, NJ: Rutgers University Press.

District of Columbia Mental Health Civil Commitment Modernization Act of 2004, 150 Cong. Rec. H8258 (daily ed. October 6, 2004) (statement of Rep. Norton). Retrieved from http://thomas.loc.gov

Domestic Violence, 148 Cong. Rec. H6921 (daily ed. March 6, 2002) (statement of Rep. Carson). Retrieved from http://thomas.loc.gov

Douglas, D. D. (2002, November/December). To be young, gifted, black and female: A meditation on the cultural politics at play in representations of Venus and Serena Williams. *Sociology of Sport Online, 5*(2). Retrieved from http://www.physed.otago.ac.nz/sosol/v5i2 /v5i2_3.html

Dowe, P. (2016). African American women: Leading ladies of liberal politics. In N. E. Brown & S. A. Greshon (Eds.). *Distinct identities: Minority women in U.S. politics* (pp. 49–62). New York: Routledge.

Drug-Free Workplace Act of 1998, 144 Cong. Rec. H4979–80 (daily ed. June 23, 1998) (statement of Rep. Millender-McDonald). Retrieved from http://thomas.loc.gov

du Cille, A. (1994). The occult of true Black womanhood: Critical demeanor and Black feminist studies. *Signs: Journal of Women in Culture and Society, 19*(3), 591–629.

Dumas, R. G. (1980). Dilemmas of Black females in leadership. In L. F. Rodgers-Rose (Ed.), *The Black woman* (pp. 203–215). Beverly Hills, CA: Sage.

Durham, Aisha. (2012). Beyoncé, Southern booty and Black femininities in music video. *Feminist Media Studies, 12*(1), 35–49.

Dvorak, P. (2009, April 3). Banita Jacks case: Lots of blame to go around in D.C. girls' deaths, report says. *Washington Post*. Retrieved from http://www.washingtonpost.com/wp-dyn /content/article/2009/04/02/AR2009040201609.html

Eagleton, T. (1991). *Ideology: An introduction.* London: Verso.

The Ebony advisor: Expert advice on love and relationships. (2003, June). *Ebony,* 25.

The Ebony story. (1995, November). *Ebony,* 80.

Edmonds, K. B., Reid, A. M., & Simons, D. (1988). Superwoman [Recorded by K. White] On *Karyn White* [CD]. Los Angeles: Warner Brothers.

Edwards Tassie, K., & Brown Givens, S. M (Eds.). 2015. *Women of color and social media multitasking: Blogs, Timelines, feeds, and community.* Lanham, MD: Lexington Books.

Elin, L. (2003). The radicalization of Zeke Spier: How the Internet contributes to civic engagement and new forms of social capital. In M. McCaughey & M.D. Ayers (Eds.), *Cyberactivism: Online activism in theory and practice* (pp. 97–114). New York: Routledge.

Ellison, R. (1995). *Invisible man.* New York: Random House.

End Domestic Violence Week, 148 Cong. Rec. E299 (daily ed. March 7, 2002) (statement of Rep. Watson). Retrieved from http://thomas.loc.gov

Ending and surviving an abusive relationship: Reports say sisters don't have to suffer in silence. (2000, October). *Ebony,* 48.

Entman, R. (1993). Framing: Towards clarification of a fractured paradigm. *Journal of Communication, 43*(4), 51–58.

Ess, C. (2002). Ethical decision-making and Internet research: Recommendations from the AoIR Ethics Working Committee. Association of Internet Researchers (AoIR).

Essence. (2010). About Essence Communications Inc. Retrieved from http://www.essence .com/about/

Essence. (2015). Media Kit. Retrieved from http://www.essence.com.

Fairclough, N. (1993). Critical discourse analysis and the marketization of public discourse: The universities. *Discourse and Society, 4*(2), 133–168.

Fairclough, N. (1995). *Critical discourse analysis.* London and New York: Longman.

Fanon, F. 1967. *Black skin, White masks.* New York: Grove Press.

Farmer, P. (2005). Pathologies of power, health, human rights, and the new war on the poor. Berkeley: University of California Press.

Feagin, J. R., & Sikes, M. P. (1994). *Living with racism: The Black middle-class experience.* Boston: Beacon.

Feist-Price, S., & Wright, L. B. (2003). African American women living with HIV/AIDS: Mental health issues. *Women & Therapy, 26*(1/2), 27–44.

Fenno, R. (2003). *Going home: Black representatives and their constituencies.* Illinois: University of Chicago Press.

Fife, D., & Mode, C. (1992a). AIDS incidence and income. *Journal of Acquired Immune Deficiency Syndromes, 5*(11), 1105–1110.

Fife, D., & Mode, C. (1992b). AIDS prevalence by income group in Philadelphia. *Journal of Acquired Immune Deficiency Syndromes, 5*(11), 1111–1115.

Fischer, F. (2003). Reframing public policy: Discursive politics and deliberative practices. New York: Oxford University Press.

Flammang, J. A. (1985). Female officials in the feminist capital: The case of Santa Clara County. *Western Political Quarterly, 38*(1), 94–118.

Flammang, J. A. (1997). Women's political voice: How women are transforming the practice and study of politics. Philadelphia: Temple University Press.

Florini, S. (2013). 'Tweets, Tweeps, and Signifyin': Communication and cultural performance on "Black Twitter." *Television & New Media, 15*(3): 223–237.

Fogg-Davis, Hawley. (2006). Theorizing Black lesbians within Black feminism: A critique of same-race street harassment. *Politics & Gender, 2*, 57–76.

Foston, Nikitta. (2002, November). Why AIDS is becoming a Black woman's disease and what we can do about it. *Ebony*, 174.

Foston, Nikitta. (2005, June). How to look better, feel better & live longer. *Ebony*, 135.

Foucault, M. (1972). *Archeology of knowledge* (A. M. Sheridan, Trans.). New York: Pantheon.

Foucault, M. (1977). *Discipline and punish: The birth of the prison* (A. Sheridan, Trans.). New York: Vintage Books.

Foucault, M. (1984). Nietzsche, genealogy, history. In P. Rabinow (Ed.), *The Foucault reader* (pp. 76–100). New York: Penguin.

Friedman, J., Hyman, P., Rich, A., & Martinelli, N. (1995). I refuse to be lonely [Recorded by P. Hyman]. On *I refuse to be lonely* [Album]. Philadelphia: Volcano Records.

Front row: Ebony on the scene. (2005, December). *Ebony*, 18.

Gaines, K. K. (1997). Uplifting the race: Black leadership, politics, and culture in the twentieth century. *Journal of Southern History, 63*(2), 443–444.

Gajjala, R. (2003). South Asian digital diasporas and cyberfeminist webs: Negotiating globalization, nation, gender and information technology design. *Contemporary South Asia, 12*(1), 41–56.

Gamble, K. (2007). Black political representation: An examination of legislative activity within U.S. House Committees. *Legislative Studies Quarterly, 32*(3), 421–447.

Gamble, K. L. (2011). Black voice: Deliberation in the United States Congress. *Polity, 43*(3), 291–312.

Gatens, M. (1996). Imaginary bodies: Ethics, power, and corporeality. New York: Routledge.

Gaunt, K. (1995). African American women between hopscotch and hip-hop: Must be the music (that's turning me on). In A. Valdivia (Ed.), *Feminism, multiculturalism, and the media: Global diversities* (pp. 277–308). Thousand Oaks, CA: Sage.

Gaventa, J. (1980). Power and powerlessness: Quiescence and rebellion in an Appalachian Valley. Urbana: University of Illinois Press.

Gay, C., & Tate, K. (1998). Doubly bound: The impact of gender and race on the politics of Black women. *Political Psychology, 19*(1), 169–184.

Gaynor, Gerren Keith. 2013. *Essence* magazine founder says he doesn't regret selling to Time Inc.: Co-founder Edward Lewis defends Time Inc. sale after criticism from former editor. *Black Enterprise: Wealth for Life*. Retrieved from http://www.Blackenterprise.com/news/edward-lewis-essence-magazine-sale-regret/.

Gelles, R. (1979). *Family violence*. Beverly Hills, CA: Sage.

Gentles, K., & Harrison, K. (2006). Television and perceived peer expectations of body size among African American adolescent girls. *Howard Journal of Communication, 17*(1), 39–55.

Giddings, P. (1984). When and where I enter: The impact of Black women on race and sex in America. New York: Quill William Morrow.

Gillum, T. L. (2002). Exploring the link between stereotypic images and intimate partner violence in the African American community. *Violence Against Women, 8*, 64–87.

Gilman, S. (1985). Difference and pathology: Stereotypes of sexuality, race, and madness. Ithaca, NY: Cornell University Press.

Gina The Blogmother. (2007, October 1). Brothers speak on WAOD: "National Domestic Violence Awareness Month"—National Day of Unity [Web blog post]. Retrieved from http://www.whataboutourdaughters.com/waod/2007/10/1/brothers-speak-on-waod-national-domestic-violence-awareness.html

Gitlin, T. (1980). *The whole world is watching: Mass media in the making and unmaking of the new left*. Berkeley: University of California Press.

Goffman, E. (1974). *Frame analysis: An essay on the organization of experience*. Cambridge, MA: Harvard University Press.

Goldstein, N. 1997. Lesbians and the medical profession: HIV/AIDS and the pursuit of visibility. In N. Goldstein and J. L. Manlowe (Eds.), *The gender politics of HI/AIDS in women: Perspectives on the pandemic in the United States* (pp. 86–112). New York: New York University Press.

Gordy, C. (2006, October). A survivor's tale. *Essence*, 220.

Gordy, C., Habrezghi, N., Hunter, L. P., Jumaralli, Z., Murray, C., Williams, M., et al. (2006, August). Essence do right men. *Essence*, 141.

Grant, G. G. (2000, May). Safe, soulful sex. *Essence*, 66.

Greene, B. (1992). Still here: A perspective on psychotherapy with African American women. In J. C. Chrisler & D. Howard (Eds.), *New directions in feminist psychology* (pp. 13–25). New York: Springer.

Grosz, E. (1994). *Volatile bodies: Toward a corporeal feminism*. Bloomington: Indiana University Press.

Guba, E. G., & Lincoln, Y. S. (1981). Effective evaluation: Improving the usefulness of evaluation results through responsive and naturalistic approaches. San Francisco: Jossey-Bass.

Guy-Sheftall, B. (Ed.). (1995). Words of fire: An anthology of African American feminist thought. New York: New Press.

Guy-Sheftall, B. (2002). The body politics: Black female sexuality and the nineteenth-century Euro-American imagination. In K. Wallace-Sanders (Ed.), *Skin deep, spirit strong: The Black female body in American culture* (pp. 13–63). Ann Arbor: University of Michigan Press.

Hall, S. (Ed.). (1997). Representation: Cultural representations and signifying practices. London: SAGE.

Halliday M. A. K (1994). *An introduction to functional grammar*, 2nd ed. London: Arnold.

Hammonds, E. (1992). Missing persons: African American women, AIDS and the history of the disease. *Radical America, 24*(2), 7–23.

Hampton, R. L., & Gelles, R. (1994). Violence towards black women in a nationally representative sample of black families. *Journal of Comparative Family Studies, 25*, 115–119.

Hancock, A. (2004). *The politics of disgust: The public identity of the welfare queen*. New York: New York University Press.

Hancock, A. (2007). When multiplication doesn't equal quick addition: Examining intersectionality as a research paradigm. *Perspectives on Politics, 5*(1), 63–79.

Harper, T. N. (1996). New Malays, new Malaysians: Nationalism, society and history in Southeast Asian affairs. Singapore: Institute of Southeast Asian Studies.

Harris, D. (2010). The state of Black women in politics under the first Black president. *The Scholar & Feminist Online, 8.3*, 1–8. Retrieved from http://www.barnard.edu/sfonline/polyphonic/harris_01.htm

Harris, D. (2011). *Black feminist politics from Kennedy to Obama.* New York: Palgrave MacMillan.

Harris, T. (1995). The disease called strength: Some observations on the compensating construction of black female character. *Literature and Medicine, 14,* 109–126.

Harris-Perry, M. (2011). *Sister citizen: Shame, stereotypes, and Black women in America.* New Haven, CT: Yale University Press.

Harrison, K. (2003). Televising viewers' ideal body proportions: The case of the curvaceously thin woman. *Sex Roles, 48*(5/6), 255–264.

Harrison, S. J., & Johnson, C. (1999, August). Her toughest case. *Essence,* 96.

Hawkesworth, M. (2003). Congressional enactments of race-gender: Toward a theory of raced-gendered institutions. *American Political Science Review, 97*(4), 529–550.

Haynie, K. L. (2001). *African American legislators in the American states.* New York: Columbia University Press.

Henderson, C. E. (Ed.). 2010. Imagining the Black female body: Reconciling image in print and visual culture. New York: Palgrave MacMillian.

Herring, S. C., Kouper, I., Scheidt, L. A., & Wright, E. (2004). Women and children last: The discursive construction of weblogs. In L. Gurak, S. Antonijevic, L. Johnson, C. Ratcliff, & J. Reyman (Eds.), *Into the blogosphere: Rhetoric, community and culture weblogs.* Retrieved from blog.lib.umn.edu/blogosphere/women_and_children.html

Herring, S. C., Kouper, I., Paolillo J. C., Scheidt, L. A., Tyworth, M., Welsch, P., . . . and Yu, N. (2005). *Proceedings of the thirty-eighth Hawai'i international conference on system sciences (HICSS-38).* Los Alamitos, CA: IEEE Press. Retrieved from http://pdf.aminer.org/000/245/349/conversations_in_the_blogosphere_an_analysis_from_the_bottom_up.pdf

Higginbotham, E. B. (1992). African-American women's history and the metalanguage of race. *Signs: Journal of Women in Culture and Society, 17*(2), 251–274.

Higginbotham, E. B. (1993). Righteous discontent: The women's movement in the Black Baptist Church, 1880–1920. Cambridge, MA: Harvard University Press.

History of Women's Rights, 149 Cong. Rec. H5462 (daily ed. June 17, 2003) (statement of Rep. Norton). Retrieved from http://thomas.loc.gov

HIV. (2004, March). *Ebony,* 140.

HIV/AIDS, 147 Cong. Rec. H3839–40 (daily ed. July 10, 2001) (statement of Rep. Clayton). Retrieved from http://thomas.loc.gov

HIV/AIDS, 152 Cong. Rec. H7504 (daily ed. September 27, 2006) (statement of Rep. Waters). Retrieved from http://thomas.loc.gov

An HIV cure? (2001, October). *Essence,* 80.

Hobson, J. (2003). The "batty" politic: Toward an aesthetic of the black female body. *Hypatia, 18*(4), 87–105.

Hobson, J. (2012). *Body as evidence: Mediating race, globalizing gender.* Albany: State University of New York Press.

Hobson, J. (2016) Black beauty and digital spaces: The new visibility politics. *Ada: A Journal of Gender, New Media, and Technology,* no. 10. Retrieved from http://adanewmedia.org/2016/10/issue10-hobson/

Hodkinson, P. (2006). Subcultural blogging? Online journals and group involvement among U.K. goths. In A. Bruns & J. Jacobs (Eds.), *Uses of blogs* (pp. 187–198). New York: Peter Lang.

Hohle, R. (2009). The body and citizenship in social movement research: Embodied performances and the deracialized self in the Black Civil Rights Movement 1961–1965. *Sociological Quarterly, 50*, 283–307.

Holland, F. L. (2007, June 13). *An essay on AfroSpear nomenclature: What we call ourselves and why* [Web log post]. Retrieved from http://francislholland.blogspot.com/2007/06/essay-of-afrospear-nomenclature-what-is.html

Holloway, L. R. (2005, October). What every woman should know about mental health ailments. *Ebony*, 154.

Honoring Asian Community Mental Health Services, 150 Cong. Rec. E1602 (daily ed. September 13, 2004) (statement of Rep. Lee). Retrieved from http://thomas.loc.gov

hooks, b. (1981). *Ain't I a woman: Black women and feminism*. Boston: South End Press.

hooks, b. (1992). *Black looks: Race and representation*. Cambridge, MA: South End Press.

hooks, b. (1993a). Male heroes and female sex objects: Sexism in Spike Lee's *Malcolm X. Cineaste, 19*(4), 13–15.

hooks, bell. (1993b). Sisters of the yam: Black women and self-recovery. Boston: South End.

hooks, b. (1994) Teaching to transgress: Education as the practice of freedom. New York: Routledge.

hooks, b. (2000). Black women: Shaping feminist theory. In Joy James & T. Denean Sharpley-Whiting (Eds.), *The Black feminist reader* (pp. 131–145). Malden, MA: Blackwell.

hooks, b. (2003). Sisters of the yam: Black women and self-recovery. Boston: South End.

hooks, b. (2009). *Belonging: A culture of place*. New York and London: Routledge.

Hookway, N. (2008). 'Entering the blogosphere': Some strategies for using blogs in social research. *Qualitative Research, 8*(1), 91–113.

Houston, M., & Davis, O. I. (2002). Centering ourselves: African American feminist and womanist studies of discourse. Cresskill, NJ: Hampton.

Howard-Hamilton, M. F. (2003). Theoretical frameworks for African American women. *New Directions for Student Services, 104*, 19–27.

Huckin, T. (2002). Textual silence and the discourse of homelessness. *Discourse and Society, 13*(3), 347–372.

Hudson, S. (1998). Re-creational television: The paradox of change and continuity within stereotypical iconography. *Sociological Inquiry, 68*(2), 242–257.

Huffaker, D. A., & Calvert, S. L. (2005). Gender, identity, and language use in teenage blogs. *Journal of Computer-Mediated Communication, 10*(2). Retrieved from http://jcmc.indiana.edu/vol10/issue2/huffaker.html

Hughes, Z. (2001, October). Depression after delivery: Black mothers and the postpartum crisis. *Ebony*, 72.

Hughes, Z. (2004, July). Why sisters are the no. 1 victims of HIV and how you can avoid it. *Ebony*, 64.

Hunt, S. A. & Benford, R. D. (2004). Collective identity, solidarity and commitment. In Snow, D.A., Soule, S. A. & Kriese, H. (Eds.), *The Blackwell companion to social movements* (pp. 433–457). Oxford: Blackwell.

Hurricane Katrina Disaster, 151 Cong. Rec. H7718 (daily ed. September 7, 2005) (statement of Rep. Lee). Retrieved from http://thomas.loc.gov

Hurston, Z. N. (1991 [1937]). *Their eyes were watching God*. Urbana: University of Illinois Press.

Hynie, M. (1998). Relational sexual scripts and women's condom use: The importance of internalized norms. *Journal of Sex Research, 35*(4), 370–380.

I like her style. (2006). Viva glam [Web log post]. Retrieved from http//stealstyle.blogspot.com

I'm living life like it's golden. (2009. March 9). The face of domestic violence [Web log post]. Retrieved from http://wisdomispriceless.blogspot.com/2009_03_01_archive.html

In These Times. (2006, February 6). Can blogs revolutionize progressive politics? Retrieved from http://www.inthesetimes.com

In Tribute to the Legal Aid Society of Milwaukee, 152 Cong. Rec. E2240 (daily ed. December 27, 2006) (statement of Rep. Moore). Retrieved from http://thomas.loc.gov

Introducing the Health Care Access Improvement Act, 143 Cong. Rec. E2182 (daily ed. November 4, 1997) (statement of Rep. Kilpatrick). Retrieved from http://thomas.loc.gov

iS iT jUsT mE? (2007, June 28). Thankful. [Web log post]. Retrieved from http://mentallyspeaking.blogspot.com/search?q=for+everything+I%27ve+been+through+in+life

Is it just me? (2008, August 28). [Web log post]. Retrieved from http://mentallyspeaking.blogspot.com

iS iT jUsT mE? (2009, June 3). Suicide is not an option! [Web log post]. Retrieved from http://mentallyspeaking.blogspot.com/2009/06/suicide-is-not-option.html?m=0

Isoke, Z. (2013). Urban Black women and the politics of resistance. New York: Palgrave Macmillan.

J. A. (1997, January). Strategies for getting out and surviving a domestic violence situation. Essence, 68.

Jackson, J. (1999) Affirmative action coverage ignores women and discrimination. Extra! 12(1), 6–8.

Jackson II, R. L. (2006). Scripting the Black masculine body: Identity, discourse, and racial politics in popular media. Albany: State University of New York Press.

Jacobs, H. ([1860] 1987). The perils of a slave woman's life. In M. H. Washington (Ed.), Invented lives: Narratives of Black women, 1860–1960 (pp. 16–67). Garden City, NY: Anchor.

James, J. (1999). Resting in the gardens, battling in the deserts: Black women's activism. In H. Boyd (Ed.), Race and resistance: African Americans in the 21st century (pp. 67–78). Cambridge, MA: South End Press.

James, M. (2009). The book of night women. New York: Riverhead Books.

Jaworski, A. (1993). The power of silence: Social and pragmatic perspectives. Newbury Park, CA: Sage Publications.

Jensen, J. V. (1973). Communicative functions of silences. ETC: A Review of General Semantics, 30, 249–257.

Jewell, K. S. (1993). From mammy to Miss America and beyond: Cultural images & the shaping of US social policy. London: Routledge.

Joe, S. (2006). Explaining changes in the patterns of black suicide in the United States from 1981–2002: An age, cohort, and period analysis. Journal of Black Psychology, 32(3), 262–284.

Johnson, A. (2013). Antoine Dodson and the (mis)appropriation of the Homo Coon: An intersectional approach to the performative possibilities of social media. Critical Studies in Media Communication, 30(2), 152–170.

Johnson, E. P. (2003). Appropriating Blackness: Performance and the politics of authenticity. Durham, NC: Duke University Press.

Johnson, M, and Carroll, S. (1978). Statistical report: Profile of women holding office, 1977. In Women in public office: A biographical directory and statistical analysis, compiled by the Center for the American Woman and Politics, Eagleton Institute, Rutgers University. Metuchen, NJ: Scarecrow.

Johnston, H., Larana, E., and Gusfield, J. R. (1994). Identities, grievances, and new social movements. In E. Larana, H. Johnston, & J. R. Gusfield (Eds.), New social movements: From ideology to identity (pp. 3–35). Philadelphia: Temple University Press.

Jones, L. (1994). Bullet proof diva: Tales of race, sex, and hair. New York: Doubleday.

Jones, M., & Alony, I. (2008). Blogs: The new source of data analysis. *Journal of Issues in Informing Science and Information Technology, 5,* 433–446.

Jones, R. (2006). Sex scripts and power: A framework to explain women's HIV sexual risk with male partners. *Nursing Clinics of North America, 41*(3), 425–436.

Jordan-Zachery, J. S. (2009). *Black women, cultural images and social policy.* New York: Routledge.

Jordan-Zachery, Julia. (2013). Now you see me now you don't: My political fight against the invisibility/erasure of Black women in intersectionality research. *Politics, Groups, and Identities, 1*(1), 101–109.

Jordan-Zachery, J., & Wilson, S. (2008). *Gender differences and policy making: An analysis of pay equity.* Paper presented at the annual meeting of the National Conference of Black Political Scientists, Atlanta, GA.

Kaiser Family Foundation. (2010). *Black Americans and HIV/AIDS.* Retrieved from HIV/AIDS Fact Sheet: http://www.kff.org/hivaids/upload/6089-08.pdf

Kanuha, V. (1994). Women of color in battering relationships. In L. Comas-Diaz & B. Greene (Eds.), *Women of color: Integrating ethnic and gender identities in psychotherapy* (pp. 428–454). New York: Guilford.

Kanuha, V. (1996). Domestic violence, racism and the battered women's movement in the United States. In J. L. Edelson & Z. C. Eisikovits (Eds.), *Future interventions with battered women and their families* (pp. 34–50). Thousand Oaks, CA: Sage.

Kaplan, E. A. (2008, November 18). First Lady got back. *Salon.* Retrieved from http://www.salon.com/life/feature/2008/11/18/michelles_booty/

Karst, K. L. (1995). Myths of identity: Individual and group portraits of race and sexual orientation. *UCLA Law Review, 43,* 263–369.

Kean, L., Prividera, L., Howard, J. W. III, and Gates, D. 2014. Health, weight, and fitness messages in *Ebony* and *Essence:* A framing analysis of articles in African American women's magazines. *Journal of Magazine & New Media Research, 15*(1): 1–25.

Keith, V. M. (2003). In and out of our right minds: Strengths, vulnerability and the mental well-being of African American women. In D. R. Brown & V. M. Keith (Eds.), *In and out of our right minds: The mental health of African American women* (pp. 277–292). New York: Columbia University Press.

Kidd, S. M. (2003). *The secret life of bees.* New York: Penguin Group.

We must be fair and non-partisan in judging our President, 105 Cong. Rec. H7612 (daily ed. September 11, 1998) (statement by Rep. Kilpatrick). Retrieved from http://thomas.loc.gov.

King, D. (1988). Multiple jeopardy, multiple consciousness: The context of a Black feminist ideology. *Signs, 14*(1), 42–72.

King, M. C. (1973). The politics of sexual stereotypes. *Black Scholar, 4*(6/7), 12–23.

Kingdon, J. W. (1984). *Agendas, alternatives and public policies.* New York: Harper Collins.

Koenig, T. (n.d.). *Reframing frame analysis: Systematizing the empirical identification of frames using qualitative data analysis software.* Retrieved from http://research.allacademic.com/meta/p_mla_apa_research_citation/1/1/0/3/1/p110319_index.html?phpsessid=a51c121dfab74433e03079e4298f0d20

Kramarae, C. (1981). *Women and men speaking: Frameworks for analysis.* Rowley, MA: Newbury House.

Kraut, R., Olson, J., Banaji, M., Bruckman, A., Cohen, J., & Couper, M. (2004). Psychological Research Online: Report of Board of Scientific Affairs' Advisory Group on the Conduct of Research on the Internet. *American Psychologist, 59,* 105–117.

Krieger, N. (1999). Embodying inequality: A review of concepts, measures, and methods for studying health consequences of discrimination. *International Journal of Health Services, 29*(2), 295–352.

Krishnan, S. P. (1997). Coverage of AIDS in popular African American magazines. *Health Communication, 9*(3), 273–288.

Kvasny, L., & Igwe, F. (2008). An African American weblog community's reading of AIDS in Black America. *Journal of Computer Mediated Communication, 13*(3), 569–591.

Kvasny, L., Payton, F. & Hales, K. (2010). Social activism in the 'Blackosphere': The Jena 6 case. In J. Park & E. Abels (Eds.), *Interpersonal relations and social patterns in communication technologies: Discourse norms, language structures and cultural variables* (pp. 18–31). Hershey, PA: IGI Global. Retrieved from http://grads.ist.psu.edu/khales/Publications /Kvasny_Payton_Hales-2009_Jena6.pdf

A Lady's Perspective. (2010). National Black HIV/AIDS Awareness Day [Web log post]. Retrieved from http://aladysperspective.blogspot.com

Lane, S. D., Rubinstein, R. A., Keefe, R. H., Webster, N., Cibula, D. A., Rosenthal, A., & Dowdell, J. (2004). Structural violence and racial disparity in HIV transmission. *Journal of Health Care for the Poor and Underserved, 15*(3), 319–335.

Lau, H. (2009) Identity scripts and democratic deliberations. *Minnesota Law Review, 94*, 897–971.

Lee, L. 2015. Virtual homeplace: (Re)constructing the body through social media. In K. Edwards Tassie & S. M. Brown Givens (Eds.), *Women of color and social media multitasking: Blogs, timelines, feeds, and community* (pp. 91–111). Lanham, MD: Lexington Books.

Lenhart, A., & Fox, S. (2006). *Bloggers: A portrait of the internet's new storytellers.* Pew Internet & American Life. Retrieved from http://www.pewinternet.org/pdfs/PIP%20Bloggers %20Report%20July%2019%202006.pdf

Leone, P., Adimora, A., Foust, E., Williams, D., Buie, M., Peebles, J., . . . Greenberg, A. (2005, February 4). *HIV transmission among Black women—North Carolina, 2004.* Centers for Disease Control and Prevention, Morbidity and Mortality Weekly Report. Retrieved from http://www.cdc.gov/mmwr/preview/mmwrhtml/mm5404a2.htm

Lewis, G. (2013) Unsafe travel: Experiencing intersectionality and feminist displacements. *Signs, 38*(4), 869–892.

Logan, S. W. (1999). *We are coming: The persuasive discourse of Nineteenth-Century Black women.* Carbondale, IL: Southern Illinois University.

Logan, T. K., Cole, J., & Leukefeld, C. (2002). Women, sex, and HIV: Social and contextual factors, meta-analysis of published interventions, and implications for practice and research. *Psychological Bulletin, 128*, 851–885.

Lorde, A. (1978). *The black unicorn.* New York: Norton.

Lorde, A. (1984). *Sister outsider: Essays and speeches.* New York: Crossing Press.

Lukes, S. (1974). *Power: A radical view.* London: Macmillan.

Macías, K. (n.d.). "Tweeting away our blues": An exploration of Black women's use of social media to combat misogynoir. Retrieved from https://www.academia.edu/8756300/ _Tweeting_Away_Our_Blues_An_Exploration_of_Black_Women_s_Use_of_Social _Media_to_Combat_Misogynoir

Madlock Gatison, A. (2016). *Health communication and breast cancer among Black women: Culture, identity, spirituality and strength.* Lanham, MD: Lexington Books.

Mansbridge, J., & Tate, K. (1992). Race trumps gender: The Thomas nomination in the Black community. *PS: Political Science and Politics, 25*(3), 488–492.

Mark L. (2007, January 27). *Stopping domestic violence in Prince George's County*. Retrieved from http://www.associatedcontent.com/article/126510/stopping_domestic_violence_in _prince.html

Marshall, P. (1983). *Praisesong for the widow*. New York: Putnam.

Martinson, L. M. (2001). An analysis of racism and resources for African-American female victims of domestic violence in Wisconsin. *Wisconsin Women's Law Journal, 16*, 259–285.

Maticka-Tyndale, E. (1991). Sexual scripts and AIDS prevention: Variations in adherence to safer-sex guidelines by heterosexual adolescents. *Journal of Sex Research, 28*(1), 45–66.

Mattis, J. S. (2002). Religion and spirituality in the meaning-making and coping experiences of African American women: A qualitative analysis. *Psychology of Women Quarterly, 26*, 309–321.

Mays, V. M., Caldwell, C. H., & Jackson, J. S. (1996). Mental health symptoms and service utilization patterns of help-seeking among African American women. In H. W. Neighbors & J. S. Jackson (Eds.), *Mental health in Black America* (pp. 161–176). Thousand Oaks, CA: Sage.

McCall, L. (2005). The complexity of intersectionality. *Signs: Journal of Women in Culture and Society, 30*(3), 1771–1800.

McCaughey, M., & Ayers, M. D. (2003). Introduction. In M. McCaughey & M. D. Ayers (Eds.), *Cyberactivism: Online activism in theory and practice* (pp. 1–24). New York & London: Routledge.

McFadden, P. (2004, June). *HIV and AIDS: Behind the iconic re-presentations of gender, race and class in southern Africa*. Paper presented at the conference Learning from our lives: Women, girls and HIV/AIDS in Africa and the Africa diaspora, Spelman College and SisterLove Inc., Atlanta, GA.

McHenry, E. (2002). Forgotten readers: Recovering the lost history of African American literary societies (New Americanists). Durham, NC: Duke University Press.

McKenna, L., & Pole, A. (2004, September). *Do blogs matter? Weblogs in American politics*. Paper presented at the annual meeting of the American Political Science Association, Chicago, IL.

McKenna, L., & Pole, A. (2008). What do bloggers do: An average day on an average political blog. *Public Choice, 134*: 97–108

McKittrick, K. (2000). 'Who do you talk to, when a body's in trouble?': M. Nourbese Philip's (un)silencing of black bodies in the diaspora. *Social & Cultural Geography, 1*(2), 223–235.

Medicare Prescription Drug Plan, 146 Cong. Rec. H6577–79 (daily ed. July 19, 2000) (statement of Rep. Carson). Retrieved from http://thomas.loc.gov

Melucci, A. (1995). The process of collective identity. In B. Klandermans & H. Johnson (Eds.), *Social movements and culture* (pp. 41–63). Minneapolis: University of Minnesota Press.

Mental Health Caucus, 149 Cong. Rec. H3853–54 (daily ed. May 8, 2003) (statement of Rep. Watson). Retrieved from http://thomas.loc.gov

Merritt, S. (1980). Sex differences in role behavior and policy orientations of suburban office-holders: The effect of women's employment. In D. W. Stewart (Ed.), *Women in local politics* (pp. 115–126). Metuchen, NJ: Scarecrow.

Mezey, S. G. (1978). Does sex make a difference? A case study of women in politics. *Western Political Quarterly, 31*, 492–501.

Mills, C. W. (1959). *The sociological imagination*. New York: Oxford University Press.

Minh-ha, Trinh T. (1990). Not you/like you: Post-colonial woman and the interlocking questions of identity and difference. In Gloria Anzaldúa (Ed.), *Making face, making soul/ haciendo caras: Creative and critical perspectives by women of color* (pp. 371–375). San Francisco: Aunt Lute Books.

Miranda, J., Chung, J. Y., Green, B. L., Krupnick, J., Siddique, J., Revicki, D. A., & Berlin, T. (2003). Treating depression in predominantly low-income young minority women: A randomized controlled trial. *Journal of the American Medical Association, 290*, 57–65.

Mishler, E. G. (1990). Validation in inquiry-guided research: The role of exemplars in narrative studies. *Harvard Educational Review, 60*(4), 415–442.

Mohanty, C. T. (2003). Feminism without borders. Decolonizing theory, practicing solidarity. Durham, NC: Duke University Press.

Monroe, S. (2006, December). Personal journeys of women with HIV/AIDS. *Ebony*, 154.

Morgan, J. (1997). "Some could suckle over their shoulder": Male travelers, female bodies, and the gendering of racial ideology, 1500–1770. *William and Mary Quarterly, 54*, 167–192.

Morrison, T. (1987). *Beloved*. New York: Knopf.

Morrison, T. (1992). Introduction: Friday on the Potomac. In T. Morrison (Ed.), Race-ing justice, en-gendering power: Essays on Anita Hill, Clarence Thomas and the construction of social reality (pp. vii–xxx). New York: Pantheon.

Motion to Instruct Conferees on H.R. 2215, the 21st Century Department of Justice Appropriations Authorization Act, 148 Cong. Rec. H1996 (daily ed. May 1, 2002) (statement of Rep. Christensen). Retrieved from http://thomas.loc.gov

Myers, G., & Margavio, A. V. (1983). The black bourgeoisie and reference group change: A content analysis of *Ebony*. *Qualitative Sociology, 6*(4), 291–307.

N. I. (2001, June). Mental health resources. *Essence*, 147.

Nash, J. (2008). Re-thinking intersectionality. *Feminist Review, 89*, 1–15.

National Alliance of State and Territorial AIDS Directors. (2008, May). *The landscape of HIV/AIDS among African American women in the United States*. Retrieved from http://www.nastad.org/Files/092557_African%20American%20Women%27s%20Issue%20Brief%20No.%201.pdf

National Alliance on Mental Illness. (2009). *African American women and depression: Fact sheet*. Retrieved from http://www.nami.org/Template.cfm?Section=Women_and_Depression&Template=/ContentManagement/ContentDisplay.cfm&ContentID=88884

National Alliance on Mental Illness. (n.d). *Mental illness*. Retrieved from http://www.nami.org/template.cfm?section=about_mental_illness

National Domestic Violence Awareness Month, 143 Cong. Rec. H8447 (daily ed. October 7, 1997) (statement of Rep. Clayton). Retrieved from http://thomas.loc.gov

Naylor, G. (1982). *The women of Brewster Place*. New York: Penguin.

Olmedo, E. L., & Parron, D. L. (1981). Mental health of minority women: Some special issues. *Professional Psychology, 12*(1), 103–111.

Opposition to H.R. 1997, the Unborn Victims of Violence Act of 2003, 150 Cong. Rec. H658 (daily ed. February 26, 2004) (statement of Rep. Jones). Retrieved from http://thomas.loc.gov

Orbe, M. (1998). Constructing co-cultural theory: An explication of culture, power, and communication. Thousand Oaks, CA: Sage.

Orbe, M. (2005). Continuing the legacy of theorizing from the margins: Conceptualizations of co-cultural theory. *Women & Language, 28*(2), 65–66.

Orey, B., & Smooth, W. (2006). Race and gender matter: Refining models of legislative policy making in state legislatures. In C. Hardy-Fanta (Ed.), *Intersectionality and politics: Recent research on gender, race, and political representation in the United States* (pp. 97–120). New York: Haworth.

Orgad, S. (2005). The transformative potential of online communication: The case of breast cancer patients' Internet spaces. *Feminist Media Studies, 5*, 141–161.

Orleck, A. (2005). Storming Caesars' Palace: How Black mothers fought their own war on poverty. Boston: Beacon.

Parker, R. G., Easton, D., & Klein, C. (2000). Structural barriers and facilitators in HIV prevention: A review of international research. *AIDS, 14*(Suppl. 1), S22–S32.

Parks, S. (2010). Fierce angles: The strong Black woman in American life and culture. New York: One World.

Pequegnat, W., & Stover, E. (1999). Considering women's contextual and cultural issues in HIV/STD prevention research. *Cultural Diversity and Ethnic Minority Psychology, 5,* 287–291.

Pedersen, S. (2007). Gender differences in British blogging. *Journal of computer-mediated communication, 12*(4), 1472–1492.

Perkins, W. E. (1996). Droppin' science: Critical essays on rap music and hip hop culture. Philadelphia: Temple University Press.

Perry, I. (2003). Who(se) am I? The identity and image of women in hip-hop. In G. Dines & J. M. Humez (Eds.) *Gender, race, and class in media: A text-reader* (2nd ed.) (pp. 136–148). Thousand Oaks, CA: Sage Publications

Perry, I. (2004). Prophets of the hood: Politics and poetics in hip hop. Durham, NC: Duke University Press.

Perry, M. (1997, September). AIDS: The second wave; COPING (as told by Teresa Wiltz). *Essence,* 130.

Peterson, C. L. (1995). "Doers of the word": African American women speakers and writers in the North (1830–1880). New Brunswick, NJ: Rutgers University Press.

Peterson, C. (2001). Eccentric bodies. In M. Bennett & V. Dickerson (Eds.), *Recovering the Black female body* (pp. ix–xvi). New Brunswick, NJ: Rutgers University Press.

Pharr, S. (2000). Homophobia and sexism. In V. Cyrus (Ed.), *Experiencing race, class, and gender in the United States* (pp. 303–307). Mountain View, CA: Mayfield.

Phillips, L., & McCaskill, B. (1995). Who's schooling who? Black women and the bringing of the everyday into academe, or why we started The Womanist. *Signs: Journal of Women in Culture and Society, 20*(4), 1007–1018.

Picard, M. (1952). *The world of silence* (Original work published 1948). (S. Godman, Trans.) South Bend, IN: Regnery/Gateway.

Places to go. (1997, June). *Essence,* 17.

Plowden, K., Fletcher, A., & Miller, J. L. (2005). Factors influencing HIV-risk behaviors among HIV positive urban African Americans. *Journal of the Association of Nurses in AIDS Care, 16*(1), 21–28.

Poole, A. (2005). "Black Bloggers and the Blogosphere." Paper presented at the *Second International Conference on Technology, Knowledge and Society,* Hyderabad, India.

Poole, A. (2007). Black bloggers and the blogosphere. *International Journal of Technology, Knowledge, and Society, 2*(6), 9–16.

Pollitt, K. (2010, May 31). What ever happened to welfare mothers? *The Nation.* Retrieved from: http://www.thenation.com/article/what-ever-happened-welfare-mothers

Potter, H. (2006). An argument for Black feminist criminology: Understanding African American women's experiences with intimate partner abuse using an integrated approach. *Feminist Criminology, 1*(2), 106–124.

Princeton Survey Research Associates. (1996, July/August). Covering the epidemic: AIDS in the news media, 1985–1996 (Special supplement). *Columbia Journalism Review, 35.*

Pulerwitz, J., Amaro, H., DeJong, W., Gortmaker, S. L., & Rudd, R. (2002). Relationship power, condom use and HIV risk among women in the USA. *AIDS Care, 14,* 789–800.

Pyett, P. M. (2003). Validation of qualitative research in the "real world." *Qualitative Health Research, 13*(8), 1170–1179.

Quinn, S. C. (1993). AIDS and the African American woman: The triple burden of race, class, and gender. *Health Education Quarterly, 20*(3), 305–320.

Randolph, M. E., Pinkerton, S. D., Somlai, A. M., Kelly, J. A., McAuliffe, T. L., & Hackl, K. (2007). Severely mentally ill women's HIV risk: The influence of social support, substance use, and contextual risk factors. *Community Mental Health, 43*(1), 33–47.

Rapp, L., Button, D. M., Fleury-Steiner, B., & Fleury-Steiner, R. (2010). The Internet as a tool for Black feminist activism: Lessons from an online antirape protest. *Feminist Criminology, 5*(3), 244–262.

Reingold, B. (2000). Representing women: Sex, gender, and legislative behavior in Arizona and California. Chapel Hill: University of North Carolina Press.

Rennison, C., & Welchens, S. (2000). *Intimate partner violence (NCJ-178247)*. Washington, DC: U.S. Department of Justice Statistics.

Renzetti, C. M. (1998). Violence and abuse in lesbian relationships: Theoretical and empirical issues. In R. K. Bergen (Ed.), *Issues in intimate violence* (pp. 117–127). Thousand Oaks, CA: Sage.

Rhodes, J. (1993). Falling through the cracks: Studying women of color in mass communication. In P. Creedon (Ed.), *Women in mass communication* (pp. 24–31). Newbury Park, CA: Sage.

Richardson, E. (2003). *African American literacies*. New York: Routledge.

Richie, B. (1996). Compelled to crime: The gender entrapment of battered Black women. New York: Routledge.

Richie, B. (2000). A Black feminist reflection on the antiviolence movement. *Signs: Journal of Women in Culture and Society, 25*, 1133–1137.

Rifaat, Y. (2008). Blogging the body: The case of Egypt. *Cynthia Nelson Institute for Gender and Women's Studies, 1*(1): 52–72. Retrieved from http://www.aucegypt.edu/GAPP/IGWS/GradCent/Documents/SurfacingVol1No1.pdf#page=59

Ristock, J. (2002). No more secrets: Violence in lesbian relationships. New York: Routledge.

Roberts, D. (1997). Killing the Black body: Race, reproduction, and the meaning of liberty. New York: Random House.

Robnett, B. (1997). How long? How long? African-American women and the struggle for civil rights. New York: Oxford University Press.

Rodriguez, B. (1997). Biomedical modes of HIV and work. In N. Goldstein & J. L. Manlowe (Eds.), *The gender politics of HIV/AIDS in women: Perspectives on the pandemic in the United States* (pp. 25–42). New York: New York University Press.

Rooks, N. (2004). Ladies pages: African American women's magazines and the culture that created them. New Brunswick, NJ: Rutgers University Press.

Rose, T. (1991). Never trust a big butt and a smile. *Camera Obscura, 23*(9): 109–131.

Rose, T. (1994). Black noise: Rap music and black culture in contemporary America. Middletown, CT: Wesleyan University Press.

Royster, J. J. (2000). Traces of a stream: Literacy and social change among African American women. Pittsburgh, PA: University of Pittsburgh Press.

Rusert, B. (2009). "A study in nature": The Tuskegee experiments and the New South plantation. *Journal of Medical Humanities, 30*(3), 155–171.

Ryan White AIDS Care Act, 151 Cong. Rec. H21592 (daily ed. September 28, 2005) (statement of Rep. Waters). Retrieved from http://thomas.loc.gov

Salber P. R, & Taliaferro, E. (1998). Domestic violence. In P. Rosen (Ed.), *Emergency medicine concepts and clinical practice*. 4th ed. Philadelphia, PA: Mosby-Year Book.

Sauda Voice (October 26, 2010). Former WNBA player killed by longtime girlfriend. [Web log post]. Retrieved from http://www.thesaudavoice.com/the_sauda_voice/2010/10/former-wnba-player-killed-by-longtime-girlfriend.html

Schable, B., Chu, S. Y., & Diaz, T. (1995). Characteristics of women 50 Years of age or older with heterosexually acquired AIDS. *American Journal of Public Health, 86*(11), 1616–1618.

Schattschneider, E. E. ([1960], 1975). *The semi-sovereign people: A realist's view of democracy in America.* New York: Harcourt Brace Jovanovich.

Schwartz-Shea, P., & Yanow, D. (2012). *Interpretive research design: Concepts and processes.* New York and London: Routledge.

Schiller, N. G., & Lewellen, D. (1994). Risky business: The cultural construction of AIDS risk groups. *Social Science Medicine, 10,* 1337–1346.

Schmidt, J. (2007). *Blogging practices in the German-speaking blogosphere. Findings from the "Wie ich blogge?!"-survey.* Research Centre "New Communication Media" working paper 07–02. Bamberg, Germany. Retrieved from http://www.fonk-bamberg.de/pdf/fonkpaper0702.pdf

Schneider, A. L., & Ingram, H. (1993). Social construction of target populations: Implications for politics and policy. *American Political Science Review, 87*(2), 334–347.

Schneider, A. L., & Ingram, H. (1997). *Policy design for democracy.* Topeka: University Press of Kansas.

Scott, K. (1991). *The habit of surviving: African American women's strategies for life.* New Brunswick, NJ: Rutgers University Press.

Scott, R. L. (1972). Rhetoric and silence. *Western Speech, 36,* 146–158.

Sesko, A. K., & Biernat, M. (2010). Prototypes of race and gender: The invisibility of Black women. *Journal of Experimental Social Psychology, 46,* 356–360.

Severin, W. J., & Tankard, J. W. (1988). *Communication theories: Origins, methods, uses.* New York: Longman.

Sharma, S. (2013). Black Twitter? Racial hashtags, networks and contagion. *New Formations, 78*(1): 46–64.

Shaw, T. C., & McDaniel, E. L. (2007, January). "Whosoever will": Black theology, homosexuality, and the Black political church. *National Political Science Review, 11,* 137–147.

Shepherd, J. M. (1980). The portrayal of Black women in the ads of popular magazines. *Western Journal of Black Studies, 4*(3), 179–182.

Sheriff, R. E. (2000). Exposing silence as cultural censorship: A Brazilian case. *American Anthropologist, 102*(1), 114–132.

Silva de Crane, R. D., & Spielberger, C. D. (1981). Attitudes of Hispanic, Black, and Caucasian university students toward mental illness. *Hispanic Journal of Behavioral Sciences, 3,* 241–255.

Simien, E. (2005). Race, gender, and linked fate. *Journal of Black Studies, 35*(5), 529–550.

Simien, E. (2006). *Black feminist voices in politics.* Albany: State University of New York Press.

Simien, E., & Clawson, R. (2004). The intersection of race and gender: An examination of black feminist consciousness, race consciousness, and policy attitudes. *Social Science Quarterly, 85*(3), 793–810.

Simon, P., Hu, D., Diaz, T., & Kerndt, P. (1995). Income and AIDS rates in Los Angeles County. *AIDS, 9*(3), 281–284.

Simon, W., & Gagnon, J. H. (1986). Sexual scripts: Permanence and change. *Archives of Sexual Behavior, 15,* 97–120.

Simone, N. (1966). Four women. On *Wild is the Wind* [Album]. New York: Philips Records.

Singer, N. (2011, October 15). Welcome, fans, to the pinking of America. *New York Times.* Retrieved from www.nytimes.com/2011/10/16/business/in-the-breast-cancer-fight-the-pinking-of-america.html

Sklar, D. (1994). Can bodylore be brought to its senses? *Journal of American Folklore, 107*(423), 9–22.

Smith, A. (2014). "African Americans and technology use." Pew Research Internet Project. Retrieved from http://www.pewinternet.org/2014/01/06/african-americans- and-technology-use/

Smith, B. (1995). Some home truths on the contemporary Black feminist movement. In B. Guy-Sheftall (Ed.), *Words of fire: An anthology of African American feminist thought* (pp. 254–268). New York: New Press.

Smith, J. A. (2004). Reflecting on the development of interpretative phenomenological analysis and its contribution to qualitative research in psychology. *Research in Psychology, 1*, 39–54.

Smith, J. A. (2008). Qualitative psychology: a practical guide to research methods (2nd ed.). Thousand Oaks, CA: Sage.

Smith, J. A., Flowers, P., & Larkin, M. (2009). Interpretative phenomenological analysis: Theory, method and research. Los Angeles: Sage.

Smith, V. (1989). Black feminist theory and the representation of the "Other." In S. Wall (Ed.), *Changing our own words: Essays on criticism, theory, and writing by Black women* (pp. 38–57). New Brunswick, NJ: Rutgers University Press.

Smith-Shomade, B. E. (2002). *Shaded lives: African American women and television.* New Brunswick, NJ: Rutgers University Press.

Smooth, W. (2006). Intersectionality in electoral politics: A mess worth making. *Politics & Gender, 2*(3): 400–14.

Smooth, W. (2013). Intersectionality from theoretical framework to policy intervention, In R. A. Wildon (Ed.), *Situating Intersectionality* (pp. 11–41). New York, NY: Palgrave.

Smooth, W. (2014). African American women and electoral politics: Translating voting power into office holding. In S. J. Carroll and R. L. Fox (Eds.), *Gender and elections: Shaping the future of American politics* (pp. 167–189). New York, Cambridge University Press.

Snow, David 2001. "Collective identity and expressive forms." Center for the Study of Democracy, University of California, Irvine eScholarship Repository. Retrieved from http://escholarship.org/uc/item/2zn1t7bj

Spates, K., & Davis, J. (2010). Hegemonic female spaces: An analysis of the covert meanings within *Ladies Home Journal* and *Ebony* magazines' advertisements. *MP: An Online Feminist Journal, 3*(2), 1–33.

Speaking Out Against Administration's Record in Combating Violence Against Women, 150 Cong. Rec. H4746 (daily ed. June 22, 2004) (statement by Rep. Majette). Retrieved from http://thomas.loc.gov

Spillers, H. (2003). Black, White and in color: Essays on American literature and culture. Chicago: University of Chicago Press.

Springer, J. T. (2008). "Roll it gal": Alison Hinds, female empowerment, and calypso. *Meridians: Feminism, Race, Transnationalism, 8*(1), 93–129.

Springer, K. (Ed.) (1999). Still lifting, still climbing: African American women's contemporary activism. New York: New York University Press.

Springer, K. (2005). Living for the revolution: Black feminist organizations, 1968–190. Durham, NC & London: Duke University Press.

Starling, K. (1998, October). New directions in Black spirituality. *Ebony*, 92.

Starling, K. (1999, May). Black women and the blues: Why so many sisters are mad and sad. *Ebony*, 140.

Starling, K. (2000, April). Why AIDS is a growing threat to Black women: Expert says disease is "An epidemic." *Ebony*, 136.

Stockett, K. (2009). *The help: A novel.* New York: Penguin.

Stone, D. (1988). *Policy paradox and political reason.* New York: Harper Collins.

Storrs, D. (1999). Whiteness as stigma: Essentialist identity work by mixed-race women. *Symbolic Interaction, 23*(3), 187–212.

Stratford, D., Mizuno, Y., Williams, K., Courtenay-Quirk, C., & O'Leary, A. (2008). Addressing poverty as risk for disease: Recommendations from CDC's consultation on microenterprise as HIV prevention. *Public Health Reports, 123*(1), 9–20.

Straus, M., & Gelles, R. (1986). Societal change and change in family violence from 1975 to 1985 as revealed by two national surveys. *Journal of Marriage and the Family, 48*, 465–479.

Strolovitch, D. Z. (2007). Affirmative advocacy: Race, class, and gender in interest group politics. Chicago: University of Chicago Press.

Sullivan, C., Tan, C., Basta, J., Rumptz, M., & Davidson, W. (1992). An advocacy intervention program for women with abusive partners: Initial evaluation. *American Journal of Community Psychology, 20*, 309–332.

Supporting the Goals and Ideals of Domestic Violence Awareness Month, 151 Cong. Rec. H8372 (daily ed. September 27, 2005) (statement by Rep. Watson). Retrieved from http://thomas.loc.gov

Supporting the Goals and Ideals of National Black HIV/AIDS Awareness Day, 151 Cong. Rec. H432 (daily ed. February 9, 2005) (statement by Rep. Lee). Retrieved from http://thomas.loc.gov

Supporting the Goals and Ideals of National Black HIV/AIDS Awareness Day, 153 Cong. Rec. H1166 (daily ed. February 5, 2007) (statement of Rep. Johnson). Retrieved from http://thomas.loc.gov

Swers, M. (2001). Understanding the policy impact of electing women: Evidence from research on Congress and state legislatures. *Political Science & Politics, 34*(2), 217–220.

Swers, M. L. (2002). The difference women make: The policy impact of women in Congress. Chicago: University of Chicago Press.

Sylvander, C. W. (1975). Ralph Ellison's *Invisible Man* and female stereotypes. *Negro American Literature Forum, 9*(3), 77–79.

Taft, C. T., Bryant-Davis, T., Woodward, H. E., Tillman, S., & Torres, S. E. (2009). Intimate partner violence against African American women: An examination of the socio-cultural context. *Aggression and Violent Behavior, 14*, 50–58.

Tannen, D. and Saville-Troike, M. (1985). *Perspectives on silence.* Norwood, NJ: Ablex.

Tate. K. (2004). Black faces in the mirror: African Americans and their representatives in the U.S. Congress. Princeton, NJ: Princeton University Press.

Taylor, S. J., & Bogdan, R. (1984). Introduction to qualitative research methods: The search for meanings. New York: John Wiley & Sons.

Taylor, S. L. (1995). *Lessons in living.* New York: Anchor.

Taylor, V., & Van Willigen, M. (1996). Women's self-help and the reconstruction of gender: The postpartum support and breast cancer. *Movements Mobilization: An International Quarterly, 2*, 123–142.

Tharps, L. L., & Cresto, A. (2004, May). Baby blues. *Essence*, 254.

Thomas, A. J. (2001). African American women's spiritual beliefs: A guide for treatment. *Women and Therapy, 23*(4), 1–12.

Thomas, S. (1994). *How women legislate.* New York: Oxford University Press.

Thompson, L. (2009). Beyond the Black lady: Sexuality and the new African American middle class. Chicago: University of Illinois Press.

Tidwell, R. (2004). The "no-show" phenomenon and the issue of "resistance" among African American female patients at an urban health care center. *Journal of Mental Health Counseling, 26*, 1–12.

Tomes, E. K., Brown, A., Semenya, K., & Simpson, J. (1990). Depression in Black women of low socioeconomic status: Psychological factors and nursing diagnosis. *Journal of the National Black Nurses Association, 4*(2), 37–46.

Townes, E. (2006). Womanist ethics and the cultural production of evil. New York: Palgrave.

Tuchman, G. (1978). The news net. *Social Research, 45,* 253–276.

U.S. Department of Commerce, Economics and Statistics Administration & Executive Office of the President, Office of Management and Budget. (2011, March). *Women in America: Indicators of social and economic well-being.* Retrieved from http://www.whitehouse.gov /sites/default/files/rss_viewer/Women_in_America.pdf

U.S. Department of Health and Human Services. (2001). *Mental health: Culture, race and ethnicity—A supplement to mental health: A report of the Surgeon General.* Rockville, MD: Substance Abuse and Mental Health Services Center for Mental Health Services.

van Dijk. T. (1986). News schemata. In C. Cooper & S. Greenbaum (Eds.), *Studying writing: Linguistic approaches* (pp. 155–186). Beverly Hills, CA: Sage.

van Manen, M. (1990). Researching lived experience: Human science for an action sensitive pedagogy. Albany: State University of New York Press.

Vanzant, I. (2004, June). When you're losing it at work. *Essence,* 108.

Vegh, S. (2003). Classifying forms of online activism: The case of cyberprotests against the World Bank. In M. M. McCaughey & M. Ayers (Eds.), *Cyberactivism: Online activism in theory and practice* (pp. 71–96). London: Routledge.

Violence Against Women, 147 Cong. Rec. H1065 (daily ed. March 22, 2001) (statement of Rep. Carson). Retrieved from http://thomas.loc.gov

The Voice of Georgia's Fourth Congressional District Is Back, 151 Cong. Rec. H3243–46 (daily ed. May 12, 2005) (statement of Rep. McKinney). Retrieved from http://thomas.loc.gov

Wade, B. (1999, April). Rx for the blues. *Essence,* 53.

Walker, A. (1982). *The color purple.* New York: Simon & Schuster.

Wallace, A. (2014). Influencing the political agenda from the outside: A comparative study of Hausa women's NGOs & CBOs in Kano, Nigeria. *National Political Science Review.*

Wallace, M. (1990). *Invisibility blues: From pop to theory.* New York: Verso.

Wallace, M. N. (1990 [1978]). *Black macho and the myth of the superwoman.* New York: Verso.

Wallace-Sanders, K. (2002a). Introduction. In K. Wallace-Sanders (Ed.), *Skin deep, spirit strong: The Black female body in American culture* (pp. 1–10). Ann Arbor: University of Michigan Press.

Wallace-Sanders, K. (Ed.) (2002b). *Skin deep, spirit strong: The Black female body in American culture.* Ann Arbor: University of Michigan Press.

Wanzo, R. A. (2009). *The suffering will not be televised: African American women and sentimental political storytelling.* Albany: State University of New York Press.

Ware, V. (1992). *Beyond the pale.* London: Verso.

Washington, H. A. (2000, May). To our health! *Essence,* 61.

Washington, M. (2010, August 10). The state of black women in the blogosphere. *The Grio.* Retrieved from http://www.thegrio.com/news/the-state-of-the-black-womens -blogosphere.php

Watkins-Hayes, C. (2008). The social and economic context of Black women living with HIV/AIDS in the US: Implications for research. In R. Reddock, S. Reid, D. Douglas, & D. Roberts (Eds.), *Sex, power, and taboo: Gender and HIV in the Caribbean and beyond* (pp. 33–66). Kingston, Jamaica: Ian Randle.

Watt, J. (2006). Blogging busts out for women. *Herizons, 20*(1), 7.

Weeks, M., Singer, M., Grier, M., & Schensul, J. J. (1996). Gender relations, sexuality and AIDS risk among African American and Latina women. In C. F. Sargent & C. B. Brettell (Eds.), *Gender and health: An international perspective* (pp. 338–370). Saddle River, NJ: Prentice Hall.

Wei, C. (2004). Formation of norms in a blog community. In L. Gurak, S. Antonijevic, L. Johnson, C. Ratliff, & J. Reyman (Eds.), *Into the blogosphere: Rhetoric, community, and culture of weblogs*. Retrieved from http://blog.lib.umn.edu/blogosphere/formation_of _norms.html

Weldon, S. L. (2006). The structure of intersectionality: A comparative politics of gender. *Politics and Gender, 2*(2), 235–248.

Welter, B. (1966). The cult of true womanhood. *American Quarterly, 18*(2), 151–174.

West, T. C. (1999). Wounds of the sprit: Black women, violence and resistance ethics. New York: New York University Press.

Whaley, A. (2001). Cultural mistrust: An important psychological construct for diagnosis and treatment of African Americans. *Professional Psychology: Research and Practice, 32*, 555–562.

Whatever happened to the Black Miss America? (2002, March). *Ebony*, 108.

Whitaker, C. (2000, July). Out of the closet: The mental health crisis in Black America. *Ebony*, 74.

White, E. (1994). Chain, chain, and change: For Black women in abusive relationships. Seattle: Seal Press.

White, E. F. (1990). Africa on my mind: Gender, counter discourse and African-American nationalism. *Journal of Women's History, 2*, 73–97.

White, E. F. (2001). Dark continent of our bodies: Black feminism and the politics of respectability. Philadelphia: Temple University Press.

Whitehead, T. (1997). Urban low-income African American men, HIV/AIDS and gender identity. *Medical Anthropology Quarterly, 11*(4), 411–447.

Williams, O. (2002, November). Breaking the cycle. *Essence*, 252.

Williams, R. Y. (2004). The politics of public housing: Black women's struggle against urban equality. New York: Oxford University Press.

Williams, T. M. (2008). Black pain: It just looks like we're not hurting. New York: Scribner.

Willis, C. J. (2010). *Exploring new boundaries: HIV/AIDS as a local crisis*. Paper presented at the annual meeting of the American Political Science Association, Washington, DC. Retrieved from http://papers.ssrn.com/sol3/papers.cfm?abstract_id=1641881

Wilson, P. (1998, December). The wall. *Essence*, 62.

Winer, D. (2003, May 23). What makes a weblog a weblog? Retrieved from http://blogs.law .harvard.edu/whatMakesAWeblogAWeblog

Winters, M., Mathers, A., Grant, A., & Haferman, H. (2010). Love the way you lie. [Recorded by Eminem & Rihanna] On *Recovery* [CD]. Santa Monica, CA: Interscope.

Wolbrecht, C. (2000). *The politics of women's rights: Parties, positions, and change*. Princeton, NJ: Princeton University Press.

Wolcott, V. W. (2001). *Remaking respectability: African American women in interwar Detroit*. Chapel Hill and London: University of North Carolina Press.

Women's Health Issues, 143 Cong. Rec. H1966 (daily ed. April 29, 1997) (statement of Rep. Millender-McDonald). Retrieved from http://thomas.loc.gov

Woodward, J., & Mastin, T. (2005). Black womanhood: Essence and its treatment of stereotypical images of Black women. *Journal of Black Studies, 36*, 264–281.

Wright, E. M. (2003). Deep from within the well: Voices of African American women living with HIV/AIDS. In D. J. Gilbert & E. M. Wright (Eds.), *African American women and HIV/AIDS: Critical responses* (pp. 29–50). Westport, CT: Praeger.

Wright, E. R., & Martin, T. N. (2003). The social organization of HIV/AIDS care in treatment programmes for adults with serious mental illness. *AIDS CARE, 15*(6), 763–773.

Wright, R. (1940). *Native son*. New York: Grosset & Dunlap.

Yancy, G. (2008a). Black bodies, White gazes: The continuing significance of race. Lanham, MD: Rowman & Littlefield.

Yancy, G. (2008b). Colonial gazing: The production of the body as "other." *Western Journal of Black Studies, 32*(1), 1–15.

Yardley, L. (2000). Dilemmas in qualitative health research. *Psychology and Health.* 15, 215–228.

Yeatman, A. (1990). Bureaucrats, technocrats, femocrats: Essays on the contemporary Australian state. London: Falmer Press.

Yee, S. (1992). *Black women abolitionists: A study in activism, 1828–1860.* Knoxville: University of Tennessee Press.

Zierler, S., Krieger, N., Tang, Y., Coady, W., Siegfried, E., DeMario, A., & Auerbach, J. (2000). Economic deprivation and AIDS incidence in Massachusetts. *American Journal of Public Health, 90*(7), 1064–1073.

INDEX

activism, 1–2, 52–53, 63, 68, 80

advertisements, 57, 59–60, 63

African Diaspora, 45–46

AfroBella, 79–80, 109, 158

agency, 6–7, 20, 68–69, 73, 156

A Lady's Perspective, 96–97, 159

A Raisin in the Sun, 44–45

ass question subscript: Black freedom movement and, 154–155; description of, 31, 40–41; domestic violence and, 109–110, 122; HIV/AIDS and, 84–85, 92–93; mental illness and, 129; *piece of ass* subscript and, 40; racial authenticity and, 40

Ass script: *ass question* subscript of, 40–41; belongingness and, 49–50, 145; dangers of, 50; description of, 15, 31, 35–41; domestic violence and, 17, 32, 50–51, 118, 121–123, 141–142; function of, 4–5, 145–146, 149; HIV/AIDS and, 32, 50–51, 83, 89–90, 100, 141–142, 152; internalization of, 49–50; mental illness and, 32, 50–51, 141–142, 153–154; presentation of, 166–67n1; sacrifice and, 150; shadow bodies and, 17–18, 50; structural violence and, 145–146; subscripts of, 35–41

Bamboozled, 61–62

Beautiful, Also, Are The Souls of My Black Sisters, 159

beauty, 35–36, 58, 70

Beloved, 44, 47

Black church, 76, 91, 118, 121, 144–145

Black congresswomen: belongingness and, 55–56; Black womanhood and, 56; characteristics of, 55; constituents of, 54–55; critiques of, 145; domestic violence and, 56, 107–108, 110–112; elections of, 11, 53; governmental response to domestic violence and, 120–121; HIV/AIDS and, 56, 77–81, 87; interpretive phenomenological analysis (IPA) and, 71; intersectionality and, 20; issues of, 54; limitations of, 56; mental illness and, 56, 126, 129–130,

135–136; personal responsibility and, 93; political strategies of, 8, 20, 54–55; racism and, 110, 132–133; self-perception of, 56; silence and, 14–15; themes and, 73–74; voiceless and, 55–56

Black female body: body parts of, 32–33, 35–37; as "the dark continent," 30; domestic violence and, 144; emergence from the shadows by, 142; "Four Women" and, 140; historical perspectives of, 33; HIV/AIDS and, 144; identity and, 28; language and, 27; mental illness and, 144; as other, 30, 34; pornotroping and, 34; power and, 145; reproduction and, 28; scripts and, 12, 15, 27–28, 142; signs and, 34; silence and, 156; as a site of knowing, 28; as a site of resistance, 28; social power and, 22; symbols and, 27, 34; as text, 34

Black feminism: Black womanhood and, 69; blogs and, 64, 66; body studies and, 15; discursive formations and, 33; diversity of Black womanhood, 25; *Ebony* and, 62–63; *Essence* and, 62–63; goals of, 19; language and, 27; muted group theory and, 15, 75; usefulness of, 29

Black freedom Movement, 25, 39, 68, 109–110, 140, 149–150, 152, 154–155

Black Girls Give Back, 97, 130, 160

Black womanhood: belongingness and, 142–143, 145; Black congresswomen and, 56; Black feminism and, 69; construction of, 5–6, 69, 75, 86, 113, 132, 135, 142, 145, 152–154; as controlling image, 69; diversity of, 13–14, 25–26, 58–60, 62–63, 82, 106–107, 135, 137–138, 141, 143–144; domestic violence and, 3, 113; *Ebony* and, 62–63; *Essence* and, 62–63; HIV/AIDS and, 3; intragroup dynamics of, 142, 145; mental illness and, 3; perceptions of, 60, 69, 142; political behavior of, 141; portrayal of, 60, 69; protectionist policies of, 92–93, 131–132, 143; shadow bodies and, 145; structural violence and, 56

ABOUT THE AUTHOR

JULIA S. JORDAN-ZACHERY is a professor of Public and Community Service and director of the Black Studies Program at Providence College (RI). Her interdisciplinary research focuses on African American women and public policy. She is the author of the award-winning book *Black Women, Cultural Images, and Social Policy* (2009, Routledge).

CPSIA information can be obtained
at www.ICGtesting.com
Printed in the USA
LVOW03s1023290917
550337LV00002B/2/P

SHADOW BODIES